# Soviet and Post-Soviet Politics and Society (SP
ISSN 1614-3515

**General Editor:** Andreas Umland,
*Stockholm Centre for Eastern European Studies*, andreas.umland@ui.se

**Commissioning**
London, mjh@ibidem.

# Soviet and Post-Soviet Politics and Society (SPPS)

Founded in 2004 and refereed since 2007, SPPS makes available affordable English-, German-, and Russian-language studies on the history of the countries of the former Soviet bloc from the late Tsarist period to today. It publishes between 5 and 20 volumes per year and focuses on issues in transitions to and from democracy such as economic crisis, identity formation, civil society development, and constitutional reform in CEE and the NIS. SPPS also aims to highlight so far understudied themes in East European studies such as right-wing radicalism, religious life, higher education, or human rights protection. The authors and titles of all previously published volumes are listed at the end of this book. For a full description of the series and reviews of its books, see www.ibidem-verlag.de/red/spps.

**Editorial correspondence & manuscripts** should be sent to: Dr. Andreas Umland, Department of Political Science, Kyiv-Mohyla Academy, vul. Voloska 8/5, UA-04070 Kyiv, UKRAINE; andreas.umland@cantab.net

**Business correspondence & review copy requests** should be sent to: *ibidem* Press, Leuschnerstr. 40, 30457 Hannover, Germany; tel.: +49 511 2622200; fax: +49 511 2622201; spps@ibidem.eu.

**Authors, reviewers, referees, and editors** for (as well as all other persons sympathetic to) SPPS are invited to join its networks at www.facebook.com/group.php?gid=52638198614
www.linkedin.com/groups?about=&gid=103012
www.xing.com/net/spps-ibidem-verlag/

## Recent Volumes

265   Леонид Люкс
К столетию «философского парохода»
Мыслители «первой» русской эмиграции о русской революции и о тоталитарных соблазнах XX века
ISBN 978-3-8382-1775-8

266   Daviti Mtchedlishvili
The EU and the South Caucasus
European Neighborhood Policies between Eclecticism and Pragmatism, 1991-2021
With a foreword by Nicholas Ross Smith
ISBN 978-3-8382-1735-2

267   Bohdan Harasymiw
Post-Euromaidan Ukraine
Domestic Power Struggles and War of National Survival in 2014–2022
ISBN 978-3-8382-1798-7

268   Nadiia Koval, Denys Tereshchenko (Eds.)
Russian Cultural Diplomacy under Putin
Rossotrudnichestvo, the "Russkiy Mir" Foundation, and the Gorchakov Fund in 2007–2022
ISBN 978-3-8382-1801-4

269   Izabela Kazejak
Jews in Post-War Wrocław and L'viv
Official Policies and Local Responses in Comparative Perspective, 1945-1970s
ISBN 978-3-8382-1802-1

270   Jakob Hauter
Russia's Overlooked Invasion
The Causes of the 2014 Outbreak of War in Ukraine's Donbas
With a foreword by Hiroaki Kuromiya
ISBN 978-3-8382-1803-8

271   Anton Shekhovtsov
Russian Political Warfare. Essays on Kremlin Propaganda in Europe and the Neighbourhood, 2020-2023
With a foreword by Nathalie Loiseau
ISBN 978-3-8382-1821-2

272   Андреа Пето
Насилие и Молчание. Красная армия в Венгрии во Второй Мировой войне
ISBN 978-3-8382-1636-2

273   Winfried Schneider-Deters
Russia's War in Ukraine
Debates on Peace, Fascism, and War Crimes, 2022–2023
With a foreword by Klaus Gestwa
ISBN 978-3-8382-1876-2

274   Rasmus Nilsson
Uncanny Allies
Russia and Belarus on the Edge, 2012-2024
ISBN 978-3-8382-1288-3

Anton Grushetsky, Volodymyr Paniotto

# WAR AND THE TRANSFORMATION OF UKRAINIAN SOCIETY (2022–23)

### Empirical Evidence

*ibidem*
Verlag

**Bibliographic information published by the Deutsche Nationalbibliothek**

Die Deutsche Nationalbibliothek lists this publication in the Deutsche Nationalbibliografie; detailed bibliographic data are available on the Internet at http://dnb.d-nb.de.

**Bibliografische Information der Deutschen Nationalbibliothek**

Die Deutsche Nationalbibliothek verzeichnet diese Publikation in der Deutschen Nationalbibliografie; detaillierte bibliografische Daten sind im Internet über http://dnb.d-nb.de abrufbar.

ISBN (Print): 978-3-8382-1944-8

ISBN (E-Book [PDF]): 978-3-8382-7944-2

© *ibidem*-Verlag, Hannover • Stuttgart 2024

Printed in the United States of America

# Contents

1.  Introduction: Information about KIIS ........................................ 9

2.  Research Methodology Problems of Conducting Surveys
    During War ........................................................................ 23
    2.1. Research methodology ...................................................... 23
        2.1.1. Four periods in the methodology of conducting
               surveys in Ukraine ................................................ 23
        2.1.2. Methodology for conducting personal (F2F)
               interviews ............................................................ 29
        2.1.3. Telephone interview methodology (CAPI).......... 33
    2.2. Problems of conducting a survey during the war.......... 36
        2.2.1. Problems with the representativeness of surveys 37
        2.2.2. Problems with the reliability of surveys ............. 39

3.  Social and Economic Changes ...................................... 47

4.  Migration and Refugees............................................... 63
    4.1. Assessment of migration ................................................ 63
        4.1.1. Method for estimating migration from the
               occupied part of Donbas in 2014-2016. ............... 64
    4.2. Migration attitudes of the population of Ukraine. ......... 67
        4.2.1. Do you plan for the future of your children or
               grandchildren in Ukraine ..................................... 67
        4.2.2. Willingness to move to the USA or the EU if you
               become a citizen of these countries ..................... 69
        4.2.3. How many refugees plan to return to Ukraine ... 72
    4.3. Attitudes of Ukrainians towards refugees and
         internally displaced persons ........................................... 76
        4.3.1. Attitudes of Ukrainians currently residing in
               Ukraine towards Ukrainian refugees in Europe . 76

4.3.2. Attitudes of Ukrainians towards internally displaced persons (IDPs). ...................................... 80

5. Geopolitical Orientations of the Population of Ukraine ......... 87
   5.1. Changes in the attitudes of the Ukrainian population towards the European Union and alliances with Russia before the start of a full-scale war in 2022 ...................... 87
       5.1.1. Changes in attitudes toward the EU and alliances with Russia .............................................. 89
       5.1.2. Changes in attitudes toward NATO .................... 97
   5.2. Changes in the attitudes of the Ukrainian population towards the EU and NATO after the outbreak of war in 2022 ................................................................................ 99
   5.3. Attitudes toward certain countries and political leaders ............................................................................. 106

6. Attitudes of Ukrainians Towards Russia and Belarus .......... 119
   6.1. Dynamics of the attitude of the population of Ukraine to Russia and the population of Russia to Ukraine before the war (2008-2021) ............................................... 119
       6.1.1. Methodology and main results ........................... 119
       6.1.2. The last joint wave (November 2021) ................. 126
   6.2. Changes in the attitude of the Ukrainian population towards Russia after the outbreak of war .......................... 134
   6.3. Changes in the attitude of the population of Ukraine to Belarus ............................................................................. 142

7. Moral and Psychological State and Readiness to Resist the Enemy ........................................................................... 149
   7.1. Introduction ....................................................................... 149
   7.2. Self-assessment of the level of happiness by the population of Ukraine ....................................................... 151
   7.3. Readiness to resist Russian aggression ........................... 155

7.4. Readiness of Ukrainians to make concessions for peace ............................................................. 163

    7.4.1. Assessing the sincerity of answers — a methodological experiment ............................... 163

    7.4.2. Readiness for territorial concessions.................. 165

    7.4.3. Willingness to refuse to join NATO.................... 177

7.5. Level of optimism .............................................. 179

8.   Formation of the Nation and Value Orientations ................. 185

8.1. Ukrainians: an unexpected nation? National and civic identification of Ukrainians............................... 185

8.2. Attitudes toward Russian language learning in Ukrainian schools .............................................. 192

8.3. The complicated relationship between Ukrainians and democracy.......................................................... 197

8.4. Which public holidays do Ukrainians like the most? ... 202

8.5. Gender balance and attitudes towards the LGBT+ community.......................................................... 203

8.6. Ukrainians' changing commitment to traditional Ukrainian values................................................ 208

8.7. Religious self-identification of the population .............. 210

8.8. Dynamics of Attitudes Toward Stalin and Perceptions of the OUN-UPA Activities during the Second World War ................................................................. 212

9.   Attitudes Towards the State, Social Institutions and Political Forces ......................................................... 219

9.1. Dynamics of attitudes towards the state and social institutions in 1991-2022 (before the invasion) .............. 219

9.2. Changes in attitudes toward the state and social institutions after the outbreak of war............................ 226

10.  Changes in Media and Internet Consumption ...................... 243

    10.1.  Changes in media consumption .................................... 243

    10.2.  Changes in Internet consumption ............................... 259

11.  Possible Social Problems of Post-war Ukraine ..................... 265

    11.1.  Methodological remarks. Bogardus scale. ................... 267

    11.2.  Russian language in Ukraine ......................................... 271

    11.3.  Russian opposition to the government ("good
        Russians") ........................................................................ 274

    11.4.  Ukrainian Russians or ethnic Ukrainians .................... 277

    11.5.  Status by behavior during the war as a new basis for
        social differentiation ....................................................... 279

    11.6.  Migrants from less developed countries ...................... 287

12.  Conclusions: The Main Trends of Changes in Ukrainian
    Society ....................................................................................... 289

    12.1.  Socio-economic changes ................................................ 290

    12.2.  Migration, refugees .......................................................... 292

    12.3.  Geopolitical orientations of the population of
        Ukraine ............................................................................... 293

    12.4.  Attitudes of Ukrainians towards Russia and Belarus. 295

    12.5.  Moral and psychological state and readiness to resist
        the enemy .......................................................................... 298

    12.6.  Value orientations and nation building ....................... 300

    12.7.  Attitudes towards the state and social institutions ..... 303

    12.8.  Changes in media and consumption ........................... 304

    12.9.  Possible social problems of post-war Ukraine ............. 306

    12.10. Summary ........................................................................... 309

Appendices ............................................................................................ 313

# 1. Introduction
## Information about KIIS

We are finishing this book in January 2024 (and are writing the introduction after having finished all the other chapters). This is the 23rd month of Russia's full-scale war against Ukraine. Despite the hypocritical statements about the brotherhood of the Ukrainian and Russian peoples, which were an important element of the discourse of the Soviet regime and post-Soviet Russian authorities, Russia's claims and manifestations of aggression against Ukraine have continued since the declaration of independence in 1991 (in the form of trade and economic warfare, political pressure, interference in internal affairs, such as elections, artificially creating pockets of instability in certain regions, etc.) However, it was only in 2014 that the war took the form of direct military intervention. Russia invaded Crimea and then eastern Ukraine, where the so-called Donetsk and Luhansk "people's republics" were created under the guise of "popular" protests and Russia actually occupied these territories, as well as Crimea. But at the time, Russia did not have the intention or resources to invade Ukraine as a whole. The full-scale invasion took place on February 24, 2022, with Russia launching what it called a "special military operation" with missile strikes on Ukraine, and troops entering through several directions, including Crimea and Belarus, and attempting to capture Kyiv. In this book, for the sake of simplicity, we will refer to the full-scale Russian invasion that began on February 24, 2022, as the war (although the actual beginning of the war is Russia's invasion of Crimea in 2014).

The authors of the book are sociologists, heads of the Kyiv International Institute of Sociology, so the impact of the war on Ukrainian society is considered from a sociological point of view. Compared to other approaches (e.g., the historical approach, which focuses on past events and the study of documents; or the economic approach, which focuses on resources and market relations), sociology focuses on people's views and values, on their behavior. We do not consider the theoretical aspects of social transformations and refer the reader to the works of the Institute of Sociology of the National Academy of Sciences of Ukraine, especially to the works of Yevhen Golovakha and his classification of social transformations[1]. Social transformation is a change in various spheres of society, primarily in people's minds. We rely on data from numerous sociological studies (mostly quantitative) to assess changes in the readiness to resist the enemy, geopolitical orientations of the population, attitudes towards the state and its social institutions, identity issues, etc. The sociological surveys we use cover the period from 1991 to December 2023 inclusive, but the main thing we are interested in is what changes have occurred since the beginning of the war in February 2022. KIIS conducts about a hundred different surveys every year (including its own surveys), which cover issues from various spheres of public life. This allows for a comprehensive assessment of the transformations that Ukrainian society is undergoing. In this book, we will mainly use data from our own surveys (and in some cases, where appropriate, data from surveys conducted by our partners and other sociological centers).

It should be noted that the history of KIIS creation and development is closely related to the history of sociological research in Ukraine. We can distinguish two periods of development of sociological surveys in Ukraine:

**1969–1990:** the period of creation and formation of sociology in Ukraine, dominance of surveys at enterprises and local surveys (within one city) by questionnaires

**1991–present:** a period of extensive growth, dominance of nationally representative surveys by interview, development of qualitative methods and integration into the world sociology.

---

1    Ye. I. Holovakha, *Transformatsiia suspilstva: Dosvid sotsiolohichnoho monitorynhu v Ukraini* (Kyiv: Fond 'Demokratychni initsiatyvy,' 1997); Ye. I. Holovakha, 'Ukrainske suspilstvo: shliakhy transformatsii.' *Ukrainskyi sotsiolohichnyi zhurnal*, nos. 1-2 (2016); *Sotsialna transformatsiia: kontseptualizatsiia, trendy, ukrainskyi dosvid*, ed. V. V. Tancher and V. P. Stepanenko (Kyiv: Instytut sotsiologii NAN Ukrainy, 2004).

**The first period (1969–1990).** is characterized by the creation of sociological laboratories at universities, sociological groups at some enterprises and research institutes. Formally in 1968, but in reality in 1969, the first scientific sociological department began to work at the Institute of Philosophy of the USSR Academy of Sciences under the leadership of V. Chornovolenko (the Department of Specific Social Research). During this period, the methodological works of Western, Polish, Russian, and later Ukrainian sociologists developed, as well as sociological classics by E. Noel, J. Szczepanski, E. Durkheim, V. Yadov, V. Zdravomyslov, H. Saganenko, B. Grushin, V. Shlyapentokh, Y. Levada, V. Maksymenko, V. Paniotto, V. Khmelko, M. Churilov, and others, who in turn were largely based on the study of Western works. The so-called "hozdogovirni" groups, commercial groups (and analogues of current survey companies), that conducted research at enterprises were widespread. For example, a commercial group of the Department of Specific Social Research of the Institute of Philosophy of the USSR Academy of Sciences conducted research at the portioning machine factory, the Radar (formerly Kommunist) factory, the Southwestern Railway, the Lviv TV factory, etc.[2] This allowed us to gain our own experience. The overwhelming majority of sociological studies were conducted at enterprises and universities, with only a few being representative of Kyiv and perhaps a few other cities with a population of over a million. In terms of content and depth of analysis, theoretical and practical sociological research was often as good as the achievements of sociology in the West (and some theoretical approaches, such as V. Khmelko's on the macrosociological dynamics of societies, were even ahead of the corresponding "discoveries" in the West), but the geography and thematic focus were, unfortunately, severely limited by the Soviet government.

**The second stage (1991–present).** The formation of international standards of sociological surveys in Ukraine began only after the

---

2    V. P. Stepanenko and K. V. Bataieva, eds., *Istoriia ukrainskoi sotsiolohii XIX–XXI* (Kyiv: Instytut sotsiolohii NAN Ukrainy, 2023).

declaration of independence in 1991[3]. However, this was not so much due to Ukraine's independence as to the processes of democratization and the development of a market economy. The transition from imitation elections in the Soviet Union to real elections caused, as it did in the United States, the need for forecasting election results and electoral research. In addition, with the development of the market economy, which also falls within this period, surveys related to marketing research emerged. Democratization and the expansion of international relations, as well as the opportunity for foreign businesses to enter the Ukrainian market, also contributed to the interest in conducting sociological research[4]. Thus, there was a demand for sociological research, a research market emerged, and the first private research companies opened (Kyiv International Institute of Sociology in 1992 and Socis in 1993). With the development of a competitive political system and market, the number of companies grew and now there are more than a hundred of them. Although the quality and integrity of research by a large number of these companies, especially in socio-political surveys, is questionable, a limited number of companies do their job properly[5].

Socis was created on the basis of the Ukrainian branch of the All-Union Public Opinion Research Center (VTsIOM), which was created in 1988. This branch began to conduct social and marketing research, but it was not representative of Ukraine as a whole and was conducted in several localities as part of an all-Union sample. KIIS was founded on the initiative of Valerii Khmelko on the basis of the research center of the Sociological Association of Ukraine in 1990, in June 1990. Khmelko became the director of this center (RNPSC — Republican Scientific and Practical Sociological Center).

---

3    V. Paniotto, 'Rozvytok metodiv sotsiolohichnykh doslidzhen v Instytuti filosifii Akademii nauk URSR (1918-2018),' in *Akademichna sotsiolohiia v Ukraini*, vol. 2 (Kyiv: Instytut sotsiolohii NAN Ukrainy, 2019), pp. 45–54.
4    O. Kutsenko and S. Babenko, 'Suchasna ukrainska sotsiolohiia: syla instytutsii, dyskursu, dii,' in *Istoriia ukrainskoi sotsiolohii XIX–XXI*, ed. V. P. Stepanenko and K. V. Bataieva (Kyiv: Instytut sotsiolohii NAN Ukrainy, 2023), pp. 530–559.
5    In Ukraine, to combat dishonest research, a database called *Ratings Sellers: Database of pseudo-sociologists and hidden PR specialists*. However, the information in the database is not exhaustive, so the problem has become less acute in recent years, but still remains.

In 1992, it was transformed into a private American-Ukrainian joint venture called the Kyiv International Institute of Sociology (KIIS), whose first founders and co-owners were V. Khmelko (1939-2021), V. Paniotto, and American sociologist and political scientist Michael Swafford (1947-2001). Thanks to the cooperation with American sociologists and thanks to Western orders, KIIS conducted the first researches that were representative of Ukraine and contributed to the establishment of standards of sociological research in Ukraine. In 1992, at the invitation of the newly restored Kyiv-Mohyla Academy (founded in 1615, but in the nineteenth century transformed by the tsarist authorities into a theological seminary, which was later liquidated by the Soviet authorities), V. Khmelko and V. Paniotto became professors at this university and founded the Department of Sociology, V. Khmelko became the head of the department, and V. Paniotto became the director of KIIS. KIIS was given premises in the Kyiv-Mohyla Academy and has been cooperating with Mohyla for over 30 years.

The requirements of Western clients revealed the shortcomings of the methodological equipment of Ukrainian sociologists:

- Lack of experience in conducting face-to-face interviews; almost all studies were conducted by questionnaires in the presence of an interviewer, not interviews;
- Lack of survey networks consisting of trained interviewers;
- Lack of standard methods for constructing representative samples;
- Lack of experience in using qualitative methods (primarily focus groups)

Cooperation with Western sociologists and, above all, customers, helped to quickly overcome these shortcomings and set standards for conducting researches that were not inferior to those of the rest of the world. Customers and partners brought the necessary literature and conducted trainings. For KIIS, for example, the key project was a joint international project with the president (at that time) of the American Sociological Association Melvin Kohn[6], the planning of which began in 1989, as well as during V. Paniotto's two month trip to the United States in 1990. The subsequent work of V. Khmelko and V. Paniotto in the United States during a semester and other numerous visits contributed to the development of new methods (e.g., Lizrel analysis). The second important stimulus to the establishment of KIIS as a real research organization was the proposal from the Radio Liberty Research Institute to create with its help an all-Ukrainian survey network that would work by personal interviews and provide data representative of the Ukrainian population. By October 1991, with the help of experienced American sociologists, Michael Haney, Slavko Martyniuk, and Michael Swafford, we had trained interviewers with the necessary qualifications to work in all regions of Ukraine. The first training for interviewers in Ukraine was conducted by Michael Haney from the Radio Liberty Research Center in 1991. The training covered four groups of 12 people, 48 interviewers in total. Slavko Martyniuk, also from the Radio Liberty Research Center, conducted the first focus groups and trained KIIS staff.

It should be noted that these trainings had consequences for the work not only KIIS, but of other companies. For example, one of the participants of these trainings, S. Stukalo, went to work for SOCIS, created a survey network there and prepared a textbook for interviewers (at KIIS, a similar textbook was prepared by D. Krakovych and A. Serdiuk). The separation of USM (later GFK) from SOCIS contributed to the dissemination of interviewing standards. Similarly, V. Paniotto's graduate student who had been trained in conducting focus groups (V. Kurakina) joined SOCIS and contributed to the development of this area in SOCIS. This became the basis for the further development of public opinion polling in

---

6    Melvin Lester Kohn (1928-2021) is a well-known American sociologist, author of classic works on the influence of social structure on personality, president of the American Sociological Association (1986-1988), and professor at Johns Hopkins University. The results of the long-term project are presented in the book: *Sotsialni struktury i osobystist: doslidzhennia Melvina L. Kona i yoho spivpratsivnykiv* (Kyiv: Kyiv-Mohyla Academy Publishing House, 2007).

Ukraine, including the emergence of branches of international organizations such as TNS and GFK, which further contributed to the improvement of national standards in this area.

In the following years (1993-1995), the sample was improved. Michael Swafford received a grant from the National Council for Soviet and East European Research, together with prominent statisticians Leslie Kish and Steven Heeringa, and with our participation and the head of Demoscope, M. Kosolapov, the KIIS sample and recommendations for sampling in post-Soviet countries were developed[7].

There were many interesting and dramatic things in the history of KIIS creation and development, but unfortunately, we did not write a book or even an article telling this story[8]. Instead, our customers and colleagues write about some of the pages of KIIS creation[9].

The first text below is an excerpt from Melvin Kohn's report presented to the annual convention of the American Sociological Association in Pittsburgh, Pennsylvania, on August 24, 1992, on the occasion of Melvin Kohn's being awarded the Cooley-Mead Prize. Kohn's work was a large comparative study that lasted a decade on the impact of social structure on personality. The research was conducted in the United States, Poland, Ukraine, Japan, and China, but this piece is only about the planning of the research in Poland and Ukraine. This research was to be conducted in parallel using the same questionnaire.

---

7     M. Swafford, M. Kosolapov, L. Kish, and S. Heeringa, *Sample Design for Republics of the Former Soviet Union* (Washington, DC: National Council for Soviet and East European Research, 1995).

8     Only a video film "KMIS: Istoriia stvorennia" was made. Part 1. https://www.youtube.com/watch?v=Xb3G50Xe_to&t=225s; Part 2. https://www.youtube.com/watch?v=cRo2ss0h7lM Accessed 10.10.2024

9     *Sotsialni struktury i osobystist*; Melvin L. Kohn, *The Development of a Theory of Social Structure and Personality* (London and New York: Anthem Press, 2019); Jaroslaw Martyniuk, *Monte Rosa: Memoir of an Accidental Spy* (Bloomington: Xlibris Corporation, 2017); R. Eugene Parta, *Under the Radar: Tracking Western Radio Listeners in the Soviet Union* (Budapest: Central European University Press, 2022).

1.    Melvin Kohn, Professor at Johns Hopkins University, President of the American Sociological Association: Conducting social research in the context of radical social change[10]

> If there is a rational basis for this article, other than to make myself forgiven for recounting some of my favorite life episodes, it is this: one can learn a lot about social and psychological phenomena by considering the problems that arise when trying to study these phenomena […].
>
> When I came to Kyiv in June 1990, my goal was to see if it was possible to make Ukrainian studies really real. From there I was going to go to Warsaw and see if there were any prospects for a new Polish study. Officially, I was in Kyiv as a representative of IREX to establish ties with the Ukrainian Academy of Sciences. This official role provided me with a room in a fairly comfortable Communist Party hotel with a guaranteed source of food, which was not easy to obtain in Ukraine even then. My role as an IREX representative also gave me access to Academy of Sciences officials, which allowed me to experience for myself how the Academy operated under the leadership of individuals whose academic and party roles were difficult to distinguish […].
>
> Meanwhile, Ukrainian sociologists created an independent sociological organization, the Sociological Association of Ukraine. Khmelko was elected its first vice president, and Paniotto was elected vice president for international relations. The Association established a research center to be funded by contracts with government organizations and foreign clients. Khmelko was appointed its director, so he got a job, albeit without any guarantees of earnings or permanent employment. Paniotto remained at the Institute of the Academy of Sciences of Ukraine for the time being, but also worked closely with Khmelko in developing the Center […].
>
> For our research — if it takes place — this change has several important implications. Any research we did would no longer be part of a larger study of the party institution. Therefore, we no longer had to squeeze our questions into a prefabricated questionnaire, and I did not have to worry about how party sponsorship might influence people's responses to our questions. However, this also meant that we no longer had a guaranteed source of funding for fieldwork. In addition, and perhaps more importantly, Khmelko and Paniotto now had to build a survey network from the ground up. This is a huge job, but it is also an opportunity to create something that hardly existed in the Soviet Union -a research center that can conduct surveys through personal, face-to-face interviews. The prospect is extremely exciting and at the same time somewhat terrifying […].
>
> …Initially, the Ukrainian study was supposed to be supported by the party institute, but Khmelko left this institute. In any case, this party and its institute ceased to exist. Then it was supposed to be supported by the Union Academy of Sciences. But Yadov's assurance of full financial support turned into symbolic support when Paniotto moved from the Ukrainian Academy

---

10    *Sotsialni struktury i osobystist.*

of Sciences to Kyiv University, and the possibility of funding research by transferring funds from the Soviet Academy to the Ukrainian Academy disappeared. Later, when the Soviet Academy was transformed into the Russian Academy, even symbolic support became impossible. The Ukrainian Academy of Sciences showed no interest in supporting my colleagues. All sources from which we hoped to receive financial support for fieldwork dried up.

However, Khmelko and Paniotto would not be themselves if they were not resourceful. They turned a research center they created into a successful polling organization. The center was a business whose first office was in the corner of Paniotto's bedroom and the second in the corner of Khmelko's living room. Its equipment consisted of a computer bought by Paniotto with money from IREX that he did not need for living expenses when he lived with my wife and me. Despite the lack of material resources, Khmelko and Paniotto conducted surveys for local authorities in Ukraine, for the Radio Liberty Research Institute, for other Western news organizations, and for the United States Information Agency. The field work in Ukraine will be funded to a very large extent by the profits Paniotto and Khmelko have made from conducting surveys for clients. They now also have financial support in the form of a grant from a newly created institution, elegantly named the Commission for Scientific and Technological Progress of the Cabinet of Ministers of Ukraine.[11] However, Khmelko and Paniotto are saving this grant to support a planned and potentially invaluable follow-up survey in a year's time. The client's surveys provided not only the financial resources for our research, but also invaluable experience in conducting surveys. In addition, by a remarkably lucky coincidence, they provided interviewer training by a highly qualified specialist in the person of Michael Haney from the research staff of Radio Liberty […].

We also needed office space in both Warsaw and Kyiv, cozy places to hold meetings, plan, and work. In Warsaw, before we received grants, we used to meet in the apartment of a staff member or in noisy cafes. The Ukrainian colleagues still work in this way (August 1992), except that in Kyiv it is much harder to find even a noisy cafe; we spent a lot of time trying to find a place to meet. The Polish group finally found a room, which was paid for from the overhead of their research grant. Soon the Ukrainian colleagues were to get an office as well. Finally, they found satisfactory office space for their research center at the Department of Sociology at the Kyiv-Mohyla Academy, where they were both appointed professors. This Academy is a medieval university that was closed in 1817 by the Russian Czar and later turned by the Communist regime into a higher school to train political workers for the Soviet Navy, and now it is again what I like to think of as a new medieval university. Amidst the institutional disarray, some things are going quite well […].

---

11    There is some inaccuracy in the author's notes here. The institution that gave the grant to support the Ukrainian research at that time (until April 1992) had a slightly different name: the Committee on Scientific and Technical Progress under the Cabinet of Ministers

We have also seen the beginning of the process of transformation of existing research institutions. A prime example is the Polish Academy of Sciences, which is making a concerted effort to reorganize itself to meet new and difficult challenges. Perhaps the most radical innovation we have seen is the revival of the Kyiv-Mohyla Academy in Ukraine. Rebuilt on a model never before seen in the former Soviet Union, this university combines teaching and research. Moreover, it has no ties to the previous regime.

2.    From the book by Gene Parta, director of Soviet Area Audience Research at Radio Free Europe/Radio Liberty (RFE/RL)[12]

Irene McKeegan from IVM Joint National Consultant was waiting for me in the hotel lobby [...]. She contacted two well-known Ukrainian sociologists on my behalf, Prof. Valerii Khmelko and Prof. Volodymyr Paniotto, who headed the Research Institute of the Ukrainian Sociological Association. Iryna met Paniotto in 1989, when he spent two months in Colombia. They were supposed to meet us for dinner that evening. Paniotto turned out to be the spitting image of Lenin. It was hard for me to hide my surprise when Irina introduced us. Despite being in the United States, his English was still shaky, so we spoke in Russian. Given that the hotel restaurant was in party mode, with an orchestra playing, couples dancing, and people at the next table treating us to sweet champagne, the introduction session was not easy. Still, I had a good first impression of both men and was confident that we could establish a strong working relationship [...]. The next day at their office, we got down to business. We decided to conduct a pilot survey with a sample of 1000 respondents. We planned to use the three methods that had been tested in Moscow, as well as try two others: direct mail and handing the questionnaire to the respondent in person to return by mail. The latter was the most common Soviet method. The results of the test would suggest which methods would work best for the larger study. This meeting was the beginning of a long and fruitful cooperation.
Volodia Paniotto and I became good friends and met regularly at ESOMAR[13] conferences over the next twenty years. He and Khmelko founded their own organization, the Kyiv International Institute of Sociology (KIIS), which became popular in November 2004. The KIIS exit polls showed that the second round of elections, which showed Yanukovych's victory over Yushchenko, was riddled with fraud. It was the spark that ignited the Orange Revolution. The Kyiv International Institute of Sociology has been widely cited in the

---

12    R. Eugene Parta, *Under the Radar: Tracking Western Radio Listeners in the Soviet Union* (Budapest: Central European University Press, 2022).

13    ESOMAR stands for the European Society for Opinion and Marketing Research. It is an international organization that brings together professionals in market research, social research, and data analytics, providing standards and ethical guidelines for the industry.

Western press for its excellent reports on Ukrainian public opinion since the Russian invasion of February 24, 2022.

Our research almost fell victim to a brutal attack when Soviet television broadcast the attack on Radio Liberty in March 1991. The main TV channel aired a movie called "Strangers' Voices" ("Vrazhdebnye golosa"), created by the KGB, and clearly labeled as such. The film was a direct attack on Radio Liberty and was mainly based on the statements of traitor Oleg Tumanov. SAAOR[14] was singled out for attack. Photos of me and Charlie Allen were shown, and our activities were condemned as an intelligence operation. The SAAOR questionnaire was analyzed on the screen and it was emphasized that while it may look like an innocent document, it was actually designed to gather intelligence.

The film was shown across the country on a Sunday evening, the best time to reach the maximum audience. I was in Warsaw when it was broadcast, and Michael Haney was in Kyiv, preparing to conduct a training for interviewers. His luggage included a fax machine, which the institute considered its "window to the world." But when the directors of the institute, Paniotto and Khmelko, saw "Strangers' Voices", they were deeply shocked. If the KGB is attacking us on television, is it wise to continue research? Paniotto's mother, who had lived through the Stalinist era, was particularly nervous [...].

The group that gathered for the Monday morning training session consisted mostly of graduate students from the university. Before the meeting, Paniotto and Khmelko told Michael that they intended to cancel the project. But when the three of them walked into the meeting room, the students stood up and burst into applause. They had seen the movie, and they insisted that the research should continue. They said that if the KGB had attacked SAAOR, the research must be important, and they wanted to be a part of it. Paniotto and Khmelko had to give in[15]. Michael held a study session and further study was scheduled. There were no consequences. The episode made it clear that the atmosphere of fear that had long pervaded the Soviet Union still lingered among the elderly, but the younger, educated generation that had grown up during perestroika was no longer in its thrall.

---

14   SAAOR—Soviet Area Audience and Opinion Research department, a department of the Radio Liberty Research Institute, which commissioned our research.

15   "Forced" ... We discussed it for a long time the day before and decided to continue, but to warn future interviewers about the risks, so that only those who are willing to take risks with us would stay. (V. P.)

3.   From the book by Slavko Martyniuk, researcher at Radio Liberty SAAOR[16]

> We launched a nationwide survey in Ukraine in October 1991, and by the end of the month we had preliminary data[17]. The results were shocking. They showed that 88 percent of the 32 million Ukrainian citizens who would vote said they would say yes to independence in a referendum. Many well-informed people at Radio Liberty found these findings unbelievable and I was tasked with investigating what could have gone wrong with this poll. After all, it was the first poll of its kind in Ukraine. Personally, I was confident that the results were quite accurate. I traveled to Ukraine to personally supervise and observe the fieldwork to make sure that the interviewers were properly trained and followed the selection and procedures developed by the Sociological Association of Ukraine. I found no errors in selecting or conducting the survey. The only thing left to do was to wait and see what the referendum results would show.
>
> On December 5, the results of the referendum were announced and, to the surprise of everyone at Radio Liberty, 90.3 percent of Ukrainians voted for independence. Still, some thought it might be a fluke. So the next step for me was to look at the results by geographic region (oblast) and demographic category. What I found was that, with the exception of Crimea and some regions in eastern Ukraine, our poll results closely matched the referendum results. Crimea was a strange case because it was the only region with a majority Russian population, but even there 54 percent voted for independence. The Center of the Sociological Association of Ukraine showed that they were competent sociologists and it was the beginning of a fruitful and grateful twenty-year relationship. Time passed and they proved to be reliable and trustworthy again and again. The following year they moved to the Kyiv-Mohyla Academy under the name of the Kyiv International Institute of Sociology.

The center created by Khmelko and Paniotto has been operating since 1990, and since 1992 it has been called the Kyiv International Institute of Sociology (KIIS). During this time, KIIS has conducted several thousand studies (before the war, it was conducting about 150 projects a year) and had several thousand clients. Among the clients are international organizations (United Nations, World Bank, USAID, DFID, ETF, IFES, IFC, TACIS, WHO and others), universities (e.g., Cambridge University (UK), The Duke University

---

16   Jaroslaw Martyniuk, *Monte Rosa: Memoir of an Accidental Spy* (Bloomington: Xlibris Corporation, 2017).

17   Radio Liberty commissioned us to do this survey, Michael Haney and Slavko Martyniuk trained interviewers from our center (which we named KIIS the following year) and supervised the survey.

(USA), The Indiana University (USA), The Johns Hopkins University (USA), London School of Economics and Political Studies (UK), The McGill University (Canada), Stony Brook University (USA) and others), ministries (Ministry of Education and Science, Ministry of Foreign Affairs, Ministry of Health, Ministry of Social Policy, etc.), media (BBC, Deutsche Welle, VOA, Radio Liberty, Inter TV Channel, ICTV, newspaper Dzerkalo Tyzhnya, etc.), commercial companies (Coca-Cola, Foyil Financial, KENSU, Kraft Foods, Kyivstar, McDonald's, Motorola, Nestle, Procter & Gamble, Raiffeisen Bank Aval, Safege, Sanofi-Aventis, Svitoch, System Capital Management and others), political parties (almost all major political parties have commissioned our research), embassies, foundations, NGOs, etc.

KIIS also founded (together with the Center for Social Indicators) and supports the National Data Bank "Kyiv Archive" and regularly submits its research to it, readers who are interested in them or other surveys can get the data set for analysis[18]. KIIS (Kyiv Archive) also submits its data to CESSDA (the Consortium of European Social Science Data Archives) and the Discuss Data project[19].

In addition to its own research, we also use the Monitoring of Social Changes in Ukrainian Society, an annual public opinion poll conducted by the Institute of Sociology of the National Academy of Sciences of Ukraine (Kyiv). This project, launched in 1992 by Natalia Panina and Yevgen Golovakha, received the State Prize of Ukraine in Science and Technology in 2014. The last two waves of this monitoring were conducted by KIIS. In addition, we used data from the Razumkov Center, the Sociological Group "Rating" and the Info Sapience Center, and some other centers.

We do not provide an overview of what you will learn from the book here, but we have made a fairly detailed table of contents that gives you an idea of what aspects of social life are described in the book and how they changed during the war.

---

18    Data Bank. 2024. survey-archive.com. Accessed August 16.
19    Discuss Data. 2024. https://discuss-data.net. Accessed August 16.

# 2. Research Methodology
## Problems of Conducting Surveys During War

## 2.1. Research methodology

In this book, we mainly use our own data, i.e. data from the Kyiv International Institute of Sociology (KIIS), obtained in surveys conducted from 1991 to 2023. Where data from other sociological centers are used, the relevant references are provided. Most of the studies we refer to were conducted using face-to-face interviews and telephone surveys. In this section, we describe the methodology of these two methods. Studies conducted by other methods (online surveys, focus groups, etc.) are described where we refer to them.

### 2.1.1. Four periods in the methodology of conducting surveys in Ukraine

There are three critical turning points for the survey methodology in Ukraine: March 2014, March 2020 and February 24, 2022. Accordingly, we can distinguish four periods that differ in terms of data collection methods and population, so studying the dynamics of certain indicators and comparing data from different periods requires taking these factors into account.

**Period 1. 1991–March 2014.** Classical period, data are representative for the entire territory of Ukraine, the main survey method is face-to-face (F2F, face-to-face or personal) interviews.

**Period 2. March 2014–March 2020.** In March 2014, the Russian Federation occupied Crimea and in the following months actually occupied certain districts of Donetsk and Luhansk regions (in Ukraine, the occupied part was called ORDLO, and unrecognized republics were created there, the so-called DPR and LPR). Although Ukraine, like almost all other countries, continued to consider these territories Ukrainian, polls were hardly ever conducted there. First of all, this was due to security issues that made it impossible to conduct high-quality surveys where interviewers could safely select respondents and the latter could answer our questions sincerely. Therefore, the data from this period is representative only for the population living in the territory controlled by Ukraine, but the main survey method remained the same: face-to-face interviews.

**Period 3. March 2020–February 24, 2022**. Until 2020, almost all surveys in Ukraine were conducted by face-to-face interviews (first using paper questionnaires, and then using tablets and CAPI (computer assisted personal interview)). At the beginning of 2020, due to the covid epidemic in Ukraine, sociologists switched mainly to computer-assisted telephone interviews (CATI), although after the epidemic subsided, a significant part of the research was also conducted by face-to-face interviews. After the outbreak of full-scale war on February 24, 2022, the use of CATI became even more relevant. The data for this period are representative only for the population living in the territory controlled by Ukraine until February 24, 2022, i.e. without ORDLO and Crimea. The main survey method is CATI (with a significant representation of personal interviews).

**Period 4. February 24, 2022–to the present** (as we finish this book, it is December 2023). The territories occupied in 2014 were supplemented by the territories occupied by Russia after February 24, 2022. In addition, about a third of the population has changed their place of residence, and the number of Ukrainian refugees is estimated by the UN to be 6-8 million (more information in the next section). Theoretically, we could survey refugees as well, but it is difficult and expensive, so most surveys are representative, first, only of the population living on the territory of Ukraine (if we use the terminology of the resident and the current population, we are talking only about the current population), and second, mainly in the territories controlled by Ukraine (more details in the next paragraph). The main survey method is CATI (with fewer face-to-face interviews than before).

Table 2.1 summarizes the characteristics of these periods.

**Table 2.1.  Periods of surveys in Ukraine**

| Period | The general population is the population of the territories: | Main survey method |
|---|---|---|
| Period 1. (1991 – March 2014) | The entire territory of Ukraine | Face-to-face interviews |
| Period 2. (March 2014 – March 2020) | Ukraine without Crimea and ORDLO | Face-to-face interviews |
| Period 3. March 2020 – February 24, 2022 | Ukraine without Crimea and ORDLO | CATI (with a significant representation of face-to-face interviews) |
| Period 4. After February 24, 2022 | Part of the territory controlled by Ukraine (without refugees) | CATI |

Studying changes in Ukraine, including changes related to the war, requires taking into account the periods when the surveys were conducted. How can this be taken into account?

First, we need to take into account changes in the population. If we want to compare two indicators from different periods, we need to see if these indicators are representative of the same population.

Consider the following example. We are interested in whether people's views on Ukraine's accession to the EU have changed. We see that in 2013, the support for joining the EU was 37%, and in 2016 it was 46%, which is an increase of 9 percentage points. If we were interested in this issue, for example, to assess the possible results of the referendum, then the issue of changes in the territories is irrelevant. If we are interested in changes in people's views, changes in "their heads," then we do not know whether they have occurred or not — it is possible that these 9.1% changes are only due to the fact that the territory has changed and that we do not conduct surveys in the least EU-oriented parts of Ukraine, i.e. in Crimea and ORDLO. One way to assess changes in people's views is to remove from the 2013 data the population of the territories that we did not survey in 2016, then the territories will be the same and we will be sure that all changes have occurred not due to changes in territory, but due to changes in views. It is difficult to remove certain regions of Donetsk and Luhansk oblasts from the 2013 data, so we will remove Donetsk and Luhansk oblasts as a whole (these two oblasts are often called Donbas). We will do the same in 2016. As we can see from Graph 2.1, the changes were 5.7%. It turns out that out of the 9% of changes, about 6% occurred "in people's minds," and 3% were due to changes in the territories.

**Graph 2.1. "What direction should Ukraine follow in its foreign policy?"** (*% of who believe that Ukraine should join the EU)*

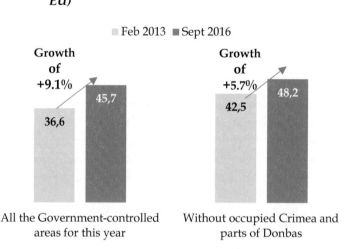

All the Government-controlled areas for this year

Without occupied Crimea and parts of Donbas

Second, we need to take into account changes **in survey methods.** How significant can the changes in the results of the study be if we use telephone interviews (CATI) instead of face-to-face interviews? Face-to-face interviews theoretically cover the entire population, but in fact they exclude those in institutional settings (hospitals, prisons, military units, etc.), as well as hard-to-reach categories, especially those from the most affluent strata of the population. Telephone interviews can reach these categories of the population as well, but do not cover the approximately 4% of respondents who do not have phones (according to the KIIS survey in July 2021). In addition, during face-to-face interviews, respondents are shown cards with a list of alternatives (for example, to determine the rating of parties, the respondent is usually shown a ballot card). In telephone interviews, the list of parties is read out and the respondent has to choose one of the parties he or she has heard about. The demographic profiles of respondents also differ. There are other features of each method that can potentially affect the results.

In the first half of December 2020, the Kyiv International Institute of Sociology, together with the Democratic Initiatives Foundation, conducted an experiment to compare party ratings obtained through personal interviews (conducted by KIIS at the request of the Foundation) and telephone interviews (KIIS's own research, Omnibus). Both surveys had the same sample size (2000 respondents each), used the same question wording and the same list of parties. The only difference is that the survey for the Democratic Initiatives Foundation was conducted by personal interviews based on random sampling at the first stages of selection with quota selection at the last stage. The KIIS survey was based on the main samples of random generation of mobile numbers (i.e., randomly generated mobile numbers, not selected from a specific database) without additional quotas, with a focus on surveying people aged 18 and older and residing in Ukraine. In Luhansk and Donetsk oblasts, the survey was conducted only on the territory controlled by the Ukrainian authorities.

Before comparing the actual ratings of the parties, the demographic profile of the respondents in both samples is compared below. For the personal interview sample, the assignment for each region, urban/rural population, gender, and age was determined in advance. The sample of the telephone survey was completely random, and after receiving the results, factors such as the participant's region, type of settlement, gender and age were brought into line with the statistics by statistical weighting. Therefore, the two samples are very close in terms of region, type of settlement, gender and age of respondents. However, more important are the differences in other characteristics, such as education and income (Table 2.2).

**Table 2.2.** Comparison of the profiles of respondents of surveys conducted by personal and telephone interviews, % (December 2020)

| | Personal interviews, DI | Telephone interviews, KIIS | The difference |
|---|---|---|---|
| **Education** | | | |
| Not higher than | 65.7 | 53.5 | +12.3 |
| Higher | 34.1 | 44.5 | -10.4 |
| Hard to say / Refusal | 0.2 | 2.1 | -1.9 |
| Total | 100.0 | 100.0 | 100.0 |
| **Financial situation of the family** | | | |
| We don't even have enough money for food | 11.7 | 7.5 | +4.2 |
| We have enough money for food, but it's hard to buy clothes | 43.7 | 35.6 | +8.1 |
| We have enough money for food and clothes, and we can save some money, but it is not enough to buy expensive things (such as a TV or refrigerator) | 35.8 | 33.2 | +2.5 |
| We can afford to buy some expensive things (such as a TV or refrigerator) | 5.5 | 16.2 | -10.7 |
| We can afford everything we want | 0.5 | 2.9 | -2.3 |
| Hard to say | 2.7 | 4.5 | -1.7 |
| Total | 100.0 | 100.0 | 100.0 |

As can be seen, respondents who participated in the telephone surveys are more educated (44.5% have higher education versus 34% in the case of respondents who took part in the survey by personal interviews) and more affluent, with 12.3% (8.1+4.2%) fewer of them lacking money for food or clothing and 10.7% more of them able to buy expensive items. Although these factors are not decisive or very strong, they are still related to political choice, so these differences in the sample affect the rating and other results of the study.

For example, P. Poroshenko's party (President of Ukraine in 2014-2019) "European Solidarity" has more educated voters, so the party received 9.5% in the study using personal interviews, and 11.9% in the study using CATI, which is 2.4% more percentage points. On the contrary, the OPFL party received less in the telephone survey, although it was within the sampling error. We do not know which method is more accurate, because no census has been conducted for 20 years and the percentage of people with higher education in the general population is unknown. In 2019, the results of the face-to-face (F2F) survey were closer to the election results than the results of the telephone survey, but the results of the telephone surveys have proven to be good. After the outbreak of the Covid epidemic, and even more so after the start of the full-scale invasion, the situation could have changed significantly, so in a situation of various limitations (for example, territorial accessibility for personal interviews given the shelling and regular air raids), it is difficult to say which method is currently preferable. In any case, our experience shows that both methods allow us to obtain high-quality information that represents the mood of the population.

### 2.1.2. Methodology for conducting personal (F2F) interviews

**Sampling.** To conduct the survey using the method of face-to-face (F2F) interviews, we used a stratified multistage sampling. This sampling procedure was developed with the participation of well-known American experts Leslie Kish[20] and Stephen Heeringa[21]. KIIS co-owner Michael Swafford received a grant to develop sampling guidelines for the former Soviet Union and we worked in a team with American statisticians[22]. Although some approaches to sampling have been modified and modernized since the early 1990s, the overall approach remains unchanged. Depending on the object and subject of the research, the sample design may vary (for example, additional "booster" interviews may be conducted for a

---

20  Leslie Kish (1910-2000) was a prominent American statistician, author of the classic work *Survey Sampling*.
21  Steven G. Heeringa is a renowned statistician and a research fellow at the University of Michigan's Institute for Social Research.
22  Swafford et al., *Sample Design for Republics of the Former Soviet Union*.

more detailed study of the population of specific territories or certain categories of Ukrainians). Below is a description of a typical nationally representative sample used by KIIS.

Our sampling begins with the stratification of the territory of Ukraine by region and type of settlement (city, urban-type settlement or village). For each stratum, the sampling task is determined proportionally to the population size to consider how many primary sampling units (PSUs) and how many interviews need to be conducted. In recent years, KIIS has proportionally distributed the PSU tasks, and then the number of interviews conducted at each point is the same (usually eight to ten interviews need to be conducted at each point, so for a sample of 2000 respondents, we select 200-250 primary sampling points).

Next, we move on to the selection of the primary sampling units (PSUs). Until the 2010s, our sample was predominantly four-stage, and we first selected settlements (in urban strata, cities and urban-type settlements, and in rural strata, rural districts) as PSUs (and then selected post offices or polling stations within the settlement). When more reliable databases of polling stations became available, we started using polling stations, and our sampling frame consists of all regular polling stations (excluding specialized stations like hospitals, prisons, etc.) based on the results of the last national elections. The last national elections were in 2019 (parliamentary elections), and our frame includes 28,621 regular polling stations in all territories controlled by the Government of Ukraine at that time. For each polling station, we know its region, administrative-territorial unit, settlement name, a complete list of boundaries (streets and houses), the number of voters, as well as the election results (which parties the voters at this polling station voted for).

Currently, our sample is a random three-stage sample. At the first stage, the required number of PSUs is selected from all PSUs of the stratum with a probability proportional to size (PPS). KIIS has developed software in R to perform the appropriate selection. At the second stage, a starting address (street, house, and for apartment buildings, also a specific apartment) is randomly selected with equal probability within each selected polling station (PSU).

At the third stage, the interviewer, starting from the initial address, selects households and respondents within them according to the developed schemes. All data on the selection of households and respondents are recorded in "interviewer diaries" (we currently use AAPOR coding).

KIIS uses various methods for selecting respondents within households. In particular, V. Paniotto and V. Khmelko developed a special procedure for selecting respondents. For example, the use of the so-called "Kish tables" (where a list of all members is made in each household and one of them is selected according to a certain principle) for selecting respondents may lead to biases, as only one respondent is interviewed in each apartment/house. In this case, the smaller the family, the more chances to be included in the sample, from families with one person, this person is included in the sample with a probability of one, where there are two people, the probability of selection of each is 0.5, etc., that is, the sample is shifted towards single people (these are primarily elderly women). To compensate for this shift, we developed a special procedure. The interviewer compiles a single list of respondents and interviews every third person along the chain. In this case, it turns out that in some households with one person and two people, the survey is not conducted, self-weighting occurs, and the probability of being included in the sample of household members with different numbers of members is the same.[23]

At the same time, KIIS applies both modified versions of "Kish tables" and the "last birthday" selection method (the problem described in the previous paragraph is then taken into account at the stage of statistical processing). In addition, KIIS has experience in applying more complex approaches. For example, in studies for WHO (Global Adult Tobacco Survey — GATS) or for the Industrial

---

23   V. Paniotto: I think in 1993 there was a meeting of the working group to develop recommendations on sample design for the CIS countries, and I was very proud of our method and told Leslie Kish about our invention. Leslie Kish said, "Yes, this is a good method, I described it in 1947, I have an article on it. It eliminates the need to reweight the array by the number of household members, but it lengthens the chain for the interviewer." I remember the year very well because it is the year of my birth. It turns out that 35 years after Leslie Kish, we have reinvented the wheel (but it's a convenient one, it reduces the sampling error).

Television Committee (Establishment Survey for forming the TV panel), after selecting polling stations, KIIS conducts enumeration, i.e., making a list of all households. Then a random selection of specific addresses that the interviewer has to visit is made.

It is worth mentioning the response rate separately. In the 1990s, it reached 90%, but then for various reasons, the rate decreased, and on the eve of the invasion in 2022, the response rate was about 30% (face-to-face surveys conducted in 2022–2023 showed that the rate only slightly decreased). However, despite the decrease in response rate, the results of KIIS pre-election surveys, for example, quite accurately reflected public sentiment. That is, although the decrease in response rate affects the accuracy of the results, the data still maintain high representativeness.

**Data Collection Method**: All our studies until 2005 were conducted using paper questionnaires, and since 2005 we have increasingly begun to use paperless surveys — computer-assisted personal interviews (CAPI). In recent years, almost all KIIS studies are conducted paperlessly (initially, we used laptops, pocket personal computers, and now tablets). We primarily use our own software (OSA CAPI), as well as ODK Collect software (and in certain projects specialized client software). The software used by KIIS allows for various randomizations (different orders of reading questions, answer options in questions, etc.) and conducting experiments, such as conjoint analysis or applying factorial design (and a number of our partners have actively used this feature in recent years).

**Survey Instrument and Pretesting**: KIIS conducts surveys in Ukrainian or Russian, at the respondent's choice. To ensure the interviewer does not influence the respondent's choice, we have developed and adhere to a special procedure. The interviewer greets the respondent with "dobryi den" or "dobryi vechir," which sounds similar in both Ukrainian and Russian. Then he asks the question in the language in which the respondent answered. If in Ukrainian, he first says in Ukrainian "Please tell me if it is easier for you to speak Ukrainian" and then switches to Russian and says the second part of the phrase in Russian "or maybe it is easier for you to speak Russian?". If the respondent says that he/she doesn't care, the interviewer asks which language he/she speaks more often at home. In complex projects or for new or specific questions, a pretest of 30-40 interviews is conducted before the fieldwork stage, and the questionnaire is refined based on the results. In some cases, cognitive interviews are conducted to test the survey instruments.

**Interviewers:** The KIIS interviewer network includes a team in each region of Ukraine (in some regions we have two or even more teams) with a total of over 300 interviewers. This allows us to conduct representative surveys both in Ukraine as a whole and in individual regions. All interviewers undergo specialized training, which includes several stages. Interviewers receive basic training as well as specific briefings and project-specific training for each project. For large-scale studies, KIIS organizes off-site sessions and intensive multi-day training programs.

**Quality Control:** We apply a multi-stage quality control system, which includes careful selection and training of interviewers, providing interviewers with detailed instructions, close supervision of data collection, reviewing field documentation of interviewers, recontacting selected respondents by an independent control department, and conducting special data checks to ensure logical consistency of respondents' answers. The use of tablets (CAPI) allows us to use GPS for control (to verify if the interviewer was in the correct location) and random recording of interview segments.

Typical control currently includes 100% verification of field documentation, GPS, and available audio recordings, as well as 100% verification of questionnaires for logical consistency. Additionally, at least 30% of interviews are selected for control through repeat visits or phone calls. In each project, the work of all interviewers is effectively covered by control measures.

### 2.1.3. Telephone interview methodology (CAPI)

Until 2017-2018, telephone surveys were not very common. We used a combination of mobile and landline phone surveys (dual frame method), which reduced sampling error. The fact is that among young people, the percentage of mobile phone users was very high, while among people over 60 years old, it was low, and with landline phones, the situation was the opposite, so the methods complemented each other. However, starting in 2012, according to the State Statistics Service, the percentage of those who had a landline phone began to decline, and our studies confirmed this. According to KIIS data, after 2018, less than 10% of the population had a landline phone, making its use unprofitable (see Table 2.3).

**Table 2.3. Decrease in the percentage of landline telephones in Ukraine, %**

|  | 2011 | 2018 | 2019 | 2020 |
|---|---|---|---|---|
| Personal mobile phone | 37 | 79 | 86 | 90 |
| Both mobile and landline phones | 41 | 11 | 8 | 6 |
| Only landline phone | 12 | 4 | 1 | 1 |
| None | 10 | 6 | 4 | 3 |
| Total | 100 | 100 | 100 | 100 |
| *Have a landline phone* | *53* | *15* | *9* | *7* |
| *Have a mobile phone* | *78* | *90* | *94* | *96* |

Thus, all telephone surveys since 2019 have been conducted using computer-assisted telephone interviews (CATI) exclusively via mobile phones. According to a KIIS survey conducted using face-to-face interviews with a random sample in July 2021, 96% of adult residents of Ukraine had personal mobile phones. Obviously, the coverage of mobile numbers continues to increase, so we only have a very small segment of the population that cannot be reached by telephone surveys.

**Sample:** For conducting telephone surveys, mobile phone numbers for all major mobile operators in Ukraine are generated entirely randomly at the initial stage (each operator has several different "prefixes", i.e. the first three digits of the number; phone numbers are generated for each "prefix"). The proportion of generated numbers for each mobile operator/"prefix" is approximately proportional to the share of total mobile numbers for each mobile operator/"prefix" (according to KIIS surveys). Phones are generated using specially developed KIIS software in R.

When generating numbers randomly, an important organizational issue arises: invalid numbers. To eliminate invalid numbers from the generated database, an "invisible" SMS is sent to the generated numbers, allowing us to determine whether the phone number is valid or not. Then, interviewers call the generated numbers and invite respondents who answered the call to participate in the survey. Usually, the survey is conducted only with respondents aged 18 and older who reside in the territory controlled by the Government of Ukraine. The response rate (as defined by AAPOR) before the invasion was 10-15%, and after it decreased to 8-12% (the cooperation rate, which is often more relevant for telephone surveys, decreased from 20-25% to 15-20%), although the available data suggest that the data maintain high representativeness.

Telephone survey datasets are subject to statistical weighting. Usually, weighting includes accounting for the probability of being included in the sample (a person with three different phone numbers has three times the probability of being included in the sample, compared to a person with only one phone number), as well as correcting for macro-region, type of settlement, gender, and age. For some more complex studies, the construction of weights is more complex, and for some, calibration is applied. For telephone surveys, the design effect is currently 1.2-1.3, so for a sample of 2000 respondents, the maximum error (at a 95% confidence level) is 2.6-2.9%.

**Data Collection Method**: For all telephone surveys, specific software is used, primarily our own (OSA CATI), which has the same wide functionality as the software for face-to-face interviews. Interviewers read the question wording from the screen and immediately record the received answer. Although KIIS also has a call center, due initially to the COVID pandemic and then after the full-scale invasion, interviewers predominantly work from home. KIIS software allows effective monitoring of the interviewer's work, even when interviews are conducted from home.

**Survey Instrument and Pretesting**: Questionnaires are programmed in Ukrainian and Russian. Interviews are conducted in

Ukrainian or Russian at the respondent's choice (using the same special procedure as described earlier for face-to-face interviews). In complex projects or for new or specific questions, a pretest of 30-40 interviews is also conducted before the field stage, and the questionnaire is refined based on the results. KIIS also has experience testing telephone interviews using cognitive interviewing methods.

**Interviewers:** The KIIS network for telephone surveys includes about 150-200 interviewers. All interviewers undergo specialized training, which includes several stages. Interviewers receive basic training as well as specific briefings and project-specific training for each project. For large-scale studies, KIIS organizes special sessions and intensive multi-day training programs.

**Quality Control:** As with face-to-face interviews, a multi-stage quality control system is applied. Control includes careful selection and training of interviewers, providing interviewers with detailed instructions, close supervision of data collection, listening to audio recordings of interviews, analyzing the response rate for each interviewer and the responses of "their" respondents, and conducting special data checks to ensure logical consistency of respondents' answers.

Currently, typical control includes selecting at least 30% of interviews for listening, as well as checking the response rate for each interviewer and the responses of "their" respondents (compared to all others). In each project, the work of all interviewers is effectively covered by control measures.

## 2.2. Problems of conducting a survey during the war

The question of whether it makes sense to conduct sociological surveys during a war is debatable. For example, Oleksandr Etkind, a psychologist and cultural expert, a researcher at the European Institute of International Law and International Relations, believes that

> [s]ociological surveys during war and open violence, internal and external, are meaningless and even harmful. Sociology is for peacetime, when there

are laws, institutions, personal security, and human rights. Sociology is historically linked to all of this and simply does not exist without it. So we can forget about polls now.[24]

This statement, however, referred mainly to polls conducted in Russia, and we, as the heads of a sociological center (KIIS) that conducts polls in Ukraine, will talk mainly about conducting polls in Ukraine. There are indeed many problems with conducting polls during the war. These include financial problems (almost all customers abandoned their projects and sociological companies did not work in Ukraine in the first months after the war began), personnel problems (due to mobilization and emigration), and technical problems (lack of electricity and internet due to missile and drone attacks). But here we will only consider methodological problems related to the war.

The main method of surveys in wartime is computer-assisted telephone interviews (CATI). The main two questions are whether we can call our data representative (whether we are interviewing all categories of the population in proportion to their size) and whether we can trust the answers of those we interview (the problem of sincerity of answers).

### 2.2.1. Problems with the representativeness of surveys

1.  Representativeness of polls during the war (coverage or frame error).

As of December 5, 2022, there were about 7.9 million refugees from Ukraine in Europe alone (although Ukrainian demographers consider this figure to be an overestimate), and according to later estimates, there were only 6.3 million refugees abroad in Ukraine as of December 19, 2023 (Ukraine Situation Flash Update #62 (December 27, 2023). According to the 11th rapid assessment of the IOM Report on Internal Displacement in Ukraine, more than 5.9 million people

---

24   'Sotsiolohiia pod dulom avtomata.' *Radio Svoboda*, March 25, 2022. https://www.svoboda.org/a/sotsiologiya-pod-dulom-avtomata-chto-dumayut-lyudi-o-voyne/31769858.html.

were displaced by the war in Ukraine[25], now (62nd rapid assessment) this figure is estimated at 3.6 million. Part of the population is in the occupied territory and part has left or has been taken to the Russian Federation (the number of people in the Russian Federation is estimated at about 2 million). Thus, the war has caused problems with surveying the following categories of the population:

1) The main group is the population that has not changed their place of residence after the outbreak of the war and is available for the survey;

2) Combatants (combatants) — approximately 2% (although they are partially available);

3) Population in the area of active hostilities on the contact line, partially accessible (1-2% of the population)

4) Refugees who have left Ukraine. We can survey them (find their new phone numbers through social networks of friends and relatives who stayed in Ukraine), but it is both expensive and irrelevant for many surveys (for example, we cannot ask them "Are you ready for possible power outages?" or "Do you agree to territorial concessions to stop the shelling?"). They are not included in our general population (but it makes sense to survey them as a separate group)

5) Internally displaced persons (IDPs) — they are fully accessible for telephone surveys.

6) Newly occupied — the population of the occupied (after February 24, 2022) territories: at the beginning of the war, they could still be interviewed, but later the occupiers disconnected Ukrainian mobile operators (3-5%)

7) Old occupied — people living in the territories occupied earlier in 2014 (Crimea and parts of Luhansk and Donetsk regions); they were not included in our general population even before the full-scale war.

---

25   'Ukraine Situation Flash Update #37 (16 December 2022).' Ukraine: ReliefWeb.

Thus, the polling data in Ukraine are representative of 91-94% of the population currently living in Ukraine. An additional systematic error of representativeness during the war can be estimated using formula (1):

$$E \text{ (error)} = (p1\text{-}p2)*IT* \, 0.01 \, (1),$$

where p1 is the percentage of this characteristic for the population of accessible areas

p2 — percentage of this characteristic for the population of inaccessible areas

IT — (inaccessible territory) percentage of the population living in areas inaccessible to the survey

Of course, we do not know p2, but sometimes we can roughly estimate the difference (p1-p2) based on pre-war data. For example, if p1-p2=20%, and we are unable to survey 7% of the population of Ukraine, then the additional representativeness error E(error)= 20%*7%*0.01=1.4%. We can see that even if the difference is quite large, 20%, but the percentage of inaccessible population is small, the additional error is no more than 1.5-2%.

## 2.2.2. Problems with the reliability of surveys

The two factors that have the greatest impact on the sincerity of respondents are administrative pressure (fear of persecution for expressing an opinion) and the so-called "spiral of silence" described by Elizabeth Noel, whereby people are not inclined to express their opinions if they feel they are in the minority.

Before the war, our population was very critical of the authorities and did not fear administrative pressure, and the results of polls very closely coincided with the election results. For example, in the first round of the last presidential election in 2019, in a poll conducted by KIIS two weeks before the election, the maximum difference from the results was only 2.6%.[26] Since the beginning of the

---

26  'Comparison of Pre-Election Polls and Exit-Polls with Election Results: President of Ukraine, 2019,' KIIS, accessed October 10, 2024, https://kiis.com.ua/ ?lang=eng&cat=reports&id=849&page=9.

war, the legislation has changed little, so we believe that the population is not afraid of administrative pressure. In particular, we ask whether potential respondents feel safe to answer the questionnaire. Usually, only a few people refused because of this.

As for the Elizabeth Noel effect, it existed before the war. For example, during the 2010 presidential election, in the western regions of Ukraine, which were predominantly supportive of Yulia Tymoshenko, Viktor Yanukovych's rating in our polls was lower than during the election, and in the eastern regions, where Yanukovych's support was dominant, our polls underestimated Tymoshenko's rating compared to the election results. With the outbreak of the war, this effect was expected to increase significantly, as the unity of opinion on some issues increased, withsupport for certain opinions reaching 70-90%. Sociologists have various methods for assessing the sincerity of answers and ways to reduce the insincerity of respondents, which we used in our surveys. Let's look at some of them:

**The percentage of those who responded** (response rate, cooperation rate). If the insincerity of answers has increased since the beginning of the war and some respondents refuse to answer, then the percentage of those who responded should have decreased. This did not happen in the first year of the invasion, although later on, indeed, fewer people agreed to be interviewed. However, we believe that this decrease is due to other factors (such as a generally higher psychological stress due to the difficult situation in the country). At the same time, we do not see a decrease in any particular category (for example, residents of certain regions), and this is a general trend for different demographic categories of the population. However, this does not prove that there is no insincerity in the answers; it is possible that the increase in those who do not want to answer is offset by the increased activity of others.

**The possibility of a decent alternative to an unpleasant answer.** In cases where there are socially desirable and socially undesirable alternatives, there may be biases, so it is important to phrase socially undesirable alternatives as neutrally as possible. In Table 2.4 there is an example of a survey of refugees.

**Table 2.4.**  **"Do you plan to return to Ukraine and when? Please select all options that apply to you." %, July-August 2022, survey by the Razumkov Center**

|  | % |
|---|---|
| Are you planning to return in the near future | 11 |
| Once you are sure that the area where you lived is safe to be in | 36 |
| After the company where you worked resumes work or you are sure that you will find another job at home | 7 |
| Immediately after the war is over | 35 |
| A year or several years after the end of the war | 13 |
| Do you plan to return to Ukraine at all? | 7 |
| I don't know, it's hard to answer | 17 |
| Total | 100 |

The option "I do not plan to return" is very sensitive during the war and was answered by only 7% of respondents. However, among the various options for returning, there is also the option to return "in a year or a few years after the end of the war," which in fact means the same thing as a person having no plans to return. Therefore, 13% of those who chose this option can be added to those who said they did not plan to return and it can be argued that at the time of the survey, approximately 20% of respondents had no plans to return to Ukraine.

## A methodological experiment to assess the sincerity of respondents

In the event of war, pro-Russian potential respondents may be reluctant to answer questions. In this case, their share should decrease in polls after the war starts. But how to determine this? The number of pro-Russian respondents has decreased, but due to what: a change in values or a refusal to participate in the survey?

To determine this, the following methodology was used (planned and conducted by A. Grushetsky). A pre-war survey of February 2022 was selected, which was completed by February 24, and included questions that allow us to calculate the number of pro-Russian respondents (survey 1, questionnaire 1). A panel survey of the same respondents was conducted on a sample of this survey (survey 2, questionnaire 2). However, some respondents refused to answer our questions. Next, we look at how the respondents of the second survey answered in the first survey, this is a projection, image of the survey 2 in the survey 1, we compare survey one with the projection of survey two in survey one by the questions of questionnaire one. And we compare the percentage of pro-Russian respondents in the entire February dataset and in the part of the dataset that is the projection of the May poll (see Graph 2.2).

**Graph 2.2. Scheme of the methodological experiment to assess the representativeness of respondents**

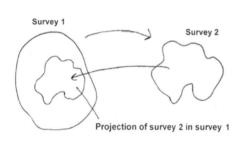

Survey 1 —
February, before the war

Survey 2 —
May, during the war

The results of the comparison are shown in Table 2.5.

**Table 2.5.** Estimation of the share of pro-Russian respondents who refuse to participate in the survey

| Indicators of pro-Russianism | February 2022 (pre-invasion) | Projection of the May 2022 poll | Difference |
|---|---|---|---|
| They have a good attitude towards Russia | 34.0 | 28.3 | 5.7 |
| Ukraine and Russia should unite | 4.5 | 2.5 | 2.0 |
| Ukraine and Russia should be independent, but without visas and customs | 47.2 | 40.0 | 7.2 |
| Independence Day is not the most important holiday | 67.1 | 60.0 | 7.1 |

As the table shows, almost 6% of those who had a good attitude toward Russia refused to participate in the May survey, as well as 2% of those who wanted to unite with Russia, 7% of those who believed that there should be special relations with Russia, without visas and customs, and 7% of those who did not indicate Ukraine's Independence Day as the most important holiday (note that these were the opinions of respondents before the war began, they have changed significantly since the war began). Thus, 6-7% of the most pro-Russian-oriented respondents did not participate in the survey. A significant part of this may be due to the inaccessibility of people because they live in the occupied territories. That is, if we talk only about the territory controlled by the government, the percentage of such potential respondents who refuse to take the survey will be lower.

The "imagined man" method as a method of increasing the sincerity of respondents was developed at KIIS by Volodymyr Paniotto in 1995. We ask the respondent to think of a person with whose activities the respondent is well acquainted, and we guarantee that we will not ask who it is. This person can be the respondent, his or her family members, friends, enemies, anyone. We believe that such an "induced" sample is also representative of the general population. Answering our questions, the respondent in most cases talks about himself, but the procedure ensures his anonymity. We used this method for the first time in a study of the shadow economy commissioned by the World Bank in 1995, as well as in other studies.

In May 2022, we asked about the readiness for territorial concessions to achieve peace as soon as possible. In July 2022, we asked this question again. At the same time, given the sensitivity of this question and the possible insincerity of some respondents, we conducted a methodological experiment. We implemented a split-sample procedure and asked half of the randomly selected respondents the same question as in May 2022. The other half was asked the question using the "imagined acquaintance" methodology.

For the "imagined acquaintance" method, respondents were asked the question "Now I'm going to ask you a slightly unusual question. Please think of someone you know well. It could be yourself, a family member, a work colleague, a friend, an enemy, etc". After the respondent replies, "yes", they are asked: "In your opinion, with which of these statements about possible compromises to achieve peace with Russia would this imaginary person agree more?". As already mentioned, this question ensures respondents' anonymity (mostly respondents conceived themselves) and ensures sincerity of answers even to questions where a sincere answer may indicate illegal activities (in particular, we have successfully studied the shadow economy). The results are shown in Graph 2.3.

**Graph 2.3. Willingness to make territorial concessions using the "direct question" method and the "imagined acquaintance" method, % (July 2022)**

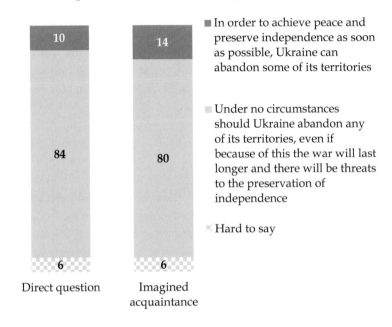

As you can see, using the "conceived acquaintance" method, we get almost the same results: 80% are against any concessions, and 14% support concessions. Although this method yields more sincere answers and we do have a slightly higher number of those who are ready for concessions, the difference is insignificant and does not actually change the overall picture of public sentiment.

To summarize, the following can be said. Methodological experiments conducted by KIIS showed that, in fact, in addition to random sampling error, there is a systematic shift in responses towards a pro-Ukrainian position. In particular, some respondents who, despite the war, sympathize with Russia, refuse to answer our questionnaire, a shift of up to 6-7% (and most likely much less if we are talking about the population of government-controlled territories). However, the changes in people's views related to the war are so significant that they cannot reduce the reliability of the results.

For example, after the start of Russia's large-scale invasion: 1) attitudes toward Russia have deteriorated sharply, with the number of those sympathetic to Russia dropping from 34% to 2%, and the vast majority feeling hatred toward Russia; 2) Ukraine's independence is supported by the vast majority of the population (over 90%); 3) trust in the President has increased dramatically from 27% to 84% (however, by the end of 2023, the level of trust had significantly decreased, although it remains quite high); 3) the Armed Forces of Ukraine are trusted by almost the entire population (96%). An increase in the systematic error of even 6-7% does not affect the reliability of all these conclusions: attitudes toward Russia have deteriorated sharply, the vast majority supports independence (if it were not 90%, but 90% - 7% = 83%, this would not qualitatively change the conclusions), and almost the entire population trusts the Armed Forces. In addition, sociologists use qualitative methods (in-depth interviews, surveys of informants, analysis of social networks, etc.), which are an additional control of the results obtained in the survey.

Thus, the systematic error associated with the sincerity of respondents increases during the war, but not enough to call into question the main results of the surveys. Sociological surveys during war are vital, as they allow us to assess the extent of damage to the population, the number of separated families, destroyed housing, the number of displaced people who plan to stay in evacuation areas, the readiness of the population to provide themselves with heat, blockades, etc. Important information is the readiness of the population to continue the struggle and support or not for territorial concessions, etc. The errors of sociological surveys during the war increase due to problems with representativeness and problems with the sincerity of answers. At the same time, sociologists can assess possible deviations and obtain reliable and valid information about the state of public consciousness and trends in its change.

# 3. Social and Economic Changes

The war in Ukraine has had a detrimental impact on the country's socio-economic situation. The enormous damage to the economy has caused serious losses and damages. The hostilities have resulted in the destruction and damage to a large amount of infrastructure, including industrial facilities, transportation routes, energy networks and communication systems. Many cities and towns have been destroyed, resulting in a significant reduction in production capacity and increased unemployment.

The losses in the economy have affected the lives of millions of Ukrainians. The social situation has deteriorated significantly, with rising unemployment and lower incomes. Many people have lost their jobs, businesses have experienced financial difficulties and a massive decline in productivity. This has led to a decline in living standards and an increase in poverty.

At the same time, the war has also caused a humanitarian crisis in the country. About one-third of the population was forced to flee their homes and become internally displaced (and often in their new location, they can only apply for less skilled and lower-paid jobs than where they lived before the invasion) or relocate to neighboring countries. The lack of stability and security has created serious obstacles to the provision of basic social services, including health care, education, and social protection. All these consequences of the war have a long-term impact on the socio-economic situation in Ukraine.

Only one episode of the war — the explosion of the Kakhovka hydroelectric power plant — led to the flooding of at least 40 settlements, more than 1,000 houses, dozens of people killed, 95,000 tons of fish killed, economic and environmental losses that are still difficult to assess.[27]

---

27  V. V. Kravtsov, 'Riven vody padaie, proiekt tymchasovoi hrebli vzhe v rozrobtsi: holovne pro pidryv Kakhovskoi HES.' *Kanal 24*, June 24, 2023, https://24tv. ua/kahovska-ges-novini-sogodni-okupanti-pidirvali-dambu_n2328730.

A World Bank press release issued on March 23, 2023[28] states that according to a joint assessment released today by the Government of Ukraine, the World Bank Group, the European Commission, and the United Nations, Ukraine's recovery and reconstruction needs have risen to $411 billion. This estimate covers only the first year of the war since Russia invaded Ukraine, from February 24, 2022 to February 24, 2023. This amount is 2.6 times the projected GDP of Ukraine in 2022.

Meanwhile, as we write this book, almost two years of war have passed, it is not known how long it will last, and it is not known what other consequences await us. The statistical information obtained from registers and government statistics is not always better than the data obtained through surveys. In addition, a significant part of state statistics in different countries, including the State Statistics Service of Ukraine (Ukrstat), obtains part of its information through surveys. For example, this is how the State Statistics Service collects information on income, expenditures, and poverty rates. Obtaining such data through surveys allows for a more accurate picture of the economic situation and social well-being of people. The US Census Bureau also conducts a large number of surveys, more than any other sociological center. This data is often more reliable than the results of statistical registrations. For example, according to police data reflected in official statistics, the percentage of rape is much lower than according to surveys. This is because a significant number of women are reluctant to report rape because they do not want this information to be publicized.

Sociologists collect both subjective information (people's psychological state, readiness to resist, willingness to compromise, geopolitical orientations, satisfaction with various aspects of life, level of happiness, etc.) and objective information (information about facts from the respondent's life) through surveys, and this generalized information is no less reliable than statistics (census type data).

---

28    World Bank Group, 'Updated Ukraine Recovery and Reconstruction Needs Assessment.' March 23, 2023, https://www.worldbank.org/en/news/press-release/2023/03/23/updated-ukraine-recovery-and-reconstruction-needs-assessment.

For example, it can be difficult to calculate the exact number of separated families through a statistical register, but a survey can provide valuable information about the real situation. People who have been separated due to war can tell about their fates, experiences and needs. This information will help to understand the size of the problem and identify the need for support and social services.

Similarly, the survey can reveal the real level of unemployment and falling incomes, as they may be underreported in official statistics. The war leads to the destruction of industrial enterprises and a decrease in production capacity, which affects employment and income. The survey will help identify the real situation on the labor market and determine the need for retraining and jobs.

Stressful situations arising from war can also be better identified through surveys. Military conflicts are accompanied by threats to life and safety, evacuations, constant worry and anxiety. These emotional and psychological conditions can leave a lasting impact on the mental health of the population. Surveys can help determine the level of stress and the impact of military events on people's psychological state, which will help organizations provide the necessary psychological support and services.

Thus, while official statistics based on registers and government sources are an important tool, they may not always provide a complete picture of the impact of war on the socio-economic situation. Surveys can complement this information by providing objective and specific data on the extent of damage, the scope of problems, and the needs and experiences of war-affected people. This will allow for a better understanding of the situation, identification of needs, and development of effective programs to support people and economic recovery.

Graph 3.1 shows the data of the research conducted by KIIS at the request of the National Democratic Institute of the United States.

**Graph 3.1. "Let's talk about the ways this war affected you. Have you faced any of the following?" % who answered "yes"**

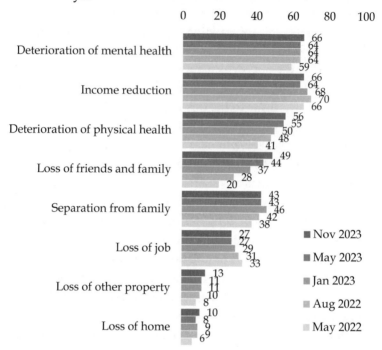

According to the survey, which covered a wide spectrum of the population, a decrease in income was one of the most common consequences of the war. At the end of 2023, 66% of respondents reported a decrease in their income (this percentage has remained virtually unchanged since May 2022). This indicates a serious impact of the war on the economic stability and financial well-being of citizens. Mental and physical health has also been significantly affected by the war. According to the survey, 66% of respondents experienced a deterioration in their mental health and 56% experienced negative changes in their physical well-being, both of which are up from May 2022. This indicates a high level of stress and traumatic experiences that affect people's overall health.

The war also led to the separation of families, with 43% of respondents reporting experiences of separation from their families.

Initially, this rate slightly increased and then stabilized. However, the most severe and traumatic consequence of the war is the loss of loved ones, which cannot be restored, and it also destroys the health and lives of loved ones. Every day of the war, they are increasing. While in May 2020, 20% of respondents had lost a friend or family member, in November 2023, the number was already 49%. In addition, 27% of respondents lost their jobs, which led to additional financial challenges and economic instability. This is the only indicator that has slightly decreased (in May 2022, it was 33%), some of those who lost their jobs managed to find another one, but a very small part (six percentage points). The population also faced the loss of property (13%) and the loss of housing (10%), this figure does not seem very high, but, firstly, it is about four million people, and secondly, this figure is underestimated because we do not survey refugees living abroad, and among them the rate of housing loss is probably higher than among the general population. The same study examined the everyday life of Ukrainians, how often they had to do without certain things or services since the outbreak of full-scale war. In the first year of the war, 50% of Ukraine's population lived without electricity many times or permanently (of course, this also affects heating, lighting, the Internet, elevators, etc.)

**Graph 3.2. "For the last 3 months, have you or anyone in your family gone without…?", % (January 2023)**

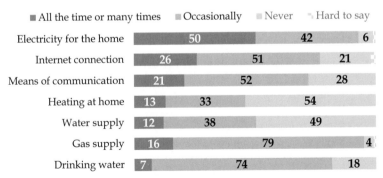

Since October 2022, Russia has conducted waves of massive and methodical missile strikes against Ukraine's critical infrastructure.

According to the then Deputy Minister of Internal Affairs Yevhen Yenin, as of the end of November 2022, the Russian military had destroyed or damaged more than 700 vital facilities, including airports, bridges, oil depots, transformer substations and power plants, etc.[29]. Russia has sent more than a thousand missiles and drones to destroy energy facilities. Millions of Ukrainians have been left without electricity and heat as winter approaches and temperatures drop below freezing.

Advisor to the Minister of Energy of Ukraine Olena Zerkal said in an interview with Radio Liberty:

> The situation is difficult, it cannot be otherwise. Because our energy system, especially the high-voltage system, has suffered very significant damage that no system in Europe has experienced since World War II. There is a constant destruction of our energy infrastructure, and the energy system is actually the backbone on which virtually all critical infrastructure, from water supply to healthcare, rests. Therefore, the destruction of our energy sector is a deliberate Holocaust in Ukraine. There is not a single thermal power plant or thermal power station that would not be hit. In addition, our high-voltage lines and substations are constantly under attack. There are some substations that have been damaged not two or three times, but seven or eight times. There are stations where all equipment is consistently destroyed. This is especially true in Kyiv and other large cities[30].

This was said in early December 2022, and the shelling continued almost every day throughout the winter. It is not surprising that under such conditions, Ukrainians in 2022 had to do without access to the Internet (26%), other means of communication (21%), and heating (13%) many times or permanently, while 33% lived without heating from time to time, and 12% often or permanently went without water supply (another 38% from time to time). In 2023,

---

29   Ye. Yenin, 'Rosiiski okypanty poshkodyly vzhe 32 tysiachi tsyvilnykh obiektiv i 700 obiektiv infrastruktury.' *Censor.net*, November 27, 2022, https://censor. net/ua/news/3383343/rosiyiski_okupanty_poshkodyly_vje_32_tysyachi_tsy vilnyh_obyektiv_i_700_obyektiv_infrastruktury_yenin.

30   Olena Zerkal, 'Vrazhaiuchi obiekty enerhetychnoi infrastruktury v Ukraini, Rosiia peresliduie dekilka tsilei.' *Radio Svoboda*, December 13, 2022, https://www w.radiosvoboda.org/a/vrazhaiuchi-obiekty-enerhetychnoi-infrastruktury-ukr ainy-rosiya-peresliduie-dekilka-tsiley/32173407.html.

Ukraine's air defense system improved, and the situation also improved. Graph 3.3 shows data on other aspects of Ukrainian life in November 2023.

**Graph 3.3. "For the last 3 months, have you or anyone in your family gone without...?", % (November 2023)**

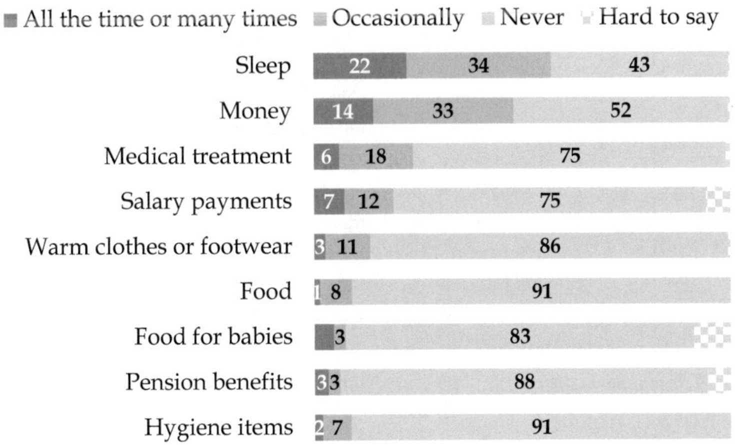

| | All the time or many times | Occasionally | Never | Hard to say |
|---|---|---|---|---|
| Sleep | 22 | 34 | 43 | |
| Money | 14 | 33 | 52 | |
| Medical treatment | 6 | 18 | 75 | |
| Salary payments | 7 | 12 | 75 | |
| Warm clothes or footwear | 3 | 11 | 86 | |
| Food | 1 | 8 | 91 | |
| Food for babies | | 3 | 83 | |
| Pension benefits | 3 | 3 | 88 | |
| Hygiene items | 2 | 7 | 91 | |

Night air raid alerts exhaust people, 22% have had to go without sleep constantly or many times, 14% have significant financial problems (another 33% from time to time), 6% have problems with medical care (another 18% from time to time).

In the survey we conducted in October after a series of daily shelling, we asked: "Recently, Russia has been actively shelling Ukrainian cities with missiles, kamikaze drones, etc. Which of these statements best describes your thoughts on this matter?". The possible responses were: "It is necessary to continue the armed response to Russian aggression, even if the shelling of Ukrainian cities continues" or "It is necessary to start negotiations to stop the shelling of cities as soon as possible, even if this requires making concessions to Russia". Of these choices, 86% chose the first option, 10% chose the second. In another study we conducted in December 2022, we asked about the stressful situations that respondents experienced over the past year.

**Graph 3.4. Stressful situations experienced by Ukrainians in 2022, % (December 2022)**

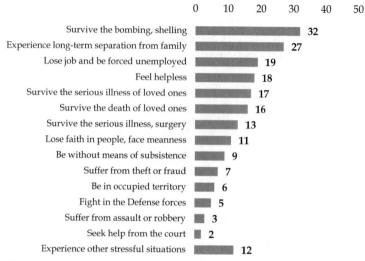

* 13% did not experience any stressful situations.

According to the study, only 13% did not experience any stressful situations, 87% experienced some kind of stressful situation during 2022, and this is the highest rate in the last 10 years of measurements. The percentage of those who have not experienced any stressful situations (Graph 3.5) can be an integral indicator characterizing the overall level of stress in society. As you can see, the situation was generally better in 2013, before the conflict in eastern Ukraine when 48% of respondents did not experience any stressful situations.

**Graph 3.5. % of respondents who did not experience any stressful situations during 2012-2023**

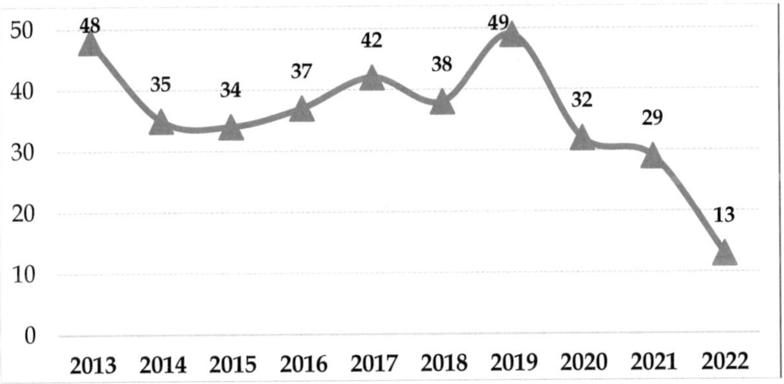

In 2014 and 2015, i.e. after the occupation of Crimea and the war in Donbas, the situation worsened, with only 35% and 34% of the population not experiencing stress, respectively (i.e. two-thirds of the population experienced at least one type of stress). In 2016 and 2017, the situation improved, the share of people who did not experience stressful situations increased to 42%, but in 2018 it decreased again (a more detailed analysis showed that the situation did not worsen for the main stressors, with a slight decrease due to "hard to say"). In 2019, this indicator went up again and amounted to 49%, meaning that 5 years after the first stage of the war, the level of stress returned to 2013. However, 2020 and the COVID pandemic brought new challenges that significantly increased the overall level of stress among Ukrainians, which was reflected in a significant drop in the proportion of those who did not experience any stress in 2020 and 2021 to 32% and 29%, respectively. Finally, in 2022, the level of stress rose sharply, with only 13% experiencing no stress and 87% experiencing at least one type of stress.

If we take only indicators of well-being, the dynamics are similar. It is worth noting that due to the difference in the wording of the questions, the percentage of those who answered that they had lost their jobs differs: in the NDI (The National Democratic Institute) study, it was 29%, and in response to the question about stress, it was 19%. In the first case, the question was asked separately for each of the items, "Have you experienced job loss?", and respondents obviously answered even about short-term job loss. In the second case, a list of 15 stressful situations was read out and the question about job loss referred to a longer-term process of "losing a job and being forced to be unemployed," so against the background of other problems, some of the short-term job loss may not have been included in the answers. Graph 3.6 shows the dynamics of the percentage of those who lost their jobs or found themselves without means of subsistence. The graph shows the sum of the percentage of those who said they were unemployed and those who said they were without means of subsistence.

**Graph 3.6.** **% of respondents who lost their jobs or found themselves without a livelihood during 2013-2022**

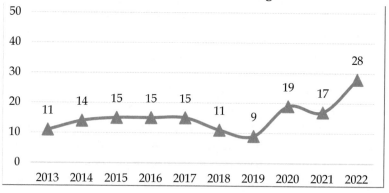

As we can see, after the annexation of Crimea and the outbreak of the war in Donbas, the number of "financially disadvantaged" increased from 11% to 15%, and only three years later the situation improved, reaching the level of 2013 in 2018, in 2019 this number decreased to 9%, but in 2020-21 it doubled to 19% and 17%, respectively due to Covid. And due to the full-scale war, by December 2022, the number of "financially disadvantaged" increased to 28%.

The sociological monitoring "Ukrainian Society" of the Institute of Sociology of the National Academy of Sciences of Ukraine also provides an opportunity to learn about the dynamics of people's assessments of Ukraine's economic situation. In Graph 3.7, we see that before the war (in November 2021), 58% assessed Ukraine's economic situation as poor and only 4% as good. And in December 2022, despite the objective deterioration of the situation, a decrease in income and an increase in the number of unemployed, the percentage of those who considered the situation to be bad decreased from 58% to 28%, and the percentage of those who considered it good increased from 4% to 18%.

**Graph 3.7. Dynamics of assessment of the economic situation in Ukraine from November 2021 to June 2023. % who assessed the situation as poor, medium, and good**

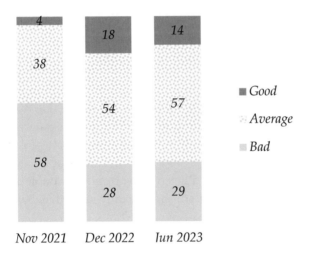

In June 2023, assessments of the economic situation deteriorated slightly, but not significantly: the percentage of those who assessed the situation as bad increased by only 1%, while those who considered it good decreased by 4%. This paradoxical situation, where the situation has objectively worsened while perceptions have improved, is also found in the analysis of other data. After the outbreak of the war, people rethought the value of the state and the situation in which Ukraine is, and the threat of losing what they had showed many that they were too critical and changed their assessment of the situation.

The data from the same project, shown in Table 3.1, shows that after the war, the amounts people consider sufficient for normal life in dollars are lower than before the war (at the beginning of the war, there was significant hryvnia inflation, so the comparison should be made in dollars, not hryvnias).

**Table 3.1.** **"How much money does your family need now per person per month to live a normal life, in your opinion?"**

|  | 2021 November | 2022 December | 2023 June |
|---|---|---|---|
| Required per month per person, median, UAH | 10,000 | 10,000 | 12,750 |
| Required per month per person, US dollars | 385 | 240 | 345 |
| Percentage of those who believe they have this amount or more | 20 | 35 | 31 |

Most importantly, the number of people who believe that they have this amount of money or more, i.e. that they can live a normal life, increased from about 20% to 35% during the war. In June 2023, the situation probably worsened and the percentage of people who have enough money to live a normal life, from their point of view, decreased to 31%, but this is still significantly more than before the war.

Finally, let's look at the results of the surveys based on the question that KIIS has been using regularly since 1994 (unfortunately, we cannot remember whether we came up with this question ourselves or took it from some American questionnaire). As you know, no one has enough money, but one person does not have enough money to eat, another to buy an Odesa port plant, and another to buy Twitter. What exactly the respondent lacks money for is a good indication of his or her financial situation. The question is "Which of the following statements most accurately describes the financial situation of your family?" with possible options:

1.  We don't have enough money even for food
2.  We have enough money for food, but it is difficult to buy clothes

3. We have enough money for food and clothes and can save some money, but it is not enough to buy expensive things (such as a refrigerator or TV)
4. We can afford to buy some expensive things (such as a TV or refrigerator)
5. We can afford to buy anything we want

The experiment showed that the answers to this question are correlated with more complex methods of assessing the well-being of the population, which means that this question, especially in the context of tracking dynamics, is a fairly reliable tool. In particular, the dynamics of changes in self-assessment of well-being in previous years coincided with the dynamics of well-being according to the World Bank methodology. This indicator is still not objective, as it includes an assessment of whether there is enough or not enough money, and, for example, the percentage of those who did not have enough money for food has always been higher according to this indicator than according to the World Bank, because the World Bank focuses on the number of calories needed to sustain life, and people assess whether they can maintain their usual diet. But this indicator is not completely subjective, because we ask about certain facts from the respondent's life. It is somewhere in between an objective and a subjective indicator.

Objectively speaking, the financial situation of Ukrainians has deteriorated dramatically since the start of the war. What are the dynamics of Ukrainians' self-assessments of well-being?

Figure 3.8 below compares the responses of respondents in February 2022 (before the invasion) with those in May 2022, December 2022, May 2023, and December 2023. For convenience, we will consider option 1 as "very low" financial situation, option 2 as "low", option 3 as "medium", and option 4 and 5 combined as "high".

As can be seen, the population's self-assessment of their well-being has not changed much since the Russian invasion and remains at approximately the same level. In particular, the share of respondents with a very low level of financial well-being was 9% before the invasion, and as of December 2023, it is 5%. However, it should be borne in mind that there are still 34% of respondents with "low" well-being, meaning that 39% of Ukrainians currently have "very low" or "low" well-being (before the invasion, the same indicator was 41%).

The share of people with "average" well-being between February 2022 and May 2023 was fairly stable at 35-39%. The share of people with "high" well-being was 22% before the invasion, dropped to 16-17% after the invasion, but as of December 2023, it returned to 21%.

Despite the objective decline in income of two-thirds of the population of Ukraine, self-assessments of well-being have hardly changed, as people's needs have significantly decreased during the war; they are more likely to be satisfied with what they have and believe that they have enough to eat or wear even with a significant decrease in income.

**Graph 3.8. Self-assessment of the family's financial situation immediately before the war (February 2022 before the war) and during the war, %**

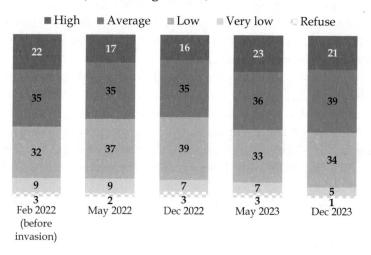

The population's self-assessment of their financial situation is an important dimension of resilience, as Russia does not abandon the idea of "organizing" a humanitarian catastrophe and socio-economic collapse in Ukraine to force surrender. However, despite a significant decline in income and an increase in unemployment, the overall self-assessment of the family's situation, as we see it, remains at the same level as before the invasion. Thanks to their own physical and emotional resources and will to win, as well as the strong support of our Western friends, Ukrainians are demonstrating resilience in enduring the difficulties of the present to achieve their cherished goal of expelling their enemies, rebuilding Ukraine and fully joining the European family.

# 4. Migration and Refugees

## 4.1. Assessment of migration

Since the beginning of the war, approximately one-third of Ukraine's population has been forced to flee their homes. This is one of the largest crises of human displacement in the modern world. According to the United Nations High Commissioner for Refugees, as of March 10, 2023, more than 8 million refugees from Ukraine (8,108,448) were registered in Europe, almost 5 million of them (4,890,639) were registered for temporary protection or similar national protection schemes in Europe. and according to later estimates, as of December 19, 2023, there were only 6.3 million refugees abroad[31]. According to the eleventh Rapid Assessment of the IOM Report on Internal Displacement in Ukraine, in December 2022, more than 5.9 million people were displaced by the war in Ukraine[32] and in December 2023[33] this figure is estimated at 3.6 million. Part of the population is in the occupied territory and part has left or has been taken to the Russian Federation (the number of people in the Russian Federation is estimated at about 2 million). Ella Libanova believed that the figure of 8 million refugees in Europe was overestimated:

> The UN High Commissioner for Refugees, as well as the Ministry of Foreign Affairs, rely on information from countries where Ukrainian 'war refugees' are staying. Since people are registered in the so-called first country after crossing the Ukrainian border (Moldova, Poland, Romania, Slovakia, Hungary), and then, if they move to another country, for example, Germany, the Czech Republic or the Netherlands, a double count occurs. In order to prevent this error in the future, it is planned to create a unified database of IDPs from Ukraine. It will combine information from all countries, not only Europe, but also Canada, the United States, Israel, etc.[34]

---

31  'Ukraine Situation Flash Update #62 (27 December 2023).' Ukraine. ReliefWeb.
32  'Ukraine Situation Flash Update #37 (16 December 2022).' Ukraine. ReliefWeb.
33  'Ukraine Situation Flash Update #62 (27 December 2023).' Ukraine. ReliefWeb.
34  Ella Libanova, 'Do 90% ukraintsiv planuiut povernutysia, ale plany mozhut zminiuvatysia.' *Ministry of Finance*, May 6, 2022, https://minfin.com.ua/ua/2022/05/06/84908432/. See also E. Libanova, 'Pidtverdzhennia otsinky pro 8 milioniv bizhentsiv z Ukrainy nemaie – dyrektorka Instytutu demohrafii.' *Suspilne*.

It is known that in January and February 2023, about 2.2 million border crossings from Ukraine to neighboring countries were recorded, while about 1.7 million border crossings back to Ukraine were noted, according to government data. This movement is pendulous, but departures exceeded returns, seemingly indicating an increase in the number of refugees fleeing shelling and rockets, power outages, and other effects of the war. On the other hand, as of December 19, 2023, there were only 6.3 million refugees abroad in Ukraine, i.e. the number of refugees decreased from 8.1 to 6.3 million[35]. Thus, it is difficult to give an accurate estimate of the number of refugees.

In our opinion, one of the most adequate estimates of the number of refugees could be an assessment that uses social media. This approach was developed by the authors in 2014 to estimate migration from Donbas. The need for migration estimates was related to the need to conduct surveys for the Industrial Television Committee and for the Rinat Akhmetov Humanitarian Center and "Dopomozhemo TV". Let's take a closer look at one of these projects.

### 4.1.1. Method for estimating migration from the occupied part of Donbas in 2014-2016.

Since September 2014, KIIS conducted regular surveys of the population of Donetsk and Luhansk oblasts to determine the need for humanitarian assistance to residents of the cities of Donetsk and Luhansk oblasts. The survey was commissioned by the Rinat Akhmetov Humanitarian Center and Dopomozhemo TV. From September to December, the Kyiv International Institute of Sociology (KIIS) conducted five waves of the survey using the computer-assisted telephone interview (CATI) method. The survey was conducted among people over the age of 18. The surveys examined the current needs of the population for food, medicines and non-food products, the situation with the work of medical and educational institutions, and communications. One of the objectives of this

---

*Novyny*, February 24, 2023. Refugees from Ukraine: sociologist tells how many people left the border because of the war (suspilne.media)

35    'Ukraine Situation Flash Update #62 (27 December 2023).' Ukraine. ReliefWeb.

study was to assess the level of migration from these cities (to more accurately assess the extent of the need for assistance).

Differing estimates of the number of internally displaced persons (IDPs) in eastern Ukraine have been the focus of attention from two ministries: the Ministry of Emergency Situations (MES) and the Ministry of Social Policy (MSP). Despite the fact that both departments share the common goal of providing assistance to IDPs in Donbas, their assessments differed significantly. For example, as of May 31, 2015. The Ministry of Emergency Situations claimed to have 874,000 IDPs, while the Ministry of Social Policy reported 1.3 million IDPs as of May 21, 2015. The difference in the estimates is more than 1.5 times, which suggests that the number of IDPs in Donbas could be much higher or lower than reported.

Our methodology is to look for those who have left through social networks. When surveying the population, we are not interested in the family being interviewed, but in its social environment and in finding out where all the family's acquaintances are, whether they are in the city or have left it. We conduct a regular stochastic sample, asking the respondent to choose five families that are closest to him or her and tell us which of them left and which stayed. This allows us to: 1) obtain information about families that have completely left and 2) increase the effective sample size by the number of people we receive information about (in particular, in the example above, we interviewed about 2011 respondents and received information about 18,318 residents of the city included in the sample).

We believe that the sample of families induced by the random sampling of our respondents is also close to stochastic. The results of the migration rate estimation are presented in Table 4.1.

**Table 4.1.  Assessment of migration from the occupied parts of Donetsk and Luhansk oblasts regions (January-February 2015)**

| | | |
|---|---|---|
| Population in Donbas as of January 1, 2014 | 6,451,691 | 100% |
| Remained | 4,655,732 | 72% |
| Left | 1,795,959 | 28% |
| From those who lef: | | |
| – internally displaced persons | 711,166 | 11% |
| – emigrants (mostly to Russia) | 1,084,793 | 17% |

Unfortunately, so far we have not been able to find funding for a more accurate assessment of the level of migration in 2022 and 2023 using this methodology, so we will rely on UN data: 5 million internally displaced persons and from 5 million (those registered for temporary protection in Europe) to 8 million (the balance of those who entered and left) refugees to Europe. To this should be added those who have left for other countries of the world (according to some estimates, 0.4 million) and Russia (according to the UN, as of August 2022, about 2 million refugees left for Russia or were illegally deported, but this figure is even more questionable than the number of refugees in Europe).

This unprecedented scale of migration can have very serious consequences. First, it is a loss of human resources. Ukraine may lose a significant number of skilled professionals and workers who contribute to the development of the economy and social sphere. This could change the balance of power in the labor market and cause labor shortages in some sectors of the economy. Second, the emigration of the most capable people may lead to a loss of the country's innovation potential and competitiveness. Thirdly, emigration can lead to the destruction of families and the loss of part of the cultural heritage. The level of migration to Ukraine from less developed regions of the world will increase. The possible consequences of all these processes are even hard to predict.

Therefore, KIIS conducted several surveys to assess the future migration attitudes of the Ukrainian population.

## 4.2. Migration attitudes of the population of Ukraine.

### 4.2.1. Do you plan for the future of your children or grandchildren in Ukraine

One of these studies was commissioned by the non-profit organization CASE Ukraine in May 2022. The respondents were asked the question: „Do you plan for the future of your children or grandchildren in Ukraine in the following scenarios in the war? If you do not have children or grandchildren, imagine that you do. The results are presented in Graph 4.1.

If the war continues as it is now, only 43% of Ukrainians plan for the future of their children and grandchildren in Ukraine. In the event of a ceasefire and postponement of the war, only slightly more (55% of residents) plan that the future of their children and grandchildren will be in Ukraine. As other surveys show, Ukrainians do not agree to a ceasefire and the start of negotiations for precisely this reason:

## Graph 4.1. "Do you plan for the future of your children or grand-children in Ukraine?", % (May 2022)

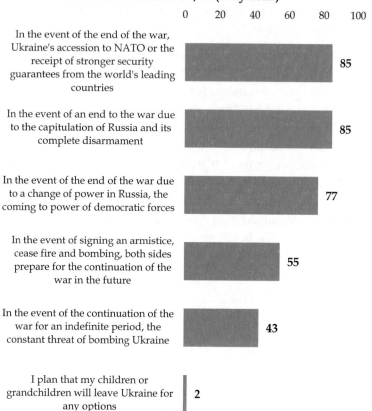

They believe that this does not provide security and only gives the enemy time to prepare a new attack, it is perceived as a continuing threat to children and grandchildren.

With the change of power in Russia to a democratic one, 77% of Ukrainians agree to plan for the future of their children and grandchildren in Ukraine. The impact of Ukraine's accession to NATO or receiving more significant security guarantees (85%) and Russia's surrender and disarmament (85%) on future planning is almost equal. We see that the main factor that influences decisions about the future in Ukraine is not the standard of living or prospects for realizing one's potential, but the problem of security, the problem of the threat from Russia. With maximum security (the last two points), only 15% of the population sees the future of their children or grandchildren abroad.

There is also some regional differentiation here. The farther to the West, the lesser the connection between insecurity and planning for the future in Ukraine. For example, in case the war continues, 35% of residents of the East, 39% of residents of the South, 45% of residents of the Central and Northern regions, and 49% of residents of Western Ukraine plan for the future of their children and grandchildren in Ukraine.

Residents of eastern Ukraine are slightly more likely to plan for the future of their children and grandchildren abroad, regardless of the course of events: 4.3% of residents of the East, 1.8% of residents of the South, 1.5% of residents of the Center, and 1% of residents of the West. But this difference is only a few percent.

### 4.2.2. Willingness to move to the USA or the EU if you become a citizen of these countries

The second study concerned the respondent himself, not his children or grandchildren. In October 2020, KIIS conducted an all-Ukrainian telephone survey, which, among other things, asked the question "If you were granted US or EU citizenship unconditionally, would you move to these countries for permanent residence?". At that time, 28% of all adult Ukrainians were ready to move abroad. In September 2022, we asked this question again and Graph 4.2 shows the answers of the respondents. As you can see, the share of those who are ready to move to the US/EU has decreased by 4 times: from 28% to 7%. At the same time, the number of those who would not want to leave even if they were granted US/EU citizenship without conditions has increased from 69% to 91%.

It should be borne in mind that about 10% of adult Ukrainians were abroad as refugees at the time of the survey. However, even if half of them had answered "yes" to this question (surveys of Ukrainian refugees at the time showed that in fact most still wanted to return home, meaning that less than half would have answered "yes"), the decline in emigration sentiment would have been significant, from 28% to about 13%.

**Graph 4.2. "Would you move to the US/EU if you were granted citizenship without conditions?", %**

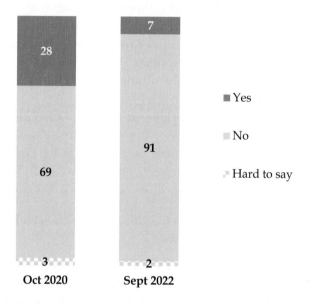

In all regions of Ukraine, the vast majority of the population (90-92%) would not like to move abroad. Also, in all regions, compared to 2020, there are significantly fewer people who would like to leave.

**Graph 4.3.** "Would you move to the US/EU if you were granted citizenship without conditions?", % by region

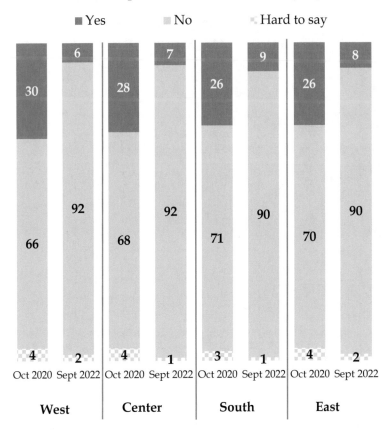

Graph 4.4 shows the results by age category. Although younger respondents are more willing to emigrate, in fact, the vast majority of all age groups (at least 84%) would not want to move to the US/EU. It is also important to note that in the case of all age groups, there is a significant decline in willingness to move to the US/EU compared to 2020. For example, in 2020, almost half (46%) of young people under 30 would like to move, while now it is 13%.

**Graph 4.4. "Would you move to the US/EU if you were granted citizenship without conditions?", % by age groups**

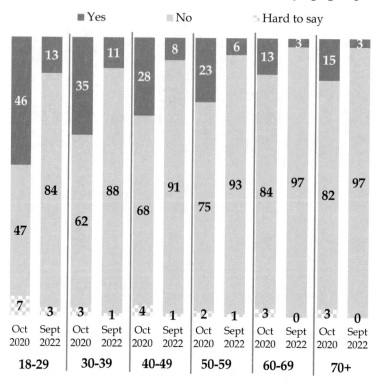

■ Yes      ■ No      ■ Hard to say

| | Oct 2020 | Sept 2022 | Oct 2020 | Sept 2022 | Oct 2020 | Sept 2022 | Oct 2020 | Sept 2022 | Oct 2020 | Sept 2022 | Oct 2020 | Sept 2022 |
|---|---|---|---|---|---|---|---|---|---|---|---|---|
| Yes | 46 | 13 | 35 | 11 | 28 | 8 | 23 | 6 | 13 | 3 | 15 | 3 |
| No | 47 | 84 | 62 | 88 | 68 | 91 | 75 | 93 | 84 | 97 | 82 | 97 |
| Hard to say | 7 | 3 | 3 | 1 | 4 | 1 | 2 | 1 | 3 | 0 | 3 | 0 |
| | **18-29** | | **30-39** | | **40-49** | | **50-59** | | **60-69** | | **70+** | |

Preserving human potential is one of the core tasks for Ukrainian society in the context of war and the period of post-war reconstruction. Traditionally, Ukraine has demonstrated fairly high rates of emigration sentiment (both in terms of polls and actual outflows). Currently, against the backdrop of general population cohesion and rather optimistic moods, in September 2022, we observed, on the contrary, an increase in the desire to stay and work in Ukraine (at the same time, 6 to 8 million Ukrainians, including both adults and children, were already abroad and we did not survey them).

### 4.2.3. How many refugees plan to return to Ukraine

If a significant number of Ukrainian refugees who fled abroad during the war do not return to Ukraine after it ends, this could lead to a number of negative consequences. In particular, Ukraine may face a serious demographic problem, as the loss of a large number of people, especially those of working age, will lead to a shrinking labor force and an increased burden on social systems. This situation could slow down the country's economic recovery after the war, as fewer workers negatively impact production capacity and tax revenues needed to rebuild infrastructure and social programs. In addition, there are many educated and skilled professionals among refugees (60% of refugees have higher education), and their non-return may cause a shortage of highly skilled labor in critical industries. According to a study by the Center for Economic Strategy: the non-return of migrants can have a major impact on the demographic situation in Ukraine for many years, even after the war is over. According to preliminary estimates within the joint project of the Center for Economic Strategy, the Center for Economic Recovery, and the Institute of Demography, the lack of an effective policy on the return of migrants could lead to a labor shortage of 3.1- 4.5 million people by 2032. Cumulative economic losses over the next ten years, according to these estimates, could reach up to $113 billion.[36] This underscores the importance of supporting Ukrainian refugees and encouraging their return home after the war.

The problem is also worsening because European countries are interested in keeping Ukrainian refugees in Europe rather than returning home. As Vasco Botelho notes in the ECB Economic Bulletin, Issue 4/2022:

> Overall, the influx of Ukrainian refugees is expected to lead to a gradual increase in the size of the euro area labor force. Based on all the details provided so far, simple calculations point to an average increase in the euro area labor force of 0.2% to 0.8% over the medium term [...]. This corresponds to an increase in the euro area labor force of between 0.3 and 1.3 million people as a result of the Ukrainian refugee crisis [...]. The increase in labor supply resulting from the influx of Ukrainian refugees may somewhat ease the tensions observed in the euro area labor market. If they are able to find work

---

36   Tsentr ekonomichnoi stratehii, 'Bizhentsi z Ukrainy: khto vony, skilky yikh ta yak yikh povernuty?' Accessed December 15, 2023, https://ces.org.ua.

without a lengthy integration process, Ukrainian refugees can help the market respond to the current strong demand for labor and address the growing skills shortage[37].

How many Ukrainian refugees will return? The situation is quite uncertain and Ukrainian demographers cannot make such an estimate. Academician Ella Libanova, Director of the Ptukha Institute for Demography and Social Studies of the National Academy of Sciences of Ukraine, hopes that 50% of refugees will return: "My dream is for 50% to return. If 60% come back, I will be the happiest person in Ukraine..."[38]. What data can be used to assess the situation? As far as we know, no standardized survey has yet been conducted that would be sufficiently representative of Ukrainian refugees (especially since estimates of their distribution in different countries are quite inaccurate). But we can provide some indicative data.

The results of the online survey conducted by 4Service Group in 39 countries in April and June 2022 and April 2023 are presented in Table 4.2.

**Table 4.2. How many Ukrainian refugees plan to return to homeland, %**

| Plans to return | April 2022 | June 2022 | April 2023 |
|---|---|---|---|
| Definitely plan to return | 75 | 66 | 52 |
| More likely to return | 14 | 18 | 20 |
| More likely not to return | 4 | 6 | 12 |
| Do not plan to return | 3 | 2 | 4 |
| Difficult to say | 4 | 8 | 11 |

The question about whether respondents plan to return to Ukraine is sensitive, there is a brutal war going on, friends and acquaintances of respondents are in the army or under enemy fire, so saying

37    Vasco Botelho, 'The Impact of the Influx of Ukrainian Refugees on the Euro Area Labour Force.' *Economic Bulletin of European Central Bank*, no. 4 (2022), https://www.ecb.europa.eu/pub/economic-bulletin/html/eb202204.en.html.

38    'Dyrektor Instytutu demohrafii prohnozuie povernennia v Ukrainu pislia viiny blyzko 50% hromadian.' *Interfax*, November 23, 2023, https://interfax.com.ua/news/general/1234567.html.

that you do not plan to return is unpatriotic. Therefore, the option "More likely to return" may be a socially desirable form for those who do not plan to return, it is better to focus on the percentage of those who definitely plan to return. We see that it has decreased from 75% to 52% during the year of war. This process is non-linear, but it is possible that by April 2024 it will decrease to 30%. But plans for return and actual behavior may differ in both directions. On the one hand, with each passing month of the war, more and more refugees adapt to the conditions of the new country, learn the language, find jobs, children make friends and get prospects for studying in European universities (this may be an important factor for mothers not to return even if they planned it for themselves). On the other hand, it depends on the immigration policies of European countries and many may not be able to stay even if they planned to.

According to an online survey conducted by Info Sapiens on behalf of the Center for Economic Strategy, as of November-December 2022, the majority of Ukrainians who were abroad planned to return to Ukraine: 50% definitely planned to return, 24% rather plan to returned than not, 8% would rather not plan to return, and about 2% definitely did not plan to return, while about 16% have not yet decided whether to return. These data more or less coincide with the data from the 4Service Group survey.

Another online survey aimed to identify the number of those who would return by asking those living in Ukraine about their relatives and friends. This approach reduces the pressure of social desirability of answers, since the respondent is not talking about himself or herself, but the information about whether his or her relative or friend is going to return comes from a relative or friend, and they too can avoid demonstrating "unpatriotic" plans. The study was conducted by the Institute for the Future in March 2023, Internet users aged 18 and older were surveyed. According to this survey, 29% of respondents said that their friends/acquaintances would definitely return to the country (they talk about it all the time), 44% said that their friends/acquaintances might return if it is safe and there is work in Ukraine, 15% said that their friends/acquaintances are unlikely to return because they are already starting to settle in a new place, 2% said that their friends/acquaintances would definitely not return, and 10% were not able to answer this question. The main reasons that influence a person's decision not to return to Ukraine are life prospects abroad (55%), security (50%), availability of work (48%), and concern for children, with the hope that their children should get a normal education and start a new life (33%).

Thus, if the war ended quickly, we could expect 30-50% of our refugees to return. But all these calculations are based on very unreliable data about people's plans, and how their own plans will change and whether they will be able to realize them depends on many factors. The main factor is the duration of the war. It is also important what compromises it will end in, how much our country will be destroyed, what kind of assistance the world will provide to rebuild Ukraine, what will be the policy of other countries, including European countries, towards refugees. So the situation is very uncertain.

## 4.3. Attitudes of Ukrainians towards refugees and internally displaced persons

### 4.3.1. Attitudes of Ukrainians currently residing in Ukraine towards Ukrainian refugees in Europe

As we have seen, the scale of migration from Ukraine is unprecedented. Ukrainian society should be very interested in this, so that at some point refugees can return, because in addition to the fact that these are our fellow citizens who deserve to return home, it is also a question of the country's post-war demographic potential and other issues that we have already discussed. Unfortunately, such large-scale social upheavals often turn into fault lines in society and become the basis for differential treatment of certain categories of people. Therefore, in addition to the security and socio-economic conditions for return, the problem of overcoming the negative attitudes of those who stayed and now live in Ukraine toward those who went abroad may become relevant. Moreover, these narratives ("they left and are enjoying Europe, while we are suffering here under shelling and blackouts") are readily broadcast by Russian propaganda, which is trying to split Ukraine.

Therefore, it is very important to foster a positive attitude toward refugees in Ukraine. This may be a necessary (though not sufficient) condition for them to return to their country after the war ends. Refugees follow the events in Ukraine very closely, they communicate with relatives, use social networks and are sensitive to how they are treated by those who stayed behind. After all, if people hear that they will be treated unfavorably, they will be less inclined to make a decision to return. It is also important to understand that refugees are people who have fled their homes because of a difficult situation, and they need support and assistance in this difficult time.

Therefore, studying how Ukrainians currently residing in Ukraine feel about their fellow citizens who have left the country is a relevant issue. An in-depth study of this issue requires specialized separate studies that could take into account different aspects and shades of the situation (e.g., voluntary departure to Europe or forced deportation to Russia, etc.). At this stage, we sought to assess the general attitude towards Ukrainian refugees. Therefore, the omnibus survey mentioned earlier in this section (regarding intentions to emigrate to the US and EU) asked only about Ukrainian refugees in Europe.

In order to study attitudes toward specific categories of refugees, we conducted a split-sample experiment. In addition to the general attitude towards Ukrainian refugees in Europe, we formulated 4 more detailed scenarios-categories of refugees, namely the attitude towards:

- "A 38-year-old woman with a minor child. They went to Europe, and her husband stayed in Ukraine."
- "A 25-year-old girl who is unmarried and has no children and who has moved to Europe."
- "A 72-year-old professor who was in Europe for personal reasons at the time of the invasion and continued to stay there."
- "A 31-year-old man who lives in Ukraine but occasionally works in Poland. At the time of the invasion, he was in Poland and decided not to return but to continue working in Poland."

Each respondent was asked only one of the five scenario questions. The question for the baseline scenario (attitudes in general) was

> As you know, many residents of Ukraine have left Ukraine and become refugees because of the Russian invasion. Some residents of Ukraine who stayed behind are sympathetic to the refugees and do not condemn them for leaving and not returning. Other people, on the contrary, are upset by this choice and condemn them for leaving and not returning. What is your general attitude towards Ukrainian refugees in Europe?.

For scenarios two to five, the question was, using scenario three as an example:

> As you know, many residents of Ukraine went abroad and became refugees because of the Russian invasion. For example, this is the case of a 25-year-old girl who is single and has no children and who went to Europe. Some residents of Ukraine who stayed behind are sympathetic to her and do not condemn her for leaving and not returning. Other people, on the contrary, are upset by this choice and condemn her for leaving and not returning. What is your attitude towards her in general?

Graph 4.5 shows the results. We can talk about the following interpretation:

- In the case of all scenarios, the attitude towards Ukrainian refugees in Europe is quite normal/positive. For example, 75-90% of Ukrainians who are currently staying in Ukraine are "understanding and do not condemn" them. At the general level (attitudes of refugees in general), 90% have a normal/positive attitude with only 5% of those who condemn them;
- However, there is still a differentiation in attitudes depending on "additional facts" about a particular category of refugees. The best attitudes are shown towards women with minor children whose husbands remained in Ukraine. In this case, the ratio of non-judgmental/judgmental attitudes — 90% to 6% — is almost completely consistent with the attitude towards refugees in general. Most likely, when respondents hear "Ukrainian refugees in Europe," they most often think of a woman with a child;

- The attitude is somewhat worse if we "remove" minor children from the description. Thus, in the case of women without children, the ratio of attitudes becomes 87% to 9%;
- Then, if we start talking about men, the attitude also becomes worse. Even if we are talking about an elderly man who was in Europe before the invasion, the ratio is 83% to 10%;
- The worst attitude (among the categories studied) is when we talk about a young man who was in Europe at the time of the invasion and stayed there. In this case, 75% do not condemn, 19% condemn.

**Graph 4.5. „And what is your general attitude towards … ?", %**
**(September 2022)**

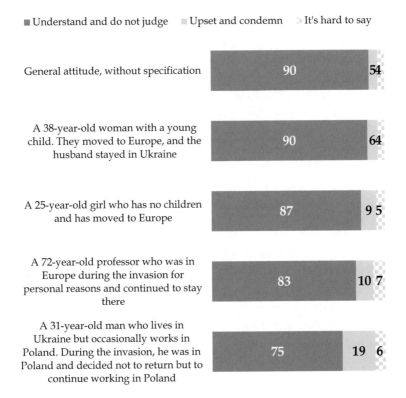

The results of the survey showed that at the time of the survey (September 2022), the attitude was generally quite normal and adequate, which creates the right background for return (when conditions are right). But the situation may change, so it is necessary to monitor this important indicator as one of the conditions for the return of Ukrainian refugees.

### 4.3.2. Attitudes of Ukrainians towards internally displaced persons (IDPs).

The attitude of Ukrainians towards internally displaced persons is also an important factor that affects the social consequences of migration processes, the adaptation of migrants in new places and the cohesion of Ukrainian society. We studied this attitude within the framework of the project All-Ukrainian survey "Local Self-Government and Territorial Organization of Power (in the Context of Full-scale Russian Invasion)" conducted by the Kyiv International Institute of Sociology in October-November 2022 at the request of the Council of Europe within the framework of the program „Decentralization and Public Administration Reform in Ukraine". Among male and female respondents, 77% did not change their place of residence after February 24, 2022. Among the remaining 23%, the distribution is as follows: moved within Ukraine but returned home – 9%, moved abroad but returned home – 3%. At the same time, 11% are those who left their settlement within Ukraine and still live in another settlement (and are actually IDPs), see Table 4.3.

**Table 4.3.  Status of the current population of Ukraine in terms of place of residence, % (October-November 2022)**

|  | % |
|---|---|
| Did not change their place of residence | 77 |
| Moved within Ukraine and returned | 9 |
| Moved abroad and returned | 3 |
| Reside in another settlement | 11 |
| Total | 100 |

It should be noted that 9 out of 10 respondents (91%) did not intend to move from their current place of residence (including 78% who definitely did not intend to move); 6% were going to move, of which 1.5% were definitely going to move. Of those who were planning to move, 71% said they would move within Ukraine (most of them to the West or "home"), and 20% said they would move abroad (another 9% were undecided). In terms of the entire population of the country currently residing in the government-controlled area, this amounts to about 1% who, at the time of the survey (November 2022), were definitely or likely planning to move abroad.

The overwhelming majority of those who have permanently resided in their current community until February 24, 2022 (72%) have a positive attitude towards IDPs in their community (Graph 4.6).

**Graph 4.6. Attitudes towards IDPs, % (October-November 2022)**

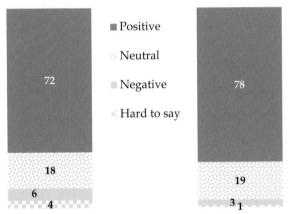

How do those who lived permanently also until 24/02/22 treat IDPs

How IDPs feel about themselves

IDPs themselves "mirrored" positive attitudes toward themselves: 77.5% of them believed that they were treated positively in the community. It can be reasonably assumed that IDPs actually felt supported, so they perceive themselves more positively. Only 6% of permanent residents had a negative attitude, and only 3% of IDPs

felt negatively about themselves (the rest had a neutral or undecided attitude).

Graph 4.7 shows the reasons for positive attitudes according
to the respondents themselves. Among those who have permanently resided in the community, the most dominant explanation
for positive attitudes is that IDPs found themselves in a difficult
situation (72% of those with positive attitudes say this). This is followed by reasons such as maintaining public order (32%), following the rules of behavior (27%), hard work (24%), and using the
Ukrainian language (23%).

**Graph 4.7. Reasons for positive attitudes towards IDPs (October-November 2022).** % out of those who has positive attitude towards IDPs / feel positive attitude

Permanent residents

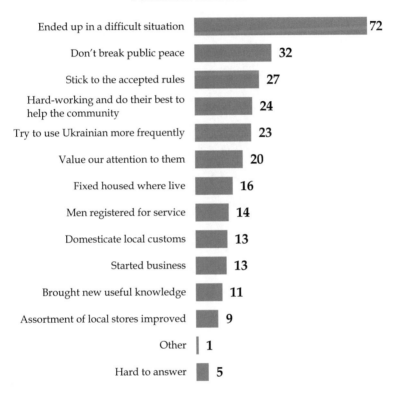

| | |
|---|---|
| Ended up in a difficult situation | 72 |
| Don't break public peace | 32 |
| Stick to the accepted rules | 27 |
| Hard-working and do their best to help the community | 24 |
| Try to use Ukrainian more frequently | 23 |
| Value our attention to them | 20 |
| Fixed housed where live | 16 |
| Men registered for service | 14 |
| Domesticate local customs | 13 |
| Started business | 13 |
| Brought new useful knowledge | 11 |
| Assortment of local stores improved | 9 |
| Other | 1 |
| Hard to answer | 5 |

IDPs

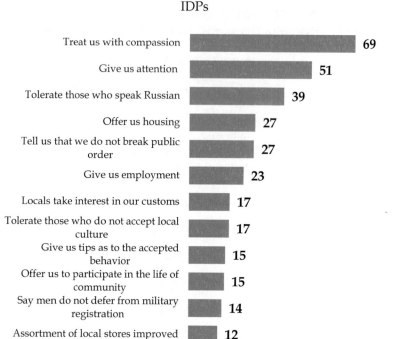

| | |
|---|---|
| Treat us with compassion | 69 |
| Give us attention | 51 |
| Tolerate those who speak Russian | 39 |
| Offer us housing | 27 |
| Tell us that we do not break public order | 27 |
| Give us employment | 23 |
| Locals take interest in our customs | 17 |
| Tolerate those who do not accept local culture | 17 |
| Give us tips as to the accepted behavior | 15 |
| Offer us to participate in the life of community | 15 |
| Say men do not defer from military registration | 14 |
| Assortment of local stores improved | 12 |
| Other | 1 |
| Hard to answer | 3 |

Among those IDPs who feel positively treated, the majority (69%) explained this by sympathy for them. This was followed by such explanations as being shown attention (51%), being tolerated for using the Russian language (39%), being offered housing (27%), not disturbing public order (27%), and being offered employment (23%).

Graph 4.8 shows the reasons for negative attitudes according to the respondents themselves. Among those who were permanent residents of the community before February 24, 2022 and had negative attitudes towards IDPs, the most common reasons were that IDPs demand free goods and services (41%) and that IDP men evade military registration (38%). This was followed by reasons such as not looking like people in difficult circumstances (28%), not wanting to work (27%), and disrupting public order (24%).

**Graph 4.8. Reasons for negative attitudes towards IDPs (October-November 2022), % out of those who has negative attitude towards IDPs / feel negative attitude**

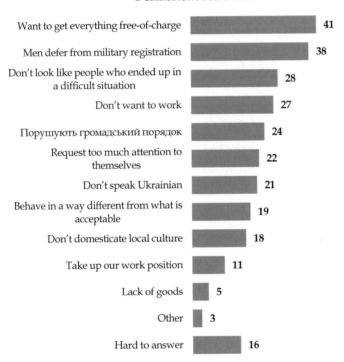

Permanent residents

| | |
|---|---|
| Want to get everything free-of-charge | 41 |
| Men defer from military registration | 38 |
| Don't look like people who ended up in a difficult situation | 28 |
| Don't want to work | 27 |
| Порушують громадський порядок | 24 |
| Request too much attention to themselves | 22 |
| Don't speak Ukrainian | 21 |
| Behave in a way different from what is acceptable | 19 |
| Don't domesticate local culture | 18 |
| Take up our work position | 11 |
| Lack of goods | 5 |
| Other | 3 |
| Hard to answer | 16 |

## IDPs

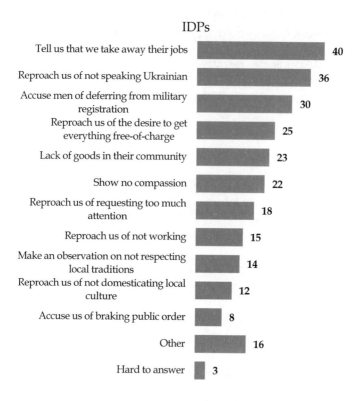

IDPs who felt negatively treated primarily said that they were reproached for allegedly "taking away their jobs" (40% of IDPs reported this reason) and for not using the Ukrainian language (36%). This is followed by being accused of not registering IDP men (30%), of wanting everything for free (25%), and of causing a shortage of goods and services (21.5%). Since only 6% of respondents have a negative attitude toward IDPs (as of November 2022), we believe that overall, the attitude toward IDPs is not a cause for concern.

# 5. Geopolitical Orientations of the Population of Ukraine

## 5.1. Changes in the attitudes of the Ukrainian population towards the European Union and alliances with Russia before the start of a full-scale war in 2022

Since Ukraine declared its independence in 1991, one of the key issues facing the country has been its major geopolitical choice. Caught between two neighbors, Russia and Europe, Ukraine had to decide which policy direction to take: rapprochement with Russia or the European Union. This question divided society and the political elite into two camps: Western-oriented and Eastern-oriented or pro-Russian. In addition to these directions, the idea that Ukraine should be a completely neutral country between "West" and "East" also flourished.

In the 1990s, Ukraine was in a difficult period of transition from a command-and-control system to a market economy, which was common to all countries of the former Soviet Union. At the same time, the country had to maintain friendly relations with both of its neighbors, including Russia, which had historically been its closest partner. The spread of European ideals in society was facilitated by Ukraine's signing of a Partnership and Cooperation Agreement with the European Union in 1994. In 2004, events took place in Ukraine that became an important moment in the country's geopolitical choice. The Orange Revolution[39], which brought pro-

---

39  One of the factors that led to the Orange Revolution was an exit poll conducted by KIIS as part of the National Exit Poll consortium. It has already been included in school textbooks. "At the end of October 2004, regular presidential elections were held in Ukraine. Out of 24 presidential candidates, Viktor Yushchenko and Viktor Yanukovych made it to the second round. According to the results of the second round of elections on November 21, independent exit polls showed that Yushchenko was leading (53% of the vote against 44% for Yanukovych). However, according to the official report of the Central Election Commission, the fig-

European politicians to power, showed that a significant part of Ukrainian society supports the course of integration with Europe (and more importantly, there has been a steady trend of growing support for European integration since the 1990s).

After the 2010 elections, politicians with pro-Russian views came to power, although they initially formally adhered to the course of European integration. Even shortly before the Revolution of Dignity, the future fugitive President Viktor Yanukovych aggressively persuaded his faction in parliament to support the Association Agreement with the EU. However, in the end, the then government abruptly changed Ukraine's course and, in particular, refused to sign the Association Agreement with the EU in November 2013. This sparked massive protests on Kyiv's Independence Square, known as the Revolution of Dignity. The Maidan protests grew in scale and turned into a national movement demanding the resignation of President Viktor Yanukovych and his entourage.

The situation on the Maidan escalated after an attempted violent crackdown on peaceful protests in February 2014, which resulted in the deaths of more than a hundred people. Yanukovych fled to Russia, and Russia began military actions against Ukraine and occupied Crimea. The situation in eastern Ukraine also escalated when Russian invaders and local separatists, openly supported by Russia, declared the so-called "Donetsk" and "Luhansk People's Republics" and began fighting government forces (it is important to emphasize that according to a KIIS poll in April 2014, when it was possible to cover the entire Donbas, the majority of its residents were against secession from Ukraine, with less than 30% of the Donbas population in favor of secession)[40]. The Revolution

---

ures were significantly different: 49.5% for Yanukovych and 46.9% for Yush-chenko. It turned out that the official results had been falsified. In protest against the election fraud, 200 thousand Kyiv residents came to Independence Square." Viktor Danylenko and Myroslava Smolnytska, *Istoriia Ukrainy: Riven standartu. Pidruchnyk dlia 11 kl. zakl. sered. osvity* (Kyiv: Heneza, 2019), 35. See also *National Exit Poll 2004* (Kyiv: Democratic Initiatives Center, 2005).

40    'Dumky ta pohliady zhyteliv pivdenno-skhidnykh oblastei Ukrainy: Kviten 2014.' Table 20.2, KIIS, https://www.kiis.com.ua/?lang=ukr&cat=reports&id =302&page=1.

of Dignity and subsequent events opened a new page in the history of Ukraine, which was forced to deal with the aggravated economic and political situation, as well as the war in the East of the country. As a result of these events, Ukraine embarked on the path of Euro-Atlantic integration, signing the Association Agreement with the European Union in 2014, and in 2017, it received a visa-free regime with the EU.

### 5.1.1. Changes in attitudes toward the EU and alliances with Russia

What were the dynamics of attitudes toward the EU and the union with Russia before the war in 2022? Graph 5.1 shows the results of answers to the questions "How do you feel about Ukraine's accession to the European Union?" and "How do you feel about joining the Union of Russia and Belarus?"[41] (interestingly, a significant number of Ukrainians simultaneously supported both joining the EU and joining the union with Russia).

---

41    The graph is based on the results of the project „Ukrainian Society: Monitoring of Social Changes" conducted by the Institute of Sociology of the National Academy of Sciences of Ukraine: 'Trydtsiat rokiv Nezalezhnosti.' *Ukrainske suspilstvo: Monitorynh sotsialnykh zmin,* no. 8(22) (2021), p. 620.

**Graph 5.1. Attitudes of the Ukrainian population towards joining the European Union and the Union of Russia and Belarus (2002-2021), % support accession**

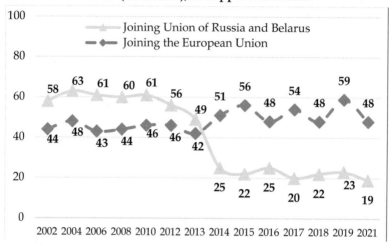

As we can see from Graph 5.1, from 2002 to 2010, the majority of Ukrainians (58%) supported Ukraine's accession to the Union of Russia and Belarus, which is significantly higher than the percentage of those who supported Ukraine's accession to the European Union (43-48%). In 2012 and 2013, support for joining the Union of Russia and Belarus began to decline. The fact is that Viktor Yanukovych pursued a controversial policy after being elected president of Ukraine in 2010. In the first year of his presidency, he was determined to strengthen relations with Russia and signed a number of agreements that promised closer cooperation between Ukraine and Russia. But already in 2011, Yanukovych began actively discussing the possibility of strengthening relations with the European Union and expressed a desire to sign the EU-Ukraine Association Agreement. In the same year, he urged the Ukrainian government to speed up the process of preparing for the signing of this agreement. As a result, the percentage of supporters of joining the Union of Russia and Belarus began to decline, from 56% in 2012 to 49% in 2013. Then Yanukovych unexpectedly refused to sign the association agreement with the EU, which triggered protests that turned into the Revolution of Dignity.

The situation in 2013 looked like a bifurcation point, if we use the concept of synergy. KIIS conducted several surveys in 2013, and support for joining the EU fluctuated. A more detailed analysis showed that one-third of the Ukrainian population was strongly oriented toward the EU, the same number was strongly oriented toward Russia, and one-third (mostly Yanukovych supporters) had no definite opinion and fluctuated depending on the government's campaigning. For example, in September and November 2013, we conducted a survey in which we used slightly different indicators. We studied attitudes towards joining the EU and attitudes towards joining the Customs Union using the following questions: "Please imagine that a referendum is being held on whether Ukraine should join the European Union. You can vote in favor of joining this union, against joining, or abstain and not participate in the vote. What is your choice?" A similar question was asked about the Customs Union.

In mid-November, just like two months ago, almost 76% of Ukrainians were ready to take part in a referendum on Ukraine's accession to the European Union or the Customs Union with Russia, Belarus, and Kazakhstan, but the shares of supporters of these two associations statistically equaled: the number of Ukrainians ready to vote for joining the European Union was almost as high as the number of those ready to vote for joining the Customs Union at about 38%.

As before, in November 2013, supporters of joining the European Union significantly outnumbered supporters of joining the Customs Union in the Western and Central regions (66% vs. 13% and 43% vs. 25%), and supporters of joining the Customs Union significantly outnumbered supporters of joining the European Union in the Southern and Eastern regions (52% vs. 27% and 61% vs. 15%). At the same time, the attitudes of Ukrainian citizens toward Ukraine's accession to the European Union and the Customs Union in November 2013 were no less controversial than in September. This evident when we ask separately about referenda on accession to the EU and on accession to the Customs Union. In the case of a referendum only on Ukraine's accession to the European Union, more Ukrainians are ready to vote in favor of joining (40%) than against it (35%).

However even in the case of a referendum only on Ukraine's accession to the Customs Union, more Ukrainians are ready to vote in favor of joining (41%) than against it (32%). In addition, the survey showed that:

- young Ukrainians (aged 18-29 and 30-39 — 51% and 41%, respectively) are more likely to vote for joining the European Union rather than the Customs Union;
- and Ukrainians of older age groups (50-59 years old — 42%, 60-69 years old — 43%, and 70 years old and older — 49%) are in favor of joining the Customs Union, not the European Union.

In 2014, Russia occupied Crimea, and a war with pro-Russian separatists organized and led by Russia broke out in eastern Ukraine. These events led to a dramatic change in the geopolitical orientation of Ukrainians. As we can see from Graph 5.1, support for the Union with Russia and Belarus fell to 19-25% in 2014-2021, while support for the EU increased to 48-59%. We can say that Ukraine has made its geopolitical choice in favor of Europe.

Let's take a closer look at the situation in 2021, the last year before the start of the war in 2022. KIIS conducted a survey of geopolitical orientations in June 2021. As of June 2021, Ukraine's accession to the European Union was supported by about half of the country's population: when asked what they would do if a referendum on whether Ukraine should join the European Union were held at that time, 52% of respondents said they would vote for Ukraine's accession to the EU, 19% voted against, and 29% were undecided or would not vote. Usually, voting surveys ask how you would vote if the voting were held on the next Sunday. In recent KIIS surveys, we do not ask about voting on the next Sunday, but ask how the respondent would vote if the voting were taking place right now, which is a kind of imitation of a referendum. Therefore, the answer "hard to say" actually means non-participation in the referendum. Assuming that undecided voters would not participate in the referendum on EU accession, 71% of all eligible voters living in the territories controlled by the Ukrainian government would participate in the vote, and the votes cast would be distributed as follows: 73% of votes in favor of joining the EU, 27% against. These indicators are closest to the possible results of the referendum if it were held in June 2021.

**Graph 5.2. Voting in the referendum on EU accession, % (June 2021)**

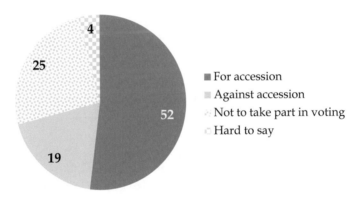

- ■ For accession
- ■ Against accession
- ⸬ Not to take part in voting
- ◫ Hard to say

The willingness of Ukrainians to vote for European Union membership had remained relatively stable in the years leading up to the invasion: about half of the population expressed readiness to vote for Ukraine's accession to the EU, while about a quarter were opposed.

**Graph 5.3. Dynamics of the population's readiness to vote for Ukraine's accession to the EU (2014-2021), %***

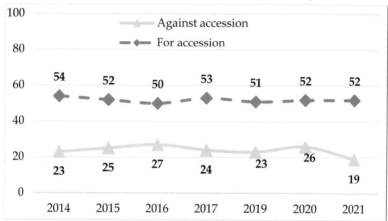

* For 2015-2017, the average annual indicator is given. The question was not asked in 2018.

As before, attitudes toward Ukraine's accession to the EU differed markedly by region: the EU accession was most strongly supported by residents of the western (70% of residents of the region are ready to vote for the EU) and central (58%) regions, and to a lesser extent by residents of the southern (39%) and eastern (29%) regions of Ukraine.

## Attitudes of Ukrainians towards Ukraine's accession to the Customs Union

The majority of Ukrainians are opposed to Ukraine's accession to the Customs Union: if a referendum on whether Ukraine should join the Customs Union were held in June 2021, 22% of Ukrainians would vote for Ukraine's accession to the Customs Union, 45% would vote against, and 33% would be undecided or would not participate in such a referendum. If those who were undecided had not come to the referendum on joining the Customs Union, about 67% of all eligible voters living in the territories controlled by the Ukrainian authorities would have participated in the vote, and the votes cast would have been distributed as follows (as noted, these indicators are the closest to the possible results of the referendum if it were held in June 2021): 33% of votes in favor of joining the Customs Union, 67% of votes against.

**Graph 5.4. Voting in the referendum on Customs Union accession, % (June 2021)**

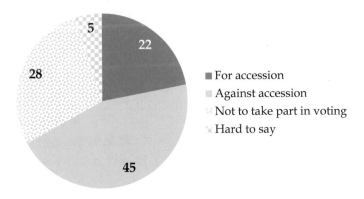

**Graph 5.5. Dynamics of the population's readiness to vote for Ukraine's accession to the Customs Union (2014-2021), %**

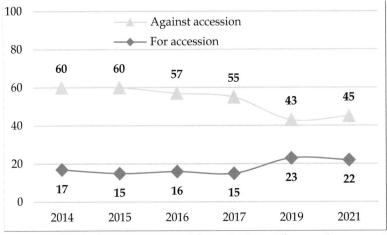

*For 2015-2016, the average annual figure is given. The question was not asked in 2018 and 2020.*

Ukraine's accession to the Customs Union was somewhat more supported by residents of the eastern and southern regions: in the western region, 8% of the population would vote for joining the Customs Union, in the central region — 18%, in the south — 33%, and in the eastern region — 41%.

## Desired direction of foreign policy

In addition to the question about possible actions in the event of referenda on accession to the European Union and the Customs Union, respondents were asked to answer which direction of foreign policy they generally consider more desirable for Ukraine. According to the results of the June 2021 poll (Graph 5.6), the majority of respondents believe that Ukraine's accession to the EU is the most desirable direction of foreign policy (51%). The course of joining the Customs Union of Russia, Belarus, Kazakhstan, Kyrgyzstan, and Armenia was considered desirable by 12% of Ukrainians. A significant number (28%) were of the opinion that Ukraine should develop independently, without joining any of these associations.

**Graph 5.6. Preferences on the direction of Ukraine's foreign policy, % (June 2021)**

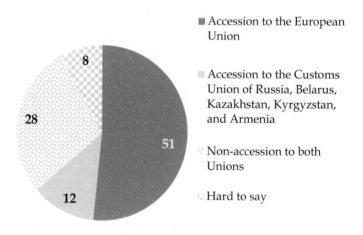

Despite some fluctuations, public opinion on the desired course of foreign policy remained virtually unchanged over the six prewar years: the majority of the population considered joining the EU to be desirable, the next most common option was neither joining the EU nor the Customs Union, and the least common was joining the Customs Union.

**Graph 5.7. Dynamics of choosing the desired direction of foreign policy (2015-2021), %**

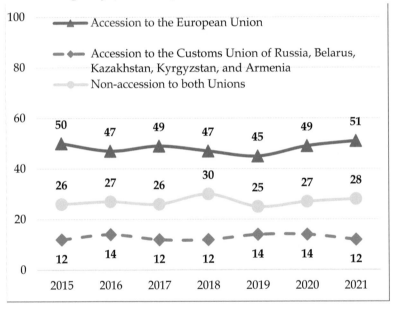

### 5.1.2. Changes in attitudes toward NATO

In June 2021, in the study we already cited when it came to the EU, almost half of the population supported Ukraine's accession to NATO: if a referendum on whether Ukraine should join NATO were held in June 2021, 48% of respondents said they would vote for Ukraine's accession to NATO, 24% voted against. The rest (28%) were undecided or would not participate in such a referendum.

Therefore, if a referendum on Ukraine's accession to NATO were held in June 2021, and all those who had made up their minds took part in the vote, the turnout would be about 72%, and the votes would be divided as follows: 66% in favor of Ukraine joining NATO, 34% against.

**Graph 5.8. Voting in the referendum on NATO membership, %**
**(June 2021)**

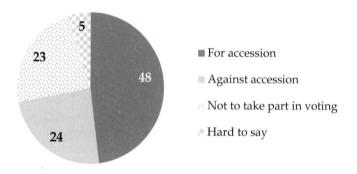

Over the past two pre-war years, readiness to vote for NATO membership has increased somewhat: the share of Ukrainians who expressed readiness to vote for NATO membership increased from 40% in 2019 to 48% in 2021.

**Graph 5.9. Dynamics of the population's readiness to vote for**
**NATO membership, % (June 2021)**

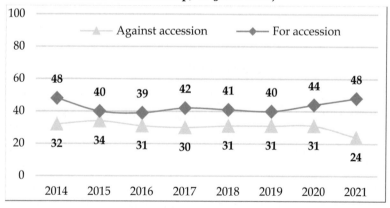

As before, there was no regional agreement on the issue of joining NATO. Residents of the western and central regions were the most supportive of joining NATO: in the western region, 66% would vote for joining NATO, and in the central region 53% would vote for joining NATO. In the Southern regions, 34% supported NATO membership while 35% were against it. In the East, the majority (47%) opposed Ukraine's accession to NATO, while 25% were in favor.

## 5.2. Changes in the attitudes of the Ukrainian population towards the EU and NATO after the outbreak of war in 2022

KIIS conducted a survey on the geopolitical orientations of Ukrainians in July 2022. In the event of a referendum on EU accession, 81% of all respondents would vote in favor of joining the EU, while 4% would vote against joining the EU. Others (15%) would not participate in the vote or do not know how to vote. Support for joining NATO is somewhat lower, but the overwhelming majority of Ukrainians would vote in favor: 71% of all respondents would vote in favor, while 7% would vote against. Against this, 22% of the population would not vote or would not know how to vote. In terms of the number of respondents who would have participated in the vote, the referendum on EU membership would have received 96% of the votes in favor, and the referendum on NATO membership would have received 91% of the votes in favor.

**Graph 5.10. "Please imagine that a referendum is being held on whether Ukraine should join ... You can vote in favor of joining, against joining, or abstain — not participate in the vote. What is your choice?", % (July 2022)**

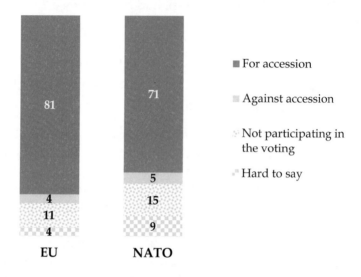

Although there is a tendency for support for joining the EU and NATO to decline from the West to the East, in all regions the majority of the population would vote in favor of joining both the EU and NATO (see Graph 5.11). Even among residents of the South and East, respectively, 77% and 71% of all respondents would support Ukraine's accession to the EU, while 65% and 56% would support joining NATO.

**Graph 5.11. Voting in the referendum on EU and NATO membership in the regional dimension, % (July 2022)**

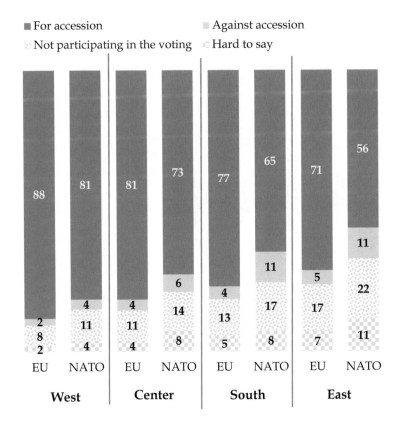

Graph 5.12 shows the results by linguistic and ethnic categories of the Ukrainian population. As can be seen, the majority of all categories support Ukraine's accession to the EU and NATO (although there is a tendency for slightly lower support among Russian-speaking citizens). Even among Russian-speaking Russians, support for joining the EU and NATO is significantly higher: 53% support EU membership, 16% do not support it; in the case of NATO, 51% support it, 27% do not support it.

**Graph 5.12. Voting in the referendum on EU and NATO membership among linguistic and ethnic categories of the population, % (July 2022)**

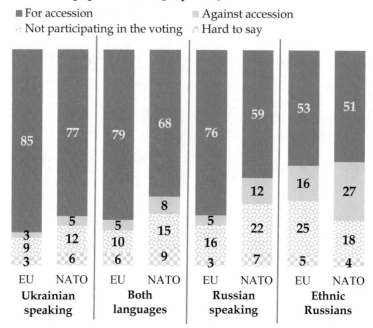

- For accession
- Not participating in the voting
- Against accession
- Hard to say

| | EU Ukrainian speaking | NATO Ukrainian speaking | EU Both languages | NATO Both languages | EU Russian speaking | NATO Russian speaking | EU Ethnic Russians | NATO Ethnic Russians |
|---|---|---|---|---|---|---|---|---|
| For accession | 85 | 77 | 79 | 68 | 76 | 59 | 53 | 51 |
| | | | | 8 | | 12 | 16 | 27 |
| | 3 | 5 | 5 | 15 | 5 | 22 | 25 | 18 |
| | 9 | 12 | 10 | 9 | 16 | 7 | 5 | 4 |
| | 3 | 6 | 6 | | 3 | | | |

## Overcoming interregional differences and consolidating public opinion of Ukrainians on Euro-Atlantic integration

Compared to June 2021, in July 2022, the share of those who support EU membership increased from 52% to 81% (see Graph 5.13). Also during this period, the share of those who support joining NATO increased from 48% to 71%. In addition, in the case of the EU, the share of those who oppose Ukraine's membership in these organizations decreased from 19% to 4%, and in the case of NATO, from 24% to 7%.

Comparing current attitudes with those before the Revolution of Dignity of 2013-2014, we can see an increase in support for EU accession after the war from 47% to 81% (and a decrease from 27% to 4% of those who oppose accession). In the case of NATO, before

2013, only 15-20% supported joining this organization (with the majority of the population opposed), while in July 2022, 71% support and only 7% oppose.

**Graph 5.13.** "Please imagine that there is a referendum on whether Ukraine should join ... . You can vote in favor of joining, against joining, or abstain — not participate in the vote. What is your choice?", %*

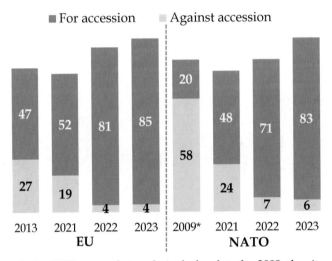

■ For accession     ▨ Against accession

* Although the KIIS's open data only includes data for 2009, the situation did not change significantly until 2013, and in 2013 (before the Revolution of Dignity) the same 15-20% of Ukrainians supported NATO membership. 2023 data is date of Rating company (July 2023).

In addition to the national level, it is important to pay attention to the evolution of public opinion in individual regions. Graph 5.14 shows the relevant data on joining the EU, and Graph 5.15 shows the data on joining NATO. In the case of EU accession in the period up to 2013, it was actually only residents of the West who mostly supported accession. In the Center, although support for EU accession prevailed, it was not a majority of the population. In the South and East, those who opposed Ukraine's membership in the EU prevailed (only a quarter would vote in favor of joining the EU in a referendum). By 2021, a clear majority of the West and Center supported EU membership. In the South, supporters of accession already prevailed, although they were less than half. In the East, opponents of accession still prevailed. By July 2022, the overwhelming majority of residents of all regions—West, Center, South, and East—supported Ukraine's accession to the EU.

**Graph 5.14. Voting in the EU accession referendum in the regional dimension, %**

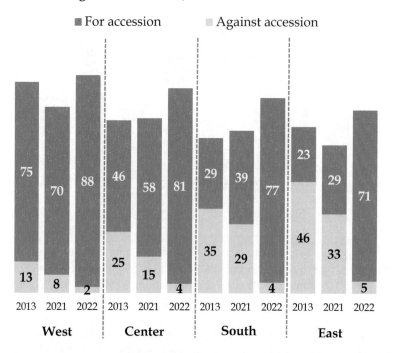

A similar trend of changes is observed in the attitude towards NATO membership, with the difference that this issue was much more polarized in the interregional dimension before 2013. Now, the majority of residents of the West, the Center, the South, and the East support joining NATO.

## Graph 5.15. Voting in the referendum on NATO membership in the regional dimension, %

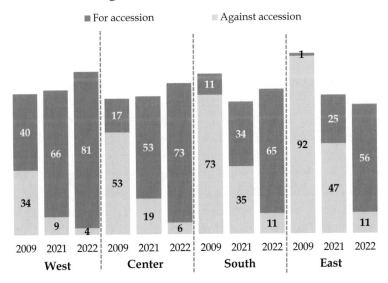

In less than 10 years, Ukraine has gone from significantly different regional views on the external vector of development to consolidation and unity in our country's Euro-Atlantic movement. Even before 2013, there was a gradual evolution of views and a growing commitment to European integration. In our polls in the 1990s, the majority was against Ukraine's membership in the EU, while in 2013 there were more people who would vote in favor of Ukraine's accession to the Union. But then there were still clear inter-regional differences, for example, a majority in the East and South would have voted against Ukraine's accession to NATO in a referendum. Although it can be said that in 2014 Ukraine made its main geopolitical choice in favor of the EU and NATO, the irreversibility of this process was questionable due to significant interregional differences. Russia's occupation of Crimea, the outbreak of the war in Donbas, and eventual the full-scale invasion in 2022 significantly accelerated the dynamics of views and led the vast majority of Ukrainians in all regions (and all linguistic and ethnic categories) to understand that Ukraine should be a member of both the EU and NATO.

## 5.3. Attitudes toward certain countries and political leaders

The geopolitical orientations of the Ukrainian population have changed over the years, reflecting the dynamic nature of international relations between countries. In the past, Ukrainians' attitudes toward different countries were shaped by historical relations, shared cultural heritage, and unresolved conflicts. However, since the outbreak of Russia's war against Ukraine in 2022, the level of support and assistance that these countries provide to Ukraine in its struggle for independence and territorial integrity increasingly determines Ukrainians' attitudes toward different countries. The attitudes of Ukrainians toward different countries have changed in the context of rising geopolitical tensions, war, and international cooperation. The interaction of past and current events plays a significant role in shaping the geopolitical orientations of the Ukrainian population, including their attitudes toward neighboring countries and global players such as the United States, Germany, the United Kingdom, and others.

Table 5.1 presents data conducted by the Razumkov Center on the attitudes of the current adult population of Ukraine (those living in Ukraine) towards different countries. This is the answer to the question: "Now I will read you the names of some countries. For each item, please tell me how positive or negative your attitude is with the following answer options: 'completely positive, mostly positive, mostly negative, completely negative and difficult to answer".

**Table 5.1.** **Attitudes of the population of Ukraine towards different countries (February-March 2023)**

*% have a positive attitude and the balance (the number of those who have a positive attitude minus the number of those who have a negative attitude)*

| | Positive attitude, % | Balance, % |
|---|---|---|
| Poland | 94 | +92 |
| United Kingdom | 91 | +87 |
| Lithuania | 91 | +87 |
| Estonia | 90 | +86 |
| Latvia | 90 | +86 |
| Canada | 90 | +85 |
| Czech Republic | 88 | +82 |
| USA | 88 | +80 |
| Netherlands | 86 | +82 |
| France | 86 | +79 |
| Germany | 85 | +76 |
| Moldova | 83 | +75 |
| Slovakia | 83 | +75 |
| Israel | 75 | +63 |
| Japan | 74 | +65 |
| Turkey | 73 | +57 |
| Georgia | 70 | +51 |
| Romania | 69 | +54 |
| Armenia | 66 | +50 |
| Azerbaijan | 65 | +51 |
| India | 46 | +14 |
| Hungary | 39 | -7 |
| China | 25 | -35 |
| Iran | 17 | -57 |
| Belarus | 12 | -68 |
| Russia | 3 | -91 |

As we can see, the leader is Poland, which immediately after the outbreak of the war opened its borders and accepted an unprecedented number of Ukrainian refugees (as of early April 2023, the number of Ukrainian refugees in Poland is the largest in Europe and is estimated by UNHCR[42] at 1.6 million). Poland has also provided significant humanitarian aid to the Ukrainian population, including food and medical supplies, military, financial assistance, and diplomatic support (Poland has been an active and consistent participant in international negotiations and cooperation with other EU and NATO countries to strengthen sanctions against Russia and support Ukraine). Poland is viewed positively by 94% of respondents and negatively by only 2%. This is followed by the United Kingdom, Lithuania, Estonia, Latvia, and Canada (approximately 90% have a positive attitude) and almost the same number in the Czech Republic and the United States (88%). The Netherlands, France, Germany, Moldova, and Slovakia also have more than 80% of supporters.

According to some reports, Germany is the second largest country in Europe in terms of the number of Ukrainian refugees (almost 1 million[43]), it is also the first in the EU in terms of military aid to Ukraine[44] and, if we take the world as a whole, it is second only to the United States and the United Kingdom in terms of military aid. In general, Germany is one of the two or three countries that provide the most assistance to Ukraine in terms of real aid. Meanwhile, the attitude towards the Baltic countries (Lithuania, Estonia, Latvia) is slightly better. The difference is statistically significant, although very small, amounting to only 5-6 percentage points. And the United States, Ukraine's main military and financial donor, is not at the top of the list. This once again confirms a pattern known to sociologists: people's behavior and attitudes toward certain objects are more influenced by the perception of reality than by reality itself. Furthermore, perception depends on reality itself, on the personal experience of a person and his or her immediate environment, and on the information space in which this person is located.

---

42   Ines Aizele, 'De zhyve naibilshe ukrainskykh bizhentsiv.' *DW*, April 12, 2023, https://www.dw.com.

43   Ibid.

44   'Viiskova dopomoha dlia Ukrainy: skilky vzhe vytratyv Zakhid?' *DW*, December 19, 2022, https://www.dw.com.

The leaders of negative attitudes are, of course, Russia (negative 94%, positive 3%, balance -91%), Belarus (balance -68%), Iran (-57%), a country which openly supports Russia and provides weapons, China (-35%), whose policy is less obvious to Ukrainians, and Hungary (positive 39%, negative 46%, balance -7%). Hungary's policy toward Russia's war with Ukraine is perceived by the Ukrainian population as contradictory and ambiguous. On the one hand, the Hungarian government has condemned Russia's attack on Ukraine and has accepted more than 300,000 Ukrainian refugees, while on the other hand, the Hungarian government has slowed down some sanctions against Russia, including energy sanctions, and has maintained seemingly friendly relations with the Putin regime. Hungarian Prime Minister Viktor Orban stated that Hungary should not be involved in this military conflict, as his priority is the security of the Hungarian people.

In January 2023, KIIS conducted a study[45] on the attitudes of the Ukrainian population toward Israel, commissioned by the Embassy of the State of Israel, which allows us to clarify the factors of this attitude. According to the survey, 48% of Ukrainians believed that Israel supports Ukraine, 8% believe that Israel supports Russia, 20% believe that Israel supports neither side, and the rest (24%) had no definite opinion on this issue. Just over half the respondents (53%) believed that Israel provides some support to Ukraine. The last question we asked (so that the answers to this question would not influence the answers to other questions) was as follows:

> At the moment, Israel does not provide military capabilities to Ukraine. The Israeli press has reported that Israeli officials are interested in supporting Ukraine and providing it with weapons, but they believe that such an action could jeopardize Israel itself. What do you think about Israel's decision?

---

45   On January 3-11, 2023, the Kyiv International Institute of Sociology interviewed 2002 respondents living in all regions of Ukraine (except for the Autonomous Republic of Crimea) by telephone using a computer. The survey was conducted with adult citizens of Ukraine (aged 18 and older) who at the time of the survey resided in Ukraine, within the borders controlled by the Ukrainian authorities until February 24, 2022.

For 33% of Ukrainians, the position of Israeli officials (that providing weapons to Ukraine could jeopardize Israel itself) is understandable and acceptable. Slightly more respondents consider the position unacceptable: 43% (of whom 17% at least understand it, while 26% both do not understand it and consider it unacceptable). In addition, a quarter of respondents (24%) have not decided on their opinion.

Another study characterizing the attitudes of Ukrainians toward Israel was completed by KIIS in early December 2023[46]. On October 7, 2023, the Hamas terrorist movement attacked Israel. In response, Israel launched a military operation in the Palestinian Gaza Strip. Many people in the world sympathized and supported both Israel and the Palestinians. KIIS asked Ukrainians who they sympathized with in the conflict: Israel or Palestine. We compare the data of our survey with the results of surveys in some other countries.[47]

---

46  Between November 29 and December 9, 2023, the Kyiv International Institute of Sociology interviewed 1,031 respondents living in all regions of Ukraine (except Crimea) by telephone using a computer. The survey was conducted with adult citizens of Ukraine (aged 18 and older) who at the time of the survey resided in Ukraine (within the borders controlled by the Ukrainian authorities until February 24, 2022).

47  Matt Haines, 'A Gaza War Divides American Opinion.' *VOA*, December 23, 2023, https://www.voanews.com/a/gaza-war-divides-american-opinion-/73 85723.html; Matthew Smith, 'Most Britons Have Sympathy for Both Sides in Israel-Palestine Conflict.' *YouGov*, November 6, 2023, https://yougov.co.uk/in ternational/articles/47784-most-britons-have-sympathy-for-both-sides-in-isra el-palestine-conflict; 'Palestino-izrailskiy konflikt: oktiabr 2023 goda.' *Levada-Center*, October 27, 2023, https://www.levada.ru/2023/10/27/palestino-izrai lskij-konflikt-oktyabr-2023-goda/.

**Table 5.2.** **"Which side of the Israeli-Palestinian conflict do you sympathize with more?" % (November–December 2023)**

| Country | Sympa-thizing with Israel | Sympathiz-ing with Palestine | Sympa-thize with both sides | Unde-cided | Total |
|---|---|---|---|---|---|
| Ukraine | 69 | 1 | 18 | 12 | 100 |
| USA | 38 | 11 | 28 | 23 | 100 |
| United Kingdom | 19 | 19 | 31 | 31 | 100 |
| Russia* | 6 | 21 | 66 | 7 | 100 |

* In Russia, the questionnaire's answer options did not include the answer "I sympathize with both sides" but "I do not sympathize with either side."

As can be seen (Table 5.2), compared to all these countries, Ukraine is the most pro-Israeli, with almost 70% of those who sympathize with Israel and only 1% with Palestine. In the United States, we see a predominance of those who sympathize with Israel, but they make up 38% (i.e., less than half). And while only 11% sympathize with Palestine, a significant number of Americans sympathize with both sides (28%) or "could not answer the question" (23%). In the United Kingdom, the share of those who sympathize with Israel and Palestine is generally the same: 19% each. Instead, 31% each either "sympathize with both sides" or "could not answer the question."

At the same time, Russia is the only one of these countries where there is significantly more sympathy for Palestine (21%) than for Israel (6%). However, the majority of Russians (66%) said that they do not sympathize with anyone at all. The positive attitude toward Israel may be due to the fact that since 2013, Israel has been perceived by most Ukrainians as a positive example of nation-building in a hostile environment of countries that are many times larger than the Jewish state in terms of population and territory. In addition, Russia has sided with the Palestinians, maintains relations with Hamas, and is an ally of Iran, Israel's main enemy. Iranian "Shaheeds" attack Ukrainian cities almost every day, so Israel is the enemy of the enemy of Ukraine.

The hierarchy of attitudes towards different countries shows that Ukrainian society is now very sensitive not only to real assistance, but also to symbolic support and to the consistency of this support. The complicated situation of interaction between different political forces in Germany, the United States, or Israel, the statements of individual politicians, and the unwillingness to provide certain types of weapons requested by Ukraine affect attitudes toward the country. The war simplifies the perception of the world, makes it contrasting, black and white, and it is difficult for people to assess the situation in terms of the balance of positive and negative, the result of different forces, and even minor negative information is perceived not as a component of the balance, but as a fly in the ointment that spoils the barrel of honey. For example, Lithuania's military or financial assistance cannot be compared to that of the United States or Germany, but consistent diplomatic efforts in support of Ukraine, the fight for sanctions against Russia, and the absence of contradictions in the statements of politicians are reflected in the high ratings of the Ukrainian population. Pre-war problems are likely to have less of an impact on the perception of certain countries. For example, relations between Ukraine and Poland have not been so rosy, with a complicated historical background of conflict and violence in the past. Some Polish politicians and public figures have expressed dissatisfaction with Ukraine's memory policy and demanded recognition of the genocide of Poles in Volyn and Galicia in 1943-1944. These issues sometimes caused tension and misunderstandings between the two countries, but after the outbreak of the war, this was not felt at all. Both attitudes toward Poland and Poles were dominated by gratitude for support in the fight against Russia. In October 2022, Poles were the closest ethnic group to Ukrainians on the social distance scale[48]. Further fluctuations in attitudes toward Poles also depend on current events (problems with the import of Ukrainian grain, blocking the border by Polish carriers).

---

48   'Inter-Ethnic Prejudice in Ukraine, September 2022.' Table 1, KIIS. Accessed December 3, 2023. https://www.kiis.com.ua/?lang=eng&cat=reports&id=1150 &page=1.

A comparison of attitudes toward some of the countries for which we found data from[49] before the war and a year after the war began (Graph 5.16) shows that attitudes toward Ukraine's main donors, the United States, the United Kingdom, and Germany, have improved significantly.

**Graph 5.16.** **Changing attitudes of Ukrainians towards certain countries (2021-2023), % who have a positive attitude towards this country**

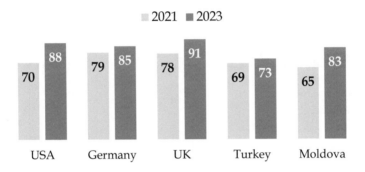

Attitudes toward Turkey have also improved somewhat. One of the significant factors that has improved Ukrainians' attitudes toward Turkey is the delivery of Bayraktar TB2 unmanned aerial vehicles (UAVs). These Turkish military drones proved to be effective and reliable in combat operations against Russian troops at the beginning of the war. However, Turkey also has its own interests in cooperation with Russia, which determine its cautious policy and less favorable assessments of Ukrainians. The significant improvement in attitudes toward Moldova is due to the fact that at the time of the 2021 survey, the president of Moldova was the pro-Russian politician Igor Dodon, and therefore only 65% of Ukrainians had a positive attitude toward Moldova. In November 2021, presidential elections were held in which pro-Western candidate Maia Sandu won, defeating pro-Russian Igor Dodon. After the outbreak of war, Moldova took a clear pro-Ukrainian position, imposed sanctions against Russia, and in January 2023, Sandu arrived in Kyiv on an

---

49   The same study by the Razumkov Center.

official visit and held talks with Zelenskyy. They signed a declaration of strategic partnership between Moldova and Ukraine. The behavior of country leaders also affects attitudes toward these countries.

Table 5.3 shows the results of a survey on the attitude of Ukrainians to political leaders[50].

**Table 5.3. Attitudes of the Ukrainian population towards the leaders of countries (February-March 2023), % who have a positive attitude and the balance (i.e. the number of those who have a positive attitude minus the number of those who have a negative attitude)**

| | Positive attitude, % | Balance, % |
|---|---|---|
| Boris Johnson | 87 | +80 |
| Andrzej Duda | 86 | +81 |
| Joe Biden | 83 | +74 |
| Ursula von der Leyen | 61 | +50 |
| Emmanuel Macron | 60 | +35 |
| Recep Erdogan | 58 | +34 |
| Justin Trudeau | 51 | +41 |
| Olaf Scholz | 50 | +23 |
| Rishi Sunak | 45 | +36 |
| Donald Trump | 29 | -20 |
| Angela Merkel | 29 | -24 |
| Viktor Orban | 14 | -45 |
| Xi Jinping | 12 | -39 |
| Alexander Lukashenko | 3 | -89 |
| Vladimir Putin | 1 | -96 |

We see that the top two positions are occupied by Boris Johnson (former British Prime Minister) and Andrzej Duda (President of Poland), the leaders of the very countries that Ukrainians view most favorably.

Boris Johnson, who was then the Prime Minister of the United Kingdom, arrived in Kyiv on Independence Day, August 24, 2022. During his visit, Boris Johnson expressed the UK's solidarity and

---

50   The same study by the Razumkov Center.

support for Ukraine's fight against Russian aggression. The visit took place despite the danger of shelling and the unpredictability of the situation. This visit emphasized the UK's determination and commitment to helping Ukraine, which could play an important role in improving the attitude of Ukrainians towards Boris Johnson as a political leader. Volodymyr Zelenskyy awarded Boris Johnson the Ukrainian Order of Freedom. Boris Johnson and Andrzej Duda are also known for their charismatic leadership style and open communication with the public. It is clear that attitudes toward these leaders in Ukraine may differ significantly from those in their home countries or other European countries.

On February 26, 2022, two days after Russia's full-scale invasion of Ukraine, Andrzej Duda reiterated his support for Ukraine's direct path to the EU. On May 22, 2022, the Polish president arrived in Kyiv for a visit and spoke at the Verkhovna Rada of Ukraine, assuring that he would make every effort to ensure that Ukraine joined the EU in the near future. Joe Biden has almost the same support for Ukrainians, thanks to the unprecedented support of Ukraine by the United States and his position and visit to Ukraine on February 20, 2023.

The leaders of the negative attitude of Ukrainians are, of course, Putin (97% have a negative attitude towards him, 1% have a positive attitude, i.e. the balance is 96%, 2% find it difficult to say) and Lukashenko (3% have a positive attitude, 92% have a negative attitude, the balance is 89%). Ukrainians also have a negative attitude towards Viktor Orban and Xi Jinping.

In general, attitudes toward countries and their leaders are co-ordinated. The exception is the more negative than positive attitude toward Angela Merkel and Donald Trump. In the case of Angela Merkel, this may be due to the fact that Angela Merkel has sought to maintain a dialogue with Russia in an effort to find diplomatic responses to crises, including the occupation of Crimea and the conflict in eastern Ukraine, which may be perceived by Ukrainians as insufficient condemnation of Russian aggression. Angela Merkel was also against granting Ukraine a NATO Membership Action Plan (MAP). She believed that this could provoke Russia and worsen the situation in Donbas. Angela Merkel also actively supported the construction and implementation of the Nord Stream Two gas pipeline between Russia and Germany. Ukrainians may perceive this as insufficient support for Ukraine and promotion of Russia's economic interests. At the same time, attitudes toward Merkel remained distinctly positive before the invasion, but changed dramatically after the invasion (especially against the backdrop of her sluggish and vague position in condemning Russia).

As for Donald Trump, during his tenure as president, Donald Trump sometimes expressed positive emotions about Vladimir Putin and Russia. Now, Donald Trump sometimes makes controversial statements about Ukraine, for example, about the need to urgently end the war even without returning some Ukrainian territories. Both Donald Trump himself and some members of the Republican Party criticize Biden and advocate for a review of the amount of aid to Ukraine. However, by the end of 2023, issues of domestic politics in the United States and preparations for the 2024 elections took precedence, and Trump influenced a number of Republicans to block aid to Ukraine.

The dynamics of changes in the attitudes of Ukrainians toward some of these politicians[51] (see Graph 5.17) is quite obvious.

---

51   The same study by the Razumkov Center.

**Graph 5.17. Changes in the attitude of Ukrainians towards certain politicians (2021-2023), % who have a positive attitude towards these politicians**

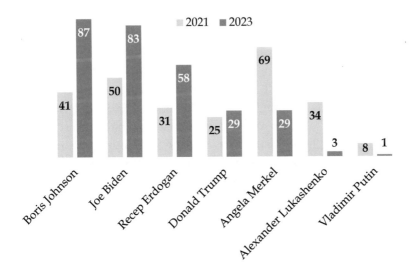

Attitudes toward Boris Johnson, Joe Biden, and Recep Erdogan have improved significantly, attitudes toward Donald Trump have not changed significantly, attitudes toward Angela Merkel have dropped significantly, attitudes toward Alexander Lukashenko have dropped from 34% to 3%, and Putin's was 8% and became 1%. As for Putin, attitudes toward him deteriorated sharply in 2014 after the annexation of Crimea and the war in Donbas; in 2013, 42% had a positive attitude toward him.

Thus, the war that began on February 24, 2022, when Russia launched its aggression against Ukraine, has had a significant impact on the foreign policy orientations of Ukrainians, their attitudes toward countries and political leaders. In this difficult period for Ukraine, the solidarity and support of the international community have become key factors shaping public opinion in the country. First, Ukrainians have become more positive about countries that actively support Ukraine and provide military, humanitarian, and economic assistance. Cooperation with the European Union,

NATO, and their member states, including the United States, the United Kingdom, Germany, Poland, and Turkey, is of particular importance to Ukrainian society. Second, attitudes toward political leaders who openly defend Ukraine have improved. Ukrainians highly appreciate the role of Boris Johnson, Andrzej Duda, Joe Biden and other politicians who visited Ukraine during the war, publicly condemned Russian aggression and stepped up international assistance. Third, negative attitudes toward Russia and its political leadership are turning into hatred because of the incredible suffering of the Ukrainian people, the killing of tens of thousands of people, the loss of loved ones, friends and acquaintances, the destruction of cities, infrastructure, housing and cultural monuments, and numerous war crimes by Russians. This affects the attitude towards those countries and leaders who assist the aggressor or even insufficiently or inconsistently condemn it.

# 6. Attitudes of Ukrainians Towards Russia and Belarus

## 6.1. Dynamics of the attitude of the population of Ukraine to Russia and the population of Russia to Ukraine before the war (2008-2021)

### 6.1.1. Methodology and main results

KIIS and the Levada Center have been measuring attitudes toward the neighboring state from time to time[52]. In 2008, V. Paniotto suggested that Levada Center deputy director Alexei Grazhdankin coordinate the wording of the questions and the timing of the survey, as well as synchronize the publication of the results. Alexei Grazhdankin supported this idea, and from 2008 to 2022 we had a joint project where we asked questions about the attitude of the population to the neighboring state, its leadership, population, and some other questions (for example, attitude to Stalin) every three months in parallel. The latest research was conducted at the end of 2021. The outbreak of war stopped this project.

During the project, 37 surveys were conducted in each country at the expense of each company, with a sample of about 2000 Ukrainians in Ukraine and about 1600 Russians in Russia (for a total of about 74,000 Ukrainians and 59,000 Russians surveyed during the project). The data are representative of the population of each country aged 18 and older. In Ukraine, after 2014, surveys were conducted only on the territory controlled by the government of Ukraine. All surveys until April 2020 were conducted by face-to-face interviews, and from April 2020, the surveys are not fully equivalent, as Russia continued to conduct the survey using face-to-face interviews, while Ukraine switched to a telephone survey (CATI).

---

52  An autonomous nonprofit organization, the Levada Center is forcibly included in the register of nonprofit organizations in Russia that perform the functions of a foreign agent.

In the course of the survey, Ukrainians were asked the question: "How do you generally feel about Russia now?" and Russians were asked: "How do you generally feel about Ukraine now?" with the options "very good," "good," "hard to say," "bad," "very bad." Let's look at the results of a series of these studies and in more detail at the results of the latest wave of these studies.

First of all, it is noteworthy that Ukrainians have had a better attitude toward Russia than Russians toward Ukraine for almost the entire period of observation (from 2008 to February 2020, except for September 2019) (see Graph 6.1). The attitude of Ukrainians toward Russia from 2008 (and possibly earlier) until May 2014 can be described as "unrequited love." In September 2019, Russians' attitudes toward Ukraine were somewhat better, perhaps because of expectations that the new Ukrainian government would change Ukrainians' attitudes toward Russia.

**Graph 6.1. Dynamics of positive attitudes of the population of Ukraine towards Russia and of the population of Russia towards Ukraine (2008-2021), % of those who have a positive or very positive attitude towards the other country**

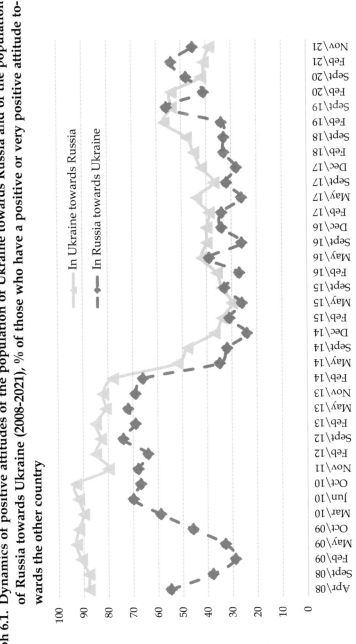

During this period, in different years, 80% to 90% of Ukrainians had a positive attitude toward Russia, while the share of Russians who had a positive attitude toward Ukraine ranged from 30% to 70%. For example, after the Russian-Georgian war in August 2008, Russian attitudes toward Ukraine deteriorated significantly; by January 2009, only 29% of Russians maintained a positive opinion of Ukraine (62% negative, 10% undecided), while 90% of Ukrainians continued to have a positive attitude toward Russia.

What could be the explanation? In our opinion, the following hypotheses can be put forward. The positive attitude of Ukrainians towards Russia from 2008 (and most likely earlier) to 2013 can be explained by the natural attitude towards the brotherly people[53] , who, prior to the historical life experience of most Ukrainians, were perceived as people of the same country in which they lived relatively recently, only 20 years ago. During this period, 15-20% of the Ukrainian population wanted to unite with Russia into one state (though mostly not in the sense of a full merger), the rest supported Ukraine's independence, but 70% wanted special relations with Russia without visas and customs.

In 2008, different political forces in Ukraine took different positions on the Russian-Georgian war, and the media (owned by different oligarchs) gave different assessments of the events, so the population of Ukraine as a whole did not change its positive attitude towards Russia. Our hypotheses about the Russian population are based on consultations with Russian sociologists and are as follows: Unlike Ukrainians, Russians, for various reasons, perceive the feeling of „belonging to a Great Country" as an essential and meaningful value; Ukraine is seen as an entity that should be part of this „Great Country"; the process of the collapse of the USSR and the

---

53   Here, the word "brotherly" is used positively. Nowadays, the word "brotherhood" in relation to Russians has a rather negative meaning for Ukrainians (especially in the combination "older brother"). One immediately associates it with the brotherhood in the story of the Ukrainian writer Felix Kryvin. "At the dawn of history, half of humanity was destroyed: Cain killed Abel. Then came the days of peace. Cain turned out to be a good owner: he quickly mastered the land and populated it with abundant offspring. And to his children, who could not appreciate all this, Cain repeatedly said: 'Take care, children, of this world for which your uncle died!'"

formation of independent states is seen, in particular, not as the creation of independent states – Ukraine and Russia – but as the separation of Ukraine from Russia. Since Ukrainians have separated from Russia, they are to some extent treated as "traitors" in the minds of most Russians, so attitudes toward Ukrainians after 1991 are worse than Ukrainians' attitudes toward Russians (and attitudes toward citizens, as will be seen below, dominate as a component of attitudes toward the country as a whole).

The second reason for the existence of "unrequited love" may be the targeted activities of the media, especially television, which for Russians (as well as for Ukrainians) was the main source of information before the pandemic. Opposition TV channels are practically absent from the daily TV viewing of the vast majority of Russians, and the remaining channels on many issues (including geopolitical ones) are controlled from one center. A well-known Russian journalist, the general director of NTV, Yevgeniy Kisilyov, who worked in Russia until 2009. says that the basic principle of reporting news about Ukraine resembles the principle of talking about the dead[54], but only in reverse: the bad elements can be discussed or nothing at all.

The collapse of Ukrainians' positive attitudes toward Russia began after the annexation of Crimea and continued after the outbreak of the war in Donbas, with only 30% of Ukrainians having a positive attitude toward Russia by March 2015. However, after the end of the "hot" phase of hostilities, the positive attitude of Ukrainians toward Russia gradually recovered, and in February 2019, 57% of Ukrainians had a positive attitude toward Russia. But from the end of 2020 and into 2021, tensions with Russia increased and the percentage of supporters of Russia dropped to about 40%. However, this may also be due to the effect of the method, as we have already mentioned, KIIS switched to telephone surveys.

In this project, we also asked the question: "How would you like to see Ukraine's relations with Russia?". There were three potential options: "1 – Ukraine's relations with Russia should be the

---

54    A well-known Russian proverb says that „One should say either good or nothing about the dead."

same as with other states—with closed borders, visas, customs";
"2—Ukraine and Russia should be independent but friendly states,
with open borders, no visas and customs" and "3—Ukraine and
Russia should unite into one state". We interpret answers 1 or 2 as
support for Ukraine's independence (although in option 2, respondents would like to have independence with special relations
with Russia, including no visas and no customs). Option 3 represents those who are against Ukraine's independence. The results
are shown in Graph 6.2.

**Graph 6.2. What kind of relations with Russia do people in Ukraine want (2008-2021), %**

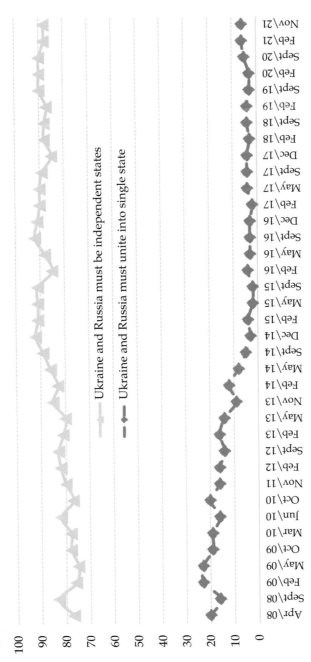

— Ukraine and Russia must be independent states

◆ Ukraine and Russia must unite into single state

\* The line in the graph "Ukraine and Russia should be independent" is the sum of the first two columns in Table D6.2 in the appendix, i.e. the percentage of those who want independence with borders and customs and those who want independence but without borders and customs.

Between 2009 and 2014, the percentage of those who support Ukraine's independence increased from 75% to 90% and remained stable thereafter. In the latest survey of the project, in November 2021, compared to February 2021, the level of support for Ukraine's independence (the percentage of those who believe that Ukraine should be independent from Russia) remained approximately the same at 88% (it was the same), this figure has remained virtually unchanged since 2014. The number of those who want closed borders with Russia is 39%, and the number of those who want independent relations, but without borders and customs, is 49%. Unification into one state would be preferable for 6%.

In Russia, in November 2021, compared to February 2021, the share of those who want to close the borders with Ukraine has not changed much (24% as opposed to 23%), but the share of those who do not want visas and borders has decreased (51% as opposed to 57%). The number of those who want to unite into one state has not changed much (17% compared to 18% before).

### 6.1.2. The last joint wave (November 2021)

Let's take a closer look at the results of the latest wave of the joint survey. In Ukraine, in November 2021, 39% of Ukrainians had a good or very good attitude toward Russia, about 47% had a bad or very bad attitude, and 12% were undecided. Compared to February 2021, there was a general deterioration in attitudes toward Russia. This may have been due to Russia's escalation of the situation on Ukraine's borders.

In Russia, 45% of the population had a good or very good attitude toward Ukraine, 43% had a poor or very poor attitude, and 12% were undecided. Compared to February 2021, attitudes have deteriorated markedly, as in February, 54% of Russians had a good attitude toward Ukraine. The attitude of Ukrainians toward Russia significantly depended on the region: 26% of respondents in the West had a positive attitude toward Russia, 35% in the Center, 49% in the South, and 52% in the East. The majority of those who had a negative attitude toward Russia were concentrated in the Western region (61%), while the lowest number of such people was in the Eastern region (30%).

To study the issue in more depth, respondents were also asked the questions "How do you generally feel about Russians (residents of Russia) now?" and "How do you generally feel about the Russian leadership now?" The results are shown in Graph 6.3.

**Graph 6.3. Attitudes of respondents towards the Government and the population of another country separately, % (November 2021)**

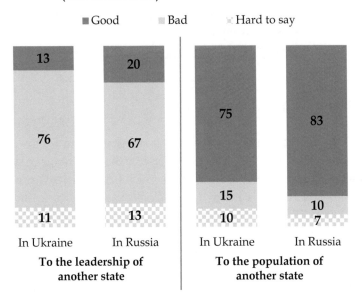

In the case of both countries, there is a similar trend where respondents have a mostly good attitude toward the population of the neighboring state and a mostly bad attitude toward the leadership of the neighboring state (in Russia, however, the attitude toward the leadership of Ukraine and Ukrainians living in Ukraine was somewhat better than in Ukraine toward the leadership of Russia and Russians living in Russia). At the same time, in the regional dimension, attitudes toward Russians living in Russia varied much less, from 71% of good attitudes in the West to 82% in the East.

Good attitudes toward the Russian leadership increased from 5% in the West to 27% in the East.

    Table 6.1 shows the percentage of Ukrainians who have a positive attitude toward Russia, its people and leadership. Three months before the outbreak of the war, three-quarters of the Ukrainian population had a good attitude toward Russians and approximately 40% had a good attitude toward Russia. This is all after the events of 2014. What could this be due to?

**Table 6.1.  Attitudes of the Ukrainian population towards Russia, Russians and the Russian leadership 3 months before the outbreak of war, % (November 2021)**

| Have a positive attitude towards... | % |
| --- | --- |
| ...to Russia | 39 |
| ...to Russians (residents of Russia) | 75 |
| ...to the Russian leadership | 13 |

As we can see, attitudes toward Russia integrate attitudes toward the population and the country's leadership; the percentage of supporters of Russia (39%) did not differ much from the average attitudes toward Russians and to the Russian leadership (The arithmetic mean of 75% and 13% is 44%, which differs from 39% by only 5%.). We can also see that positive attitudes toward Russia are mainly associated with positive attitudes toward Russians. Figure 6.4 shows how those who have a generally good or poor attitude toward Russia view the Russian leadership and Russians. Among Ukrainian respondents who have a generally good attitude toward Russia, almost all (95%) have a good attitude toward Russians living in Russia. At the same time, only 29% of them have a good attitude toward the Russian leadership. Among Ukrainian respondents who have a generally poor attitude toward Russia, 95% have a poor attitude toward the Russian leadership, but 59% have a good attitude toward Russians living in Russia. Obviously, for some respondents, the question about their general attitude toward Russia primarily evokes associations with the Russian leadership, and as a result, these respondents are more likely to report a poor attitude. For the other part of respondents, "Russia" is primarily associated with ordinary Russians, so they are more likely to have a generally good attitude toward Russia.

**Graph 6.4. Attitudes of Ukrainians toward the Russian leadership and Russians living in Russia depending on their overall attitude toward Russia, % (November 2021)**

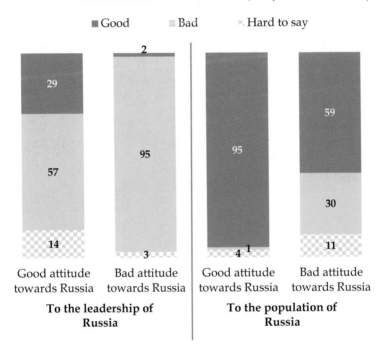

If a good attitude toward Russia is primarily related to a good attitude toward Russians, then perhaps this is a consequence of family and friendship ties? In the same November 2021 survey, we asked whether respondents had close relatives in Russia. Of those surveyed, 43% of respondents said they had close relatives in Russia (another 14% said they had relatives in Russia but did not consider them close). The share of respondents who have such relatives increases from 33% in the West to 53% in the East (Graph 6.5).

**Graph 6.5. "Do you have close relatives in Russia?", % total and by regions (November 2021)**

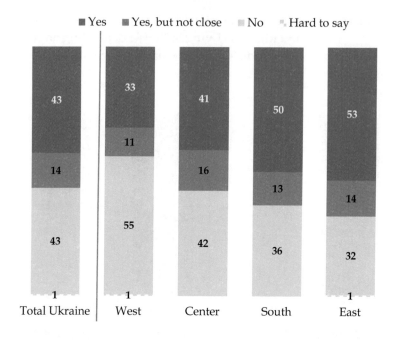

■ Yes   ■ Yes, but not close   ■ No   ▪ Hard to say

Graph 6.6 shows how those with and without close relatives view Russia in general. As can be seen, first, those who have relatives have a better attitude toward Russia in general. At the same time, this trend persists within each region separately. Both in the West and in the East, respondents who have close relatives in Russia have a better attitude toward Russia in general than other residents of the same region who do not have such relatives. Secondly, even after taking this factor into account, the tendency remains that attitudes toward Russia improve from West to East.

**Graph 6.6. Attitudes of Ukrainians towards Russia in terms of having close relatives in Russia, % (November 2021)**

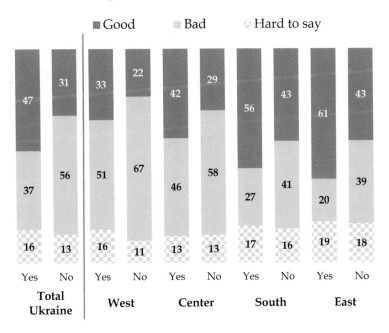

Another factor in the positive attitude toward Russians could be the perception that they may not support the leadership's policy, but they do not have any influence on it. We asked the question, "Do you think ordinary Russians have any influence on the policy of the Russian leadership towards Ukraine?" The vast majority of Ukrainians (76% overall, 73-77% depending on the region) believed that ordinary Russians have no influence on the policy of the Russian leadership, see Graph 6.7.

**Graph 6.7. "Do you think ordinary Russians have any influence on the policy of the Russian leadership towards Ukraine?", % total and by regions (November 2021)**

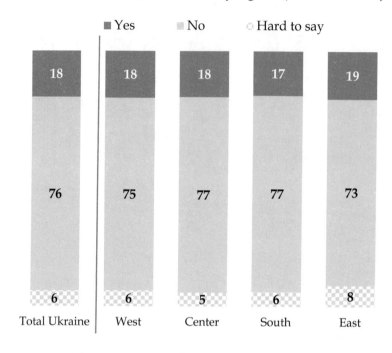

Graph 6.8 shows how Russia is generally viewed by those who believe that ordinary Russians have influence over Russia's leadership, as well as by those who believe that ordinary Russians do not have influence over Russia's leadership. In general, the results show that this factor has an impact, but not a very large one. In the West and in the Center, there is a tendency for a slightly better attitude among those who do not believe that ordinary people have influence. At the same time, in the South and East, the trend is reversed: those who believe that ordinary people have influence have a slightly better attitude.

Graph 6.8. Attitudes of Ukrainians towards Russia in terms of whether ordinary Russians have an influence on the policy of the Russian leadership, % (November 2021)

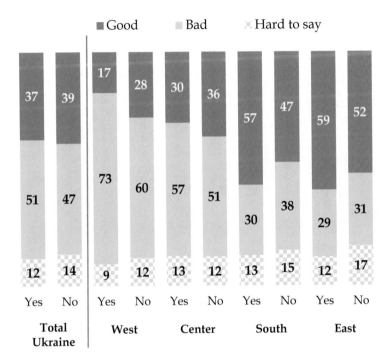

Graph 6.9 shows the relationship with attitudes toward Russians living in Russia. In this case, the tendency is more pronounced in the West and Center: those who believe that ordinary residents have influence on the leadership have a worse attitude toward Russians living in Russia.

**Graph 6.9. Attitudes of Ukrainians towards Russians living in Russia in terms of whether ordinary Russians have an influence on the policy of the Russian leadership, % (November 2021)**

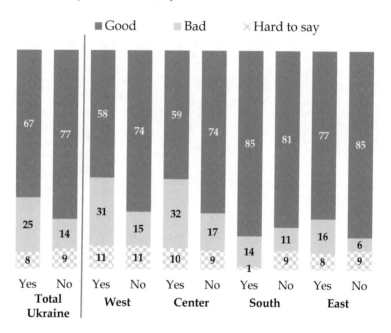

## 6.2. Changes in the attitude of the Ukrainian population towards Russia after the outbreak of war

In Chapter 6.1, we analyzed the dynamics of Ukrainians' attitudes toward Russia and Russians' attitudes toward Ukraine from 2008 to the end of 2021 based on the results of a joint project with the Levada Center. After the project was terminated, we only have data on Ukrainians' attitudes toward Russia. Graph 6.10 shows the same data on positive attitudes of Ukrainians toward Russia as in Figure 6.1 for the period 2008-2010 (but without the attitudes of Russians toward Ukraine), but it is supplemented with data from 2022 and data on negative attitudes toward Russians.

As we can see, over the past three years before the full-scale invasion, there was a gradual decline in positive attitudes towards

Russia, but even despite several months of escalation near Ukraine's borders, 34% of the Ukrainian population had a good attitude towards Russia in early February 2022 (mainly due to positive attitudes towards Russians). We conducted the first survey of Ukrainians' attitudes towards Russia after the outbreak of war in May 2022. As we can see, after the outbreak of the war, attitudes toward Russia have deteriorated dramatically, which is understandable. only 2% of citizens had a good attitude toward Russia, while 92% had a bad attitude. However, it is important to understand that 2% is about 500,000 people, which means that a rather significant number in absolute terms still maintains a positive attitude towards the aggressor despite the obvious facts. And while before the invasion 75% had a good attitude toward "ordinary Russians," in May 2022, 82% had a bad attitude toward "ordinary Russians."

**Graph 6.10. Dynamics of good and bad attitudes of the population of Ukraine towards Russia (2008-2022), %**

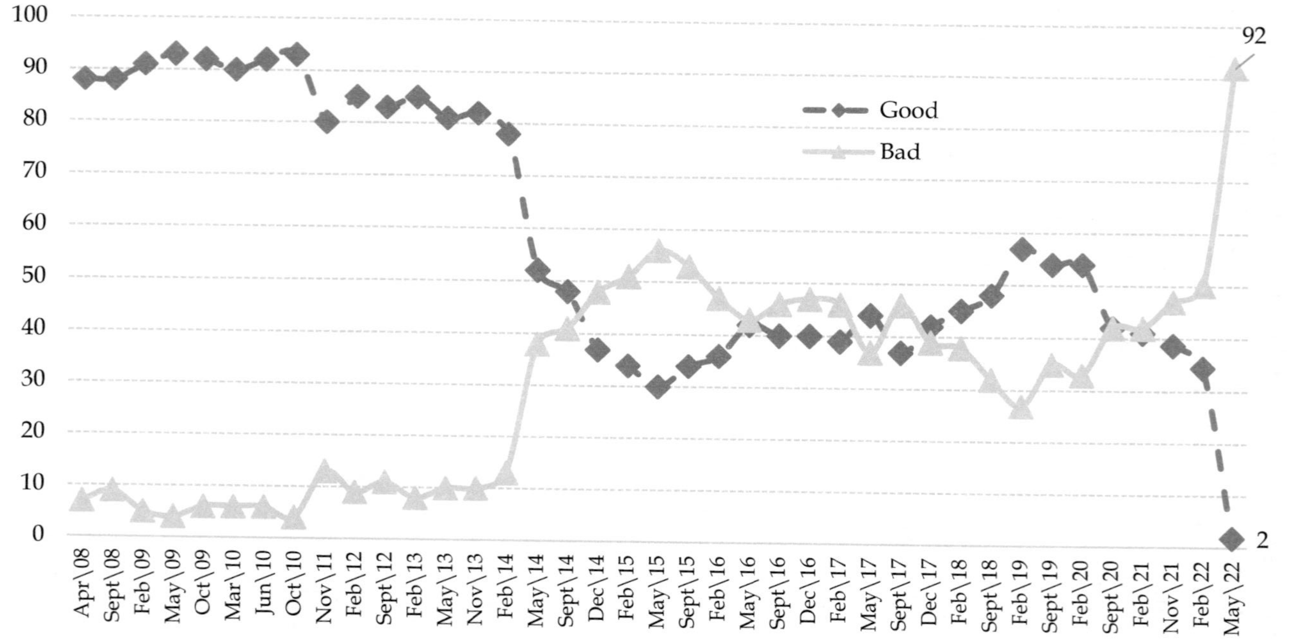

In addition to these data, it is important to see changes at the individual level. As part of a methodological experiment, we re-interviewed 513 respondents who participated in our Omnibus survey conducted in early February 2022, before the full-scale invasion. For these respondents, we knew what their attitude toward Russia was in early February, and now we repeated the same question. As you can see in Graph 6.11, among those who had a bad attitude towards Russia before, 97% continue to have it (although 3% now chose the option "hard to say"). The change in the views of those who had a good attitude toward Russia and those who had an undecided attitude toward it is dramatic. Thus, 80% of those who used to have a good attitude toward Russia, in May 2022 have a bad attitude toward it. Less than one in ten has maintained a positive attitude toward Russia, although another 12% have now decided to answer "undecided." Among those who had an undecided attitude toward Russia, 97% have already begun to have a bad attitude toward it two months into the war.

**Graph 6.11. In May 2022, how did those who had a good / bad / undecided attitude towards Russia in early February 2022 feel about it, %**

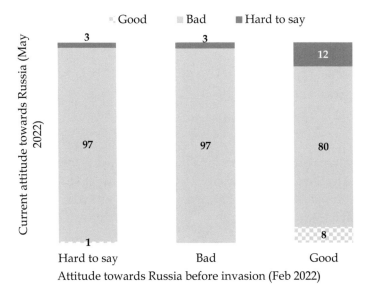

In all regions of Ukraine, the vast majority of residents already had a bad attitude towards Russia in May 2022 (see Graph 6.12), in particular, 90% in the South had a bad attitude, and 85% in the East (while in early February, respectively, 45% and 53% had a good attitude towards Russia). Relatively the highest number of those who continued to have a good attitude toward Russia was recorded in the East at 4%.

**Graph 6.12. Attitudes towards Russia by regions, % (May 2022)**

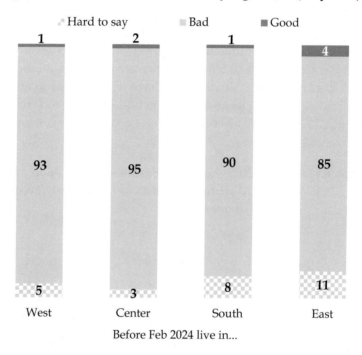

Before Feb 2024 live in...

The vast majority of citizens (82%) who continued to live in the occupied territories after February 24, 2022 had a negative attitude toward Russia, and only 6% had a positive attitude toward it (Graph 6.13).

**Graph 6.13. Attitudes towards Russia depending on where the respondent currently lives, % (May 2022)**

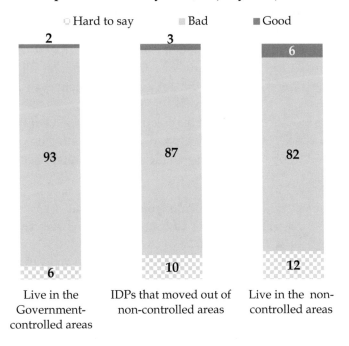

The outbreak of a full-scale war also had an extremely negative impact on attitudes toward Russians. While before, and even after 2014, a significant number of Ukrainians believed that Russians were mostly hostages of their government and against the war with Ukraine, these illusions disappeared during the war. According to the Rating company, as early as August 2022, 81% of Ukrainians had a negative attitude toward Russians (in April 2022 this was 69%, and in April 2021 this was 41%), 14% were neutral, and only 3% were positive.

In Chapter 11 ("Possible Social Problems of Postwar Ukraine"), we examine the attitudes of the Ukrainian population toward various ethnic groups using the Bogardus Social Distance Scale. Among these groups are Russians. Back in 2013, the attitude of Ukrainians toward Russians and Belarusians was better than toward all other ethnic groups. It should be noted that it has been the best over the entire period of observation, for more than 25 years; even after 2013, the social distance to Russians and Belarusians was the smallest after Ukrainians, they ranked second and third in terms of social distance after Ukrainians. The situation changed only after the full-scale invasion of February 2022. In October 2023, the attitude toward Russians was the worst among all ethnic groups: 80% of respondents did not want to see them even as tourists.

We also tried to capture the emotional background of the Russian invasion. The question we asked was "What emotions do you feel about Russia's war against Ukraine?" The results are shown in Graph 6.14.

**Graph 6.14. "What emotions do you feel about Russia's war against Ukraine? Choose up to 3 answers from the list.", % (May 2022)**

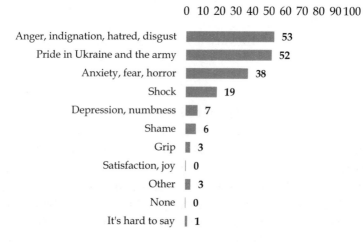

The top emotions that Ukrainians feel about Russia's war against Ukraine are: anger/indignation/hate/disgust (53%), pride in Ukraine/army (52%), and anxiety/fear/terror (38%). Table 6.2 presents the data on emotional background in a regional dimension. Although the overall situation is similar, there is a tendency for anxiety/fear/terror and shock to increase from West to East.

**Table 6.2.  Emotions by regions, % (May 2022)**

| | Until February 24, 2022, they lived in the region... | | | |
|---|---|---|---|---|
| | West | Center | South | East |
| Anger, indignation, hatred, disgust | 56 | 55 | 53 | 46 |
| Pride in Ukraine and the army | 51 | 56 | 49 | 45 |
| Anxiety, fear, horror | 34 | 39 | 38 | 41 |
| Shock | 16 | 18 | 20 | 26 |
| Depression, numbness | 6 | 7 | 7 | 10 |
| Shame | 7 | 6 | 4 | 8 |
| Grip | 5 | 2 | 2 | 1 |
| Satisfaction, joy | 1 | 0 | 1 | 0 |
| Other | 4 | 4 | 2 | 3 |
| None | 0 | 0 | 0 | 0 |
| It's hard to say | 2 | 1 | 1 | 2 |

Table 6.3 shows the data depending on where the respondent lived at the time of the survey. It is important to see that even among those living under occupation, 41% feel proud of Ukraine and its army.

**Table 6.3.  Emotions by where the respondent currently lives, %**
**(May 2022)**

|  | Live in the Government-controlled areas | IDPs that moved out of non-controlled areas | Live in the non-controlled areas |
|---|---|---|---|
| Anger, indignation, hatred, disgust | 54 | 51 | 46 |
| Pride in Ukraine and the army | 53 | 37 | 41 |
| Anxiety, fear, horror | 37 | 45 | 39 |
| Shock | 19 | 19 | 22 |
| Depression, numbness | 7 | 10 | 11 |
| Shame | 6 | 3 | 5 |
| Grip | 3 | 0 | 2 |
| Satisfaction, joy | 0 | 0 | 0 |
| Other | 3 | 2 | 0 |
| None | 0 | 0 | 1 |
| It's hard to say | 1 | 0 | 3 |

# 6.3. Changes in the attitude of the population of Ukraine to Belarus

To understand the situation before the war, we will look at the results of a joint project of the Kyiv International Institute of Sociology, the Russian non-governmental research organization Levada Center, and the Belarusian sociological company Novak. All three companies conducted the surveys in May 2014. All questions asked to respondents in each country were identical, which makes it possible to make a correct comparison of the attitudes of citizens of these countries toward their neighbors. The results are shown in Graph 6.15.

**Graph 6.15. % of adults in each country who have a good or very good attitude toward a given country (May 2014)**

*the direction of the arrow indicates the direction of the relationship (to whom)*

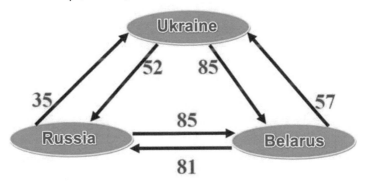

As we can see, the closest relations were between Russia and Belarus, and in 1999 the Treaty on the Establishment of the Union State between Russia and Belarus was signed, which aimed to strengthen political, economic and social ties between the two countries. Belarus was viewed positively by 85% of Russians and positively by 81% of Belarusians.

As we have seen in both Graph 6.1 and Graph 6.15, before Russia's occupation of Crimea, approximately 80% of Ukrainians had a positive attitude toward Russia, and after the annexation of Crimea and the hostilities in Donbas, the percentage of supporters of Russia fell rapidly: 52% in May 2014; 48% in September 2014; 37% in December 2014; 34% in February 2015, and 30% in May 2015. In May 2014, 52% of the Ukrainian population had a positive attitude toward Russia, although only 35% of Russians shared these positive feelings toward Ukraine. As we can see, Ukrainians were generally more friendly toward their neighbor to the east than the Russian population was toward Ukraine. This may be due to the strong efforts of Russian propaganda to foster negative attitudes toward Ukraine before the seizure of Crimea. In late 2013 and early 2014, Russian propaganda skillfully used a variety of tools to foster negative attitudes toward Ukraine. One of the most common tools was television talk shows, which actively contributed to the spread of disinformation and manipulation of public opinion. These talk shows were used to disseminate provocative statements and stereotypes that contributed to inciting hostility towards Ukraine. The talk show "Evening with Vladimir Solovyov", programs by Dmitriy Kiselyov, Margarita Simonyan, Olga Skabeeva were entirely devoted to Ukraine, while in Ukraine, there were practically no programs of this type devoted entirely to Russia. No wonder Vladimir Putin awarded 300 journalists with Russian state awards "for objectivity in covering the events in Crimea"[55]. The result of this propaganda campaign was a significant decrease in the number of people who had a positive attitude toward Ukraine. The percentage of Russians who had a positive attitude toward Ukraine decreased from 70% in November 2013 to 35% in May 2014. This demonstrated the effectiveness of Russian propaganda in manipulating public opinion and forming a negative stereotype of Ukraine among a large part of the population.

The same May 2014 survey in Russia and Ukraine examined not only attitudes toward the countries as a whole, but also separately toward the countries' residents and the countries' leadership. 80% of the population of Ukraine had a generally good attitude toward Russians (32% very good and 48% mostly good) while 13.5% had a generally bad attitude. Of those surveyed, 81% of the population of Russia had a generally good attitude toward Ukrainians (22% very good and 59% mostly good) while 12% had a generally bad attitude. The opposite situation is evident in the attitude of the population of Ukraine to the leadership of Russia and the population of Russia to the leadership of Ukraine: 71% of the population of Ukraine had a generally poor attitude toward the Russian leadership (56% very poor and 15% mostly poor), 19% had a generally good attitude (10% undecided). Of those surveyed, 79% of the population of Russia had a generally poor attitude toward the leadership of Ukraine (29% very poor and 50% mostly poor), while 11% had a generally good attitude, with 10% undecided.

---

55   'Putin tayno nagradil 300 zhurnalistov za "obektivnoe osveshchenie sobytii v Krymu".' *Wikinews*, May 5, 2014, https://www.wikinews.org.

Ukraine's relations with Belarus were even more positive, with 85% of Ukrainians feeling good about Belarus, while only 57% of Belarusians felt sympathy for Ukraine. Once again, Ukrainians showed more goodwill toward their neighbors than the population of these countries toward Ukraine. This may also be due to the influence of Russian propaganda, as Russian television is popular in Belarus.

Ukrainians' sympathies for Belarus were tested in 2020. On August 9, 2020, presidential elections were held, which became one of the most important events in the country's political history. Alexander Lukashenko, who had been president since 1994, ran for a fifth term. The election process was subject to criticism and accusations of undemocratic practices and irregularities. Most of the opposition candidates were excluded from running in the elections or were subjected to pressure and harassment during the campaign. The official election results showed a landslide victory for Alexander Lukashenko with an extremely high level of support. However, these results were questionable, suspicious, independent sociological surveys or exit polls were banned and these results triggered mass protests in many cities of Belarus, where people expressed their dissatisfaction with the electoral process and demanded new, fair and just elections. The protests that followed the announcement of the results lasted for a long time, involving millions of people. This led to the reaction of the government of Alexander Lukashenko in the form of a brutal crackdown and mass detentions of protesters. The fact of mass detentions, beatings and ill-treatment of arrested protesters became common knowledge. There have been reports of the use of inadequate force by law enforcement agencies, such as police and special forces. The violent dispersal of the demonstrations resulted in violations of human rights, including freedom of speech, freedom of assembly and freedom of expression. Many protesters were subjected to systematic beatings, deprivation of liberty and threats in prisons. A large number of people were detained and prosecuted for their participation in the protests. In September 2020, KIIS conducted a nationwide survey of the Ukrainian population, which studied the attitude of Ukrainians to the events in Belarus. During the interview, respondents were asked the question: "As you know, there are mass protests in Belarus against Lukashenko's government. Who do you support more: the protesters or Lukashenko?". According to the survey, 45% of all Ukrainians supported the protesters. Lukashenko was supported by 31% of respondents. It should be noted that before these events, Lukashenko was very popular in Ukraine. According to the Rating Center[56], in October 2019, 67% of Ukrainians had a positive attitude towards him while only 15% had a negative attitude, and in August 2020, only 45% had a positive attitude while 42% had a negative attitude. In September 2021, 34% had a positive attitude and 59% had a negative attitude, meaning that the vast majority already had a negative attitude towards Lukashenko.

With the beginning of a new stage of the war in February 2022, the situation in the attitudes of Ukrainians toward Russia and Belarus has changed radically. Changes in attitudes toward Russia were discussed at the beginning of this section. As for Belarus, not only did it not condemn Russia's attack on Ukraine, but it actually became an accomplice in Putin's invasion of Ukraine, serving as a staging ground for Russian military units attacking Ukraine from the north. Thanks to this support, Russian troops approached Kyiv in two days, took Chornobyl and other cities in northern Ukraine. Belarus provided its infrastructure to the Russian army. Missiles were fired from Belarusian territory towards Ukraine, and Belarusian railways and medical infrastructure were used in the attack. It is clear that this has led to a significant deterioration in the attitudes of Ukrainians toward Belarusians and Belarus (as we know, attitudes toward a country integrate attitudes toward the population and the country's leadership).

In a survey conducted by KIIS in May 2022, we asked "Do you think Belarus is an accomplice to the military conflict in Ukraine?" 84% of Ukrainians answered this question in the affirmative, while only 10% answered "no". Another question was "How has your attitude toward Belarusians changed since Russia attacked Ukraine on February 24, 2022?". Of those surveyed, 68% answered that "It

---

56   'Otsinka obranoi mizhnarodnoi polityky. Pytannia.' September 2-4, 2021, v.paniotto@gmail.com (Google).

has worsened"; 24% that "it has not changed" and 3% that "it has improved". When asked about their attitude toward Belarusians, 43% had a positive attitude, while 48% had a negative attitude.

According to the above-mentioned research by the Rating Company, in August 2022, 52% of the Ukrainian population had a negative attitude toward Belarusians (in April 2022 it was 33%, in April 2021 it was 4%), 34% had a neutral attitude, and 10% had a positive attitude.

Regarding attitudes toward Belarus, data conducted in February-March 2023 is available from the Razumkov Center. Thus, according to the Razumkov Center, only 12% of Ukrainians had a positive attitude towards Belarus (81% had a negative attitude). This was a sharp drop compared to the 85% positive attitude we recorded in 2014 (only 6% had a negative attitude then), see Graph 6.16.

**Graph 6.16. Changes in the attitude of Ukrainians towards Belarus from 2014 to 2023, %**

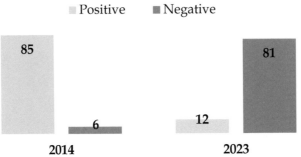

As noted above, in Chapter 11 we examine the attitudes of the Ukrainian population toward various ethnic groups using the Bogardus social distance scale. Among these groups are Russians. Attitudes toward Belarusians have been the best after those toward Ukrainians and Russians over the entire period of observation, more than 25 years, even after 2013. But after the outbreak of the war in 2022, the situation changed dramatically. In October 2023, attitudes toward Belarusians are almost the worst among all ethnic groups (46% of respondents do not want to see them even as tourists). All these data show the deep disappointment of Ukrainians with the position of Belarus and Belarusians in the Russian-Ukrainian conflict.

# 7. Moral and Psychological State and Readiness to Resist the Enemy

## 7.1. Introduction

The moral and psychological state of the population is always an important characteristic of the state of society, but it is especially important in times of war. Understanding the moral and psychological state of the population and its readiness to resist determines the strategy and tactics of warfare, the prioritization of assistance to civilians, and the formation of foreign policy. It is immeasurably important to understand the psychological mood of society, its pain points, aspects of resilience[57] and resistance to the current aggressor. This makes it possible not only to build an effective military strategy, but also to provide the population with the necessary assistance, support and resources. The moral and psychological state of the population is a critical factor in the context of any military conflict, especially during a full-scale war. It affects the readiness for self-defense, the will to win, and patience under stress and unusual circumstances. Changes in this state can determine the direction of events, the resilience of society in the face of threats, and its ability to recover from a crisis. Readiness to resist the enemy is not only the physical ability to fight. It is a psychological readiness to sacrifice one's own life for the freedom of one's country, it is the cohesion of society, and it is cooperation at various levels, from the public to the state. In this section, we attempt to address these questions based on the results of sociological research conducted in Ukraine before and during the war. We examine how the war affected the moral and psychological state of the population, their readiness to resist, their attitudes toward various aspects of the military conflict, and their sense of personal belonging to the resistance.

---

57 Resilience is the ability of a person to cope with difficult life events and recover from difficulties or stress. It includes psychological resilience, stress resistance, etc.

A large project for a comprehensive assessment of the resilience of the population was conducted by KIIS for Chemonics International Inc. with the support of the Partnership for a Stronger Ukraine (PFRU) and the Center for Sustainable Peace and Democratic Development (SeeD). At the time of writing, two waves have been conducted (and KIIS is preparing to conduct the third wave in 2024). The first wave of the SHARP project (Comprehensive Assessment of Resilience of the Population using the SCORE methodology) was conducted in the fall of 2022 with more than 4,300 respondents interviewed, and the second wave was conducted in the summer of 2023 with almost 5,000 respondents interviewed.

SHARP (SCORE-inspired Holistic Assessment of Resilience of Population) is a population survey aimed at obtaining data on the resilience of Ukraine through quantitative assessment of social cohesion, resilience and needs of people. The name is an acronym for SCORE-inspired Holistic Assessment of Resilience of Population (SHARP). The study covered indicators such as social cohesion, trust in institutions, service delivery, access to basic needs, community cooperation, civic engagement, and civil resistance.

The research methodology includes the assessment of certain phenomena or characteristics in terms of points. The scores range from 0 to 10, where 0 means that the phenomenon measured by this indicator is not observed at all in the context under study, and 10 means that it is clearly and universally observed. A score of 10 does not always mean something good, and a score of 0 does not always mean something bad. The interpretation of the value of an indicator depends on whether the phenomenon it measures is desirable or undesirable. A score of 10 for "Personal Safety" is very good, while a score of 10 for "Aggression" is very bad[58].

Graph 7.1 shows the level of social cohesion and its individual components and the dynamics from the fall of 2022 to the summer of 2023. According to the researchers:

---

58    Personal safety is the extent to which a person feels safe from violence in everyday life and believes that the police can protect them.

The state of social cohesion is high throughout Ukraine. However, there is a slight deterioration in vertical cohesion (between citizens and the government), which is related to the measurement of trust in state institutions and figures. With the exception of trust in institutions, other elements of social cohesion have remained relatively stable since the first wave of SHARP in the fall of 2022. Trust in institutions has declined markedly. The identification dimension of social cohesion, namely the sense of belonging to the country and pluralism, are the strongest elements. They are followed by orientation towards the common good.[59]

**Graph 7.1. Elements of social cohesion, %**

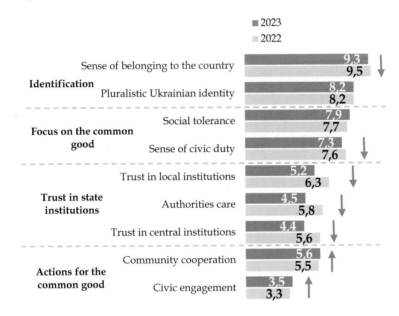

## 7.2. Self-assessment of the level of happiness by the population of Ukraine

Another very important indicator of the state of society is subjective: life satisfaction or the level of happiness in society. Happiness is an important indicator of the well-being of society. It is a comprehensive indicator that includes both tangible and intangible aspects

---

59    'Results of the Second Wave of Research "Comprehensive Assessment of Population Resilience" (SHARP).' *KIIS*, https://kiis.com.ua/?lang=eng&cat=news &id=1363&page=4.

of life, including health, education, social relations, political stability, economic situation, and more. Self-assessment of happiness is sensitive to the slightest changes in these areas, and therefore can serve as a reliable indicator of the general state of society.

In times of war, the study of happiness becomes even more important. This is a period when the pressure on society increases and resources become limited. The level of happiness can reflect how well a society is coping with these challenges and where it may need help. A decline in happiness can be a signal of psychological stress, social or economic instability. Understanding how war affects people's happiness helps governments and non-profit organizations better target their resources to provide the support they need and cope with the challenges.

For over 20 years, KIIS has been asking Ukrainians the question: "Do you consider yourself a happy person?". In particular, we asked this question in December 2021, two months before the full-scale Russian invasion; in September 2022, after the invasion; as well as in May and December 2023. Accordingly, we have the opportunity to assess the dynamics of the situation with happiness in Ukraine.

In December 2021, on the eve of the invasion, 71% of Ukrainians considered themselves happy, while 15% did not. In May 2023, despite more than a year of full-scale war, the figures remained almost the same: 70% of Ukrainians considered themselves happy, and 15% did not consider themselves happy. At the same time, by December 2023, the figure had slightly decreased to 64%, although it remains high given the difficult end of 2023.

**Graph 7.2. "Do you consider yourself a happy person?" (2001–2023), %**

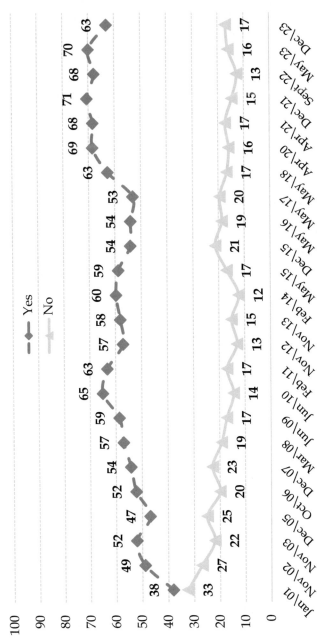

As we saw in Chapter 3, the Russian invasion had many negative consequences for ordinary Ukrainians. Therefore, it is crucial that the happiness index has remained virtually unchanged both overall and among certain categories of the population. Despite the sea of difficulties and challenges of today, Ukrainians are finding ways to adapt to the complex reality and move forward.

The results of our research look unexpected. How can people be happy when there is a terrible war going on? There are several reasons for this. First, the mechanism of happiness formation is not simple and linear. For example, an increase in income does not always lead to an increase in happiness. In the United States, real income doubled between 1985 and 2005, but the level of happiness remained unchanged. The fact is that the level of happiness can be represented as a fraction, with the level of achievements in the broad sense (level of material security, creative work, a loved one, etc.) in the numerator and the level of aspirations (claims) in the denominator (for example, what level of material security a person considers sufficient).

$$\text{Happiness} = \frac{\text{level of achievements}}{\text{level of aspirations (claims)}}$$

The level of aspirations itself is formed depending on the level of achievement of the respondent's reference group. As the American happiness researcher R. Layard wrote, people do not become happier when their entire society becomes richer, people become happier when they become richer than their neighbors[60]. In times of war, when millions of people are suffering, the level of aspirations (the denominator of the happiness formula) is significantly reduced, and this compensates for the hardships that people are experiencing. It is clear that those who are in the war zone become unhappy, but they make up only a few percent.

---

60   R. Layard, *Happiness: Lessons from a New Science* (New York: Penguin Books, 2006).

Secondly, many factors influence the level of happiness, such as children's behavior, intimate relationships, relationships with friends, etc. Although material living conditions have deteriorated significantly and many people are suffering from separation from their families, there are factors that increase the level of happiness. The cohesion of our society has grown significantly, regional differences have decreased, the value of the state for the population of Ukraine has increased, mutual support has grown, and the social and psychological climate has improved. All this increases the level of happiness of Ukrainians.

## 7.3. Readiness to resist Russian aggression

We started researching the readiness of Ukrainians to resist Russian aggression before the war began. According to Western media, citing intelligence sources, in November 2021, Russia deployed a group of about 100,000 troops near Ukraine's border, which was seen as preparations for an attack on Ukraine, although Russia itself has repeatedly denied accusations of preparing an invasion at various levels. However, tensions were rising. Our surveys in December 2021 and January 2022 showed that about half of Ukrainians believed that the accumulation of Russian troops on Ukraine's border posed a real threat of invasion, while about 40% believed that there would be no invasion.

However, people did not feel any increase in tension during the month, and the indicators did not change from December to January. It should be noted that even those who believed that the accumulation of Russian troops on Ukraine's border was a real threat of invasion, in many cases did not believe that the invasion would be full-scale with an attempt to capture Kyiv and merciless massive rocket attacks on civilian infrastructure, people were thinking about the east of Ukraine and, at most, an attempt to create a land corridor to Crimea.[61]

---

61  We cannot refer to quantitative data, but only to our own observations of numerous statements by different categories of the population in the media and social networks.

In December 2021, KIIS asked respondents the following question as part of the Omnibus survey: "In the event of an armed intervention by Russia in your city or village, would you take any action and, if so, what actions?". In February 5-13, we repeated the survey and published the results on February 15, 9 days before the war started. In general, the survey results showed that Ukrainians were going to resist the Russian interventionists (Table 7.1).

**Table 7.1.  What actions are Ukrainians ready to take in case of Russian armed intervention in their locality (multiple answers were possible), %**

| | December 2021 | February 2022 |
|---|---|---|
| **Resist (select one of the two options below or both):** | 50 | 58 |
| *To provide armed resistance* | *33* | *37* |
| *Resist by participating in civil resistance actions such as demonstrations, protests, marches, boycotts, strikes, civil disobedience* | *22* | *25* |
| Leave for a safer region of Ukraine | 15 | 12 |
| Going abroad | 9 | 8 |
| I would not do anything | 19 | 18 |
| I don't know | 12 | 8 |
| Refusal to answer | 1 | 1 |
| Total | 100 | 100 |

At the same time, since December 2021, despite Russia's continued aggressive escalation of the situation in Ukraine, readiness to resist has increased: from 33% to 37%, readiness to resist armed resistance has increased. In addition, the readiness to resist by participating in civil resistance actions increased from 22% to 25%. In general, 58% of Ukrainians were ready to resist in one way or another in February compared to 50% in December. Other options included moving to a safer region (12%); going abroad (7.5%); doing nothing (18%). Another 7.6% have not decided on the answer, and 1.2% refused to answer the question.

In the regional dimension, readiness to resist varies from 72% in the West to 30.5% in the East. Readiness to resist armed resistance ranges from 45% in the West to 18% in the East. In the West and in the Center, the readiness to resist has increased. In the South, compared to December, the difference is within the margin of error, but with a tendency to a slight increase in readiness to resist. In the East, on the contrary, the difference is also within the margin of error compared to December, but there is a tendency to lower readiness to resist. Men were more ready to resist (72%, including 60% ready for armed resistance), but this figure was also high among women (46% ready to resist, including 18% ready to resist armed).

In September 2015, KIIS conducted a public opinion poll of Ukrainian residents on methods of resistance to interventionists/occupiers at the request of the Center for Strategic Studies and the Agency for Nonviolent Solutions (the results are available at http://www.kiis.com.ua/?lang=ukr&cat=reports&id=546). In particular, the respondents were asked the question "What actions would you prefer to take in the event of a foreign armed intervention in your city or village?". According to the results of the survey, 23.8% of respondents said they would resist armed resistance, 28.6% said they would participate in civil resistance actions such as demonstrations, protests, marches, boycotts, strikes, civil disobedience. Overall, 52.4% of respondents would resist in one way or another.

Do these intentions correspond to the actual behavior of respondents after the outbreak of war? A more accurate answer to this question would require a panel study, but we do have some indicators of actual behavior. A study conducted by KIIS at the request of the National Democratic Institute in August 2022 asked respondents what they did after the outbreak of a full-scale war: "Have you done any of the following since the outbreak of full-scale war? If no: Would you do it if you had the opportunity or would you never do it?". The answer options are "yes", "no, but I would do it or would do it if I had the opportunity", "no, I would never do it". The results are shown in Graph 7.3.

It is clear that attitudes toward Russia, Russians, everything Russian, Russian culture, and the Russian language have deteriorated dramatically, with Russia's actions causing anger, hatred, and contempt (we discuss these changes in other sections), 84% of respondents began to speak Ukrainian more, and 55% wear national symbols and colors. Support for the Armed Forces has increased, with 81% indicating that they have donated money to the Armed Forces, and 21% joining the Armed Forces (or the Territorial Defense, which is also part of the Armed Forces). Before the war, 37% of respondents said they were ready to resist armed resistance (and even 60% among men), but before the war we asked about their readiness to resist in case of armed intervention by Russia in your city or village, and Russia was engaged in military operations and captured about 20% of Ukraine's territory. Many people are involved in volunteering, mutual aid, and helping internally displaced persons (IDPs). For example, 63% donated clothes or other items to IDPs, 60% donated money for humanitarian needs, and 54% sheltered or helped IDPs in other ways.

**Graph 7.3. "Have you done any of these since the start of full-scale war?", % (August 2022)**

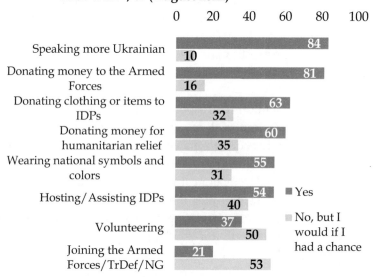

A number of surveys conducted after February 24, 2022, show that the vast majority of Ukrainians are involved in the fight against the aggressor in one form or another. In addition to participating in the resistance, according to a survey in May 2023, 78% of Ukrainians stated that they "have close relatives or friends who were injured /

killed as a result of the Russian invasion of Ukraine after February 24, 2022." In actual practice, during this period, the war has truly become a national war for Ukrainians. At the same time, it is also important to look at the resistance from a slightly different perspective: whether Ukrainians feel that they are part of the resistance to the enemy on a subjective level.

In October 2022, we asked respondents the question "To what extent do you personally feel that you are part of the national resistance to the enemy?" and respondents had to answer on a scale from 0 to 10, where a score of 0 meant I do not feel this at all, a score of 5 meant I partly feel it, partly no, it is difficult to say for sure, and a score of 10 meant I fully feel part of the national resistance. On this scale, answers 7-10 can be interpreted as including oneself or feeling a sense of attraction to the feeling of being part of the national resistance. At the same time, answers 0-3, on the contrary, meant that the respondent did not consider himself or herself part of the resistance. The intermediate answers 4-6 indicated a partial attribution of oneself to the national resistance.

As can be seen in Graph 7.4, the majority of Ukrainians, at 60%, feel part of the national resistance (43% of them feel completely part of it, and 17% rather feel part of it). Another 32% feel at least partially involved in the resistance to the enemy. At the same time, only 4% of respondents rather or absolutely do not feel part of the resistance to the enemy.

**Graph 7.4. Feeling of belonging to the national resistance to the enemy, % (October 2022)**

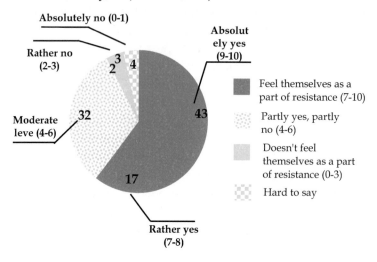

From the West to the East, the share of those who felt part of the national resistance decreases from 68% to 48%. This is due to an increase from 26% to 38% in the share of those who gave intermediate estimates of a partial sense of involvement. In other words, in all regions, the majority felt at least partially part of the national resistance, and no more than 6% did not feel this way. Among those who chose Ukrainian for the interview, 63% felt part of the resistance, compared to 42% of those who chose Russian. At the same time, among the latter, the number of those who felt partial belonging was higher: 45% vs. 30%. And in both categories, an absolute minority (4% and 7%, respectively) do not feel that they belong to the national resistance. That is, both among respondents who chose Ukrainian for the interview and among respondents who chose Russian, the majority feel at least partially affiliated with the national resistance. Many Ukrainian and foreign politicians and experts have noted the cohesion of Ukrainian society, which manifested itself in various forms of mass support for the Defense Forces and in general resilience to difficult circumstances.

At the same time, it is also important that by living this experience, most Ukrainians feel on a subjective level not just that they are live observers of the events, but real participants in the national resistance. This shared experience is now and will continue to be a social "glue" for maintaining cohesion, continuing the formation of a civil political nation, and overcoming various problems. It is important that the narrative of resistance as a national phenomenon and the involvement of everyone (to whatever extent this is possible) in repelling the aggressor be broadcast at various levels, both inside and outside the country.

To what extent will Ukrainians have the strength and readiness to continue the war if the war continues and the situation deteriorates? This is a difficult question to answer, but so far, almost two years into the war, the deteriorating situation has not had a significant impact on the readiness of the resistance. Since October 2022, Russia has launched systematic and targeted attacks on Ukraine's energy infrastructure to cause humanitarian damage. The shelling led to widespread power outages across the country. From October 10 – 18, 2022, one third of power plants in Ukraine were destroyed as a result of Russian attacks[62]. The purpose of these attacks was likely to be that the power outages, combined with the cold winter weather and damaged civilian buildings, would increase the suffering of the Ukrainian civilian population in the winter and lead to public pressure on the Ukrainian leadership to achieve a speedy peace. From October 21 – 23, KIIS conducted a survey to find out how the shelling affected the readiness of Ukrainians to resist. The results of the survey are shown in Graph 7.5

---

62  Anastasiia Pecheniuk, 'Ne pidirve voliu Ukrainy: ISW pro naslidky atak RF po tsyvilnii infrastrukturi.' *UNIAN Information Agency*, October 23, 2022, https://www.unian.ua/war/yakimi-budut-naslidki-atak-rf-po-infrastrukturi-ukrajini-zvit-isw-12020571.html.

**Graph 7.5. "Recently, Russia has been actively shelling Ukrainian cities with missiles, kamikadze drones, etc. Which of the following statements best describes your thoughts on this matter?", % (October 2022)**

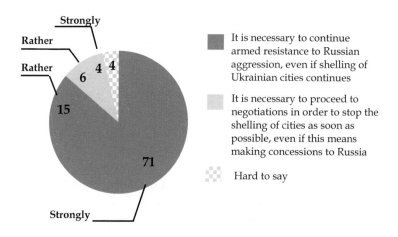

Despite the Russian shelling, which destroys infrastructure and takes lives, 86% of respondents said that the armed struggle should continue even if the shelling continues. In particular, 71% of them strongly agree with this opinion (the remaining 16% rather agree). Instead, only 10% of respondents said that it was necessary to start negotiations to stop the shelling as soon as possible, even if Russia has to make concessions. Although the share of those who are ready for concessions is increasing from West to East, in all regions the majority of people believe that armed resistance should be continued. Even in the East, 69% share this opinion (this is the response of people living in Kharkiv and Donetsk regions, which are subject to constant rocket and artillery attacks). Among the respondents who chose Russian for the interview, the vast majority (66%) also believe that armed resistance should continue even if the shelling continues (and only 29% believe that negotiations should begin, even if concessions are made).

As you can see, during the first year of the war (and indeed other studies suggest during the first 18 months of the war), the

Russian strategy to force Ukrainians to surrender did not work. Yes, the terror continued, people were killed or injured, and Ukrainian families were forced to spend their evenings in the dark. However, the nationwide pain of loss and destruction did not intimidate people, but was channeled "into anger and malice toward enemies." The Ukrainian people remained united and resilient and were ready to continue the struggle until victory.

## 7.4. Readiness of Ukrainians to make concessions for peace

### 7.4.1. Assessing the sincerity of answers – a methodological experiment

Since May 2022, KIIS has been regularly asking questions about the readiness of the population to make territorial concessions to achieve peace and preserve independence as soon as possible. In Section Two, we have already discussed the peculiarities of the survey during the war, the possible effect of the Elizabeth-Noel spiral of silence and respondents' perceptions of what answer is more or less patriotic. Taking into account the possible sensitivity of this question and the possible insincerity of some respondents, we conducted a methodological experiment to assess the sincerity of respondents. We implemented the split-half sample procedure and asked half of the randomly selected respondents a direct question about their readiness for concessions in the wording as it was in May 2022. The other half was asked a question using the "intended acquaintance" methodology, which was developed at KIIS in 1995 and has proven to be a good tool for studying sensitive issues (i.e., questions that respondents may not want to answer sincerely) both in KIIS research over the years and in the research of some of our colleagues. For the method of "conceived acquaintance", respondents were asked the question: "Now there is going to be a slightly unusual question. Please think of someone you know well – it could be yourself, a family member, a work colleague, a friend, an enemy, etc". After the respondent replied "Yes", they are asked: "In your opinion, which of these statements about possible compromises to achieve peace with Russia would this imaginary person agree with more?". Our previous experiments have shown that this question ensures respondents' anonymity (mostly respondents imagined themselves) and ensures sincerity of answers even for questions where a sincere answer may indicate illegal activities (in particular, we have successfully studied the shadow economy). The results of comparing direct questions with the "imagined friend" method are shown in Graph 7.6.

**Graph 7.6. Willingness to make territorial concessions using the "direct question" method and the "imagined acquaintance" method, % (July 2022)**

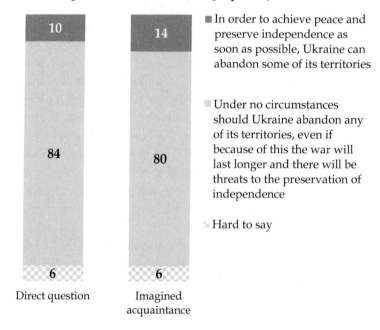

- In order to achieve peace and preserve independence as soon as possible, Ukraine can abandon some of its territories

- Under no circumstances should Ukraine abandon any of its territories, even if because of this the war will last longer and there will be threats to the preservation of independence

- Hard to say

As you can see, the "imagined acquaintance" method yields almost the same results: 80% are against any concessions, and 14% support concessions. Although this method gives us a slightly higher number of those who are ready for concessions, the difference is insignificant and does not actually change the overall picture of public sentiment.

**7.4.2. Readiness for territorial concessions**

From May 2022 to December 2023, KIIS conducted eight waves of surveys on the readiness of the population to make territorial concessions to achieve peace and preserve independence as soon as possible, which allows, in particular, to understand how the views of the population have changed since the invasion. Graph 7.7 shows the respondents' answers.

**Graph 7.7. "Which of the following statements about possible compromises to achieve peace with Russia do you agree with to the greatest extent?" (2022-2023), %**

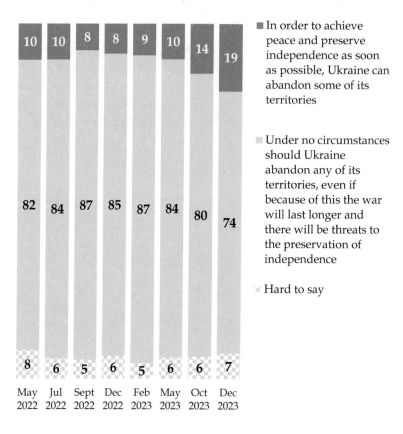

In order to achieve peace and preserve independence as soon as possible, Ukraine can abandon some of its territories

Under no circumstances should Ukraine abandon any of its territories, even if because of this the war will last longer and there will be threats to the preservation of independence

Hard to say

In the period from May 2022 to May 2023, the situation was relatively stable: about 8-10% of respondents were ready for territorial concessions, and the vast majority (82-87%) consistently opposed any concessions. After May 2023, there has been a gradual increase in the share of those who are ready for territorial concessions: from 10% in May, to 14% in October, and to 19% in December. At the same time, there is a downward trend in the share of those who oppose territorial concessions (from 84% in May to 80% in October and to 74% in December), although as of December 2023, a clear majority of Ukrainians still believe that Ukraine should not give up any of its territories.

In Ukraine, after the full-scale invasion, there was a surge of optimism, which, in particular, was accompanied by categorical statements on territorial concessions. It was natural to expect that the longer the war lasted, the more we would see the indicators "return" to somewhat lower levels. For some time, optimism was supported by bright victories in the north of Ukraine, Kharkiv and Kherson regions, but against the backdrop of a difficult 2023, we see downward trends. Expectations of a counteroffensive by Ukraine in 2023 were not realized, and this affected the mood of Ukrainians. Given the high level of uncertainty, it is difficult to say what the trajectory will be in the future. It is possible that the willingness to make concessions will increase slightly, but then stabilize (with a predominance of those who oppose any concessions).

Let's look at regional differences. Starting in May 2022, KIIS used the region where respondents lived before February 24, 2022, to analyze regional differences. Graph 7.8 shows the dynamics in this dimension. At the same time, Graph 7.9 below shows the data by the region where respondents lived at the time of the survey.

While between May and October 2023, the increase in the share of those who are ready for territorial concessions was mainly due to responses from the South and East, the increase between October and December was due to responses from the West and Center. Thus, in the West, the share of such respondents increased from 9% in October to 20% in the Center — the share of such respondents increased from 10% to 15%. In the South and East, changes in the share of those who are ready for concessions are much less noticeable, although there are also negative trends, in terms of a decrease in the share of those who are against any concessions. At the same time, in all regions, a clear majority of respondents (from 68% and 69% in the South and East to 76% and 79% in the West and Center, respectively) still oppose Russia's territorial concessions.

### Graph 7.8. Readiness for territorial concessions by place of residence by February 24, 2022, %

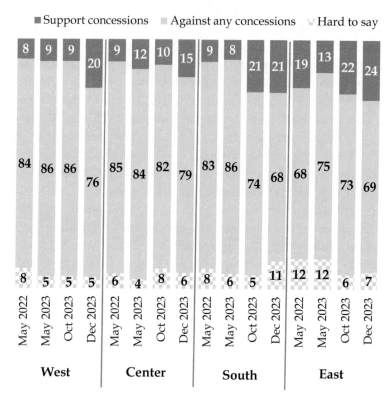

When analyzed by region of residence as of the time of the interview (i.e., December 2023), similar trends are observed (Figure 7.9). Even among residents of the South and East, who are closest to the combat zone, 67% oppose any territorial concessions, while 22% of those living in the South and 25% of those living in the East are ready for concessions. The situation among the residents of the West and Center is only slightly different, with a slightly lower readiness for territorial concessions.

**Graph 7.9. Readiness for territorial concessions by place of residence as of December 2023, %**

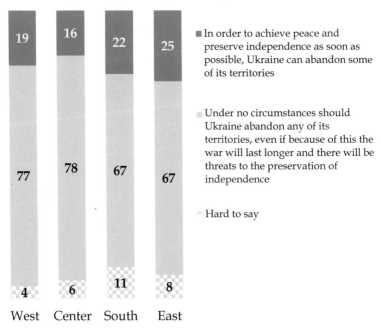

It is clear that now, when two years of war have not yet passed, we do not know what will happen next and how the mood of Ukrainians will change. It all depends on the course of the war. In addition, our question concerns the general attitude towards territorial compromises. A more detailed study of different variants of the situation shows that different experiences of war affect people's willingness to compromise. This is demonstrated by the questions in the KIIS omnibus, which we inserted at the request of John O'Locklin, Gerard Toal and Christine M. Bakke in May 2023. The researchers were interested in whether there is a difference in attitudes towards the de-occupation of the territories if it happened eight years ago, in 2014 or in 2022. The question was as follows: "Any choice about what to do during the current Russian aggression has a significant but different price. Knowing this, which of the following four choices should the Ukrainian government make at this time?". Options and results are shown in Graph 7.10.

**Graph 7.10. "Which of the following four options should the Ukrainian government adopt at this point?", % (May 2023)**

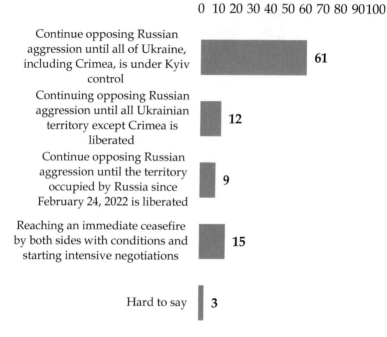

The researchers write:

> These ratios of support for different territorial compromises reveal more nuance among the Ukrainian population than the usual all-or-nothing options that dominate political discourse. Existing research suggests that we should expect some people to not tell the truth in telephone surveys when patriotic feelings are high.

When the question about compromises was formulated in more detail, the regional differences were somewhat larger than with the binary question: in the West of the country, 65% would like to continue fighting compared to only 45% in the East. However, the biggest differences in attitudes toward compromises were related to the sense of security and future well-being that families would have as a result of the war. The researchers asked the respondents the following question: "How secure do you feel about your own and your family's well-being (such as safety, shelter, food, income, etc.) in the near future (i.e., over the next 6 months)?". The scale for the assessment was from "very safe" to "very unsafe". Graph 7.11 shows the distribution of the territorial compromise option by self-assessed family safety and well-being.

**Graph 7.11. Readiness for territorial concessions depending on the perception of security for one's family in the next 6 months, % (May 2023)**

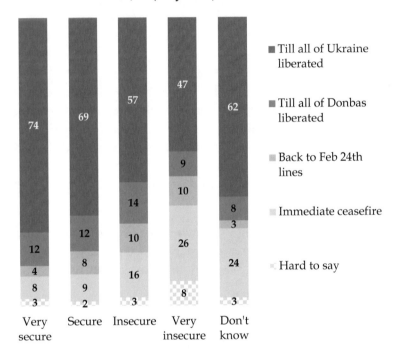

Respondents who feel the most secure about their family's future are significantly more willing to fight until all of Ukraine is regained (about 75%) than those who feel the least secure (about 46%). The researchers point out that families who feel insecure are more likely to have moved as a result of the conflict (29%) and live mainly in the East and South of the country, while "more secure" families are mainly in the Center and West, with only 6% of them reporting that they have moved since the beginning of the current conflict.

As for Crimea, KIIS conducted a separate study in February 2023. Some politicians believe that the issue of Crimea is "special". From their point of view, Crimea is one of Putin's main "achievements" in the eyes of the Russian population, and that for Putin, Crimea is something sacred and so important that he will stop at nothing to preserve it, including the use of nuclear weapons. Therefore, it is in the interests of Ukraine and the world to stop Ukrainian attempts to liberate Crimea. In the context of these discussions, the well-known British scholar Timothy Garton Ash suggested that KIIS ask another question about the possible military liberation of Crimea. Respondents were offered two scenarios, one of which included Western assistance to liberate and secure all territories, including Donbas, but without Crimea. According to this scenario, Ukraine refrains from military liberation. The second scenario is attempts to liberate Crimea militarily, but with the understanding that the West may reduce its assistance and the war may drag on. Among all respondents, 8% could not answer, other answers are shown in Graph 7.12

**Graph 7.12. "Which of the following statements do you agree with to the greatest extent?", % (February 2023)**

0   10  20  30  40  50  60  70  80  90 100

We can refrain from trying to liberate Crimea militarily if Ukraine gets a firm Western commitment to help liberate and defend the rest of Ukraine's sovereign territory, including Donbas

 68

We should continue to try to liberate all of Ukraine, including Crimea, even if that means a longer war with Russia and diminishing help from the West

 24

As we can see, this approach does indeed expand the space for finding "compromises" and more people are ready to accept this format of action. However, at the same time, the majority of respondents (at 64%) believe that Ukraine should try to liberate the entire territory, including Crimea, even if there is a risk of reduced Western support and a risk of a longer war. In contrast, 24% are more inclined to the option that in exchange for the liberation and protection of all territories including Donbas (but excluding Crimea), Ukraine can refrain from military action in Crimea. Regional differentiation is not very significant, and in all regions the vast majority insist on the liberation of all territories, including Crimea. Support for a "compromise" is no more than 27%, depending on the region. However, by the end of 2023, given the difficulties and unfulfilled expectations, the readiness for a "compromise" may have become higher. However, other related results show that Ukrainians are still likely to insist on the liberation of all territories, primarily for security reasons. In the same survey in February 2024, KIIS for the Sakharov Center posed several other scenarios of "compromise" around Crimea. The only scenario that had quite significant support was that Crimea would be neither under the control of Ukraine nor under the control of Russia, but would have a separate status under the control of the UN. In fact, this means the demilitarization of the peninsula. This scenario was supported by 41% of Ukrainians (and by the end of 2023, support for this scenario was likely to be even higher). It is important to understand the content of this "compromise" and why many Ukrainians are ready to support it. First, Russia will not control Crimea (for Ukrainians, even those who are ready for territorial losses, official recognition remains mostly unacceptable, i.e., it is rather a readiness to actually recognize Russia's control). Secondly, Ukrainians, having had the bitter experience of the occupation of the South by Crimea in 2022, want to have guarantees that this will not happen again, so the issue of demilitarization of the peninsula may be the cornerstone of a "compromise."

After February 24, 2022, KIIS (like other reputable sociological companies) conducted dozens of all-Ukrainian polls, in which various stakeholders—Western scholars, analysts, journalists, etc.—often tried to "feel" the limits of acceptable compromises for Ukrainians using different wording and methods. However, the results of the surveys conducted by KIIS and other companies are unanimous: regardless of the wording of the questions, Ukrainians are not interested in "peace". Ukrainians realize that without additional serious conditions, a mere ceasefire will only postpone further Russian aggression, so the fight must continue and there can be no concessions.

At the same time, additional conditions in Ukraine's favor may push Ukrainians to discuss certain "compromises." It should be understood that to a large extent, the approval of certain "compromises" by the Ukrainian public depends on trust in Western partners in their implementation. Although Ukrainians certainly support the movement towards Europe, many Ukrainians also react emotionally to the way the West, often with difficulty, made and still makes decisions on arms supplies and sanctions against Russia. This is despite the fact that many Ukrainians are aware on a rational level of the complex context in which Western governments operate. Uncertainty remains about Ukraine's membership in NATO and on credible "security guarantees." Ukrainians have learned the hard way from the Budapest Memorandum. Therefore, many Ukrainians simply do not yet see convincing evidence that the West can provide genuine security guarantees and guarantees in other areas (e.g., reconstruction) that would be worth considering in the context of possible "compromises."

Let us consider the issue of Western assistance in more detail. At the end of 2023

the US Congress has blocked the allocation of additional assistance to Ukraine[63], and there are constant problems with receiving adequate assistance from other Western partners. In a KIIS survey for the European Union Advisory Mission in September 2023, 75% of Ukrainians recognized the EU's assistance to Ukraine as useful, but 56% called it insufficient (and this issue has only worsened by the end of 2023). According to our previous polls, from September

---

63   Valerii Saakov, 'Baiden nazvav "shantazhem" blokuvannia dopomohy SShA Ukraini.' *Deutsche Welle*, December 7, 2023.

2022 to October 2023, the number of those who believe that the West is tired of Ukraine and wants Ukraine to make concessions to Russia increased from 15% to 30%. Also, from February 2023 to October 2023, the number of those who believe that Russia has too many resources and can wage war against Ukraine for a long time increased from 22% to 49%. Although Ukrainians remain optimistic, this optimism appears to be becoming more and more restrained. In early December 2023, KIIS asked Ukrainians whether, with proper Western support (weapons, finance, sanctions), Ukraine could succeed at all. Or, conversely, does Russia have too many resources regardless of Western support? The vast majority of Ukrainians (87%) believe that if the West properly supports Ukraine with weapons, finance, and sanctions, Ukraine will be able to cause Russia to fail and achieve an acceptable result. Of those surveyed, 7% believe that Russia is too strong regardless of Western support. The remaining 6% have not decided on their opinion.

What should be done in the event of a significant reduction in Western support? The graphs below show how respondents answered these questions depending on whether they were ready for or opposed to territorial concessions. Respondents who support territorial concessions are indeed more pessimistic in their outlook: 22% of them believe that Russia is too strong and that even proper Western assistance will not help. However, the majority (71%) of those who are ready for territorial concessions believe that with proper Western support, Ukraine will be able to make progress. Among those who oppose territorial concessions, 93% are confident of success with proper support from the West.

**Graph 7.13. Possibility of Ukraine's success with proper support from the West depending on readiness for territorial concessions, % (December 2023)**

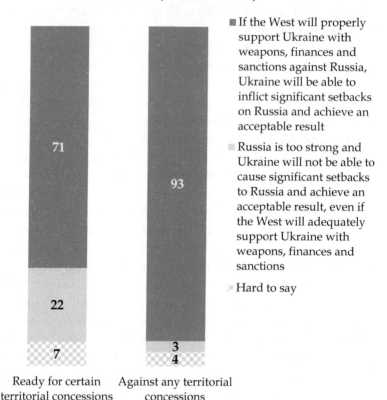

- If the West will properly support Ukraine with weapons, finances and sanctions against Russia, Ukraine will be able to inflict significant setbacks on Russia and achieve an acceptable result

- Russia is too strong and Ukraine will not be able to cause significant setbacks to Russia and achieve an acceptable result, even if the West will adequately support Ukraine with weapons, finances and sanctions

- Hard to say

Ready for certain territorial concessions

Against any territorial concessions

Instead, the categories of respondents who are ready for territorial concessions have opposing views on the strategy of action in the event of a significant decline in Western support. Among respondents who are ready for territorial concessions, 69% would consider it appropriate to end hostilities with serious security guarantees (28% are in favor of continuing hostilities). At the same time, among respondents who are against any territorial concessions, even with a significant limitation of aid, 70% are in favor of continuing the hostilities (and 22% are in favor of ending them).

**Graph 7.14. Actions in case of a significant reduction in Western aid depending on the readiness for territorial concessions, % (December 2023)**

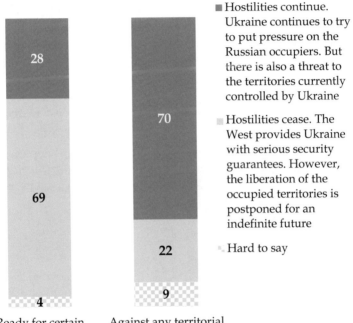

■ Hostilities continue. Ukraine continues to try to put pressure on the Russian occupiers. But there is also a threat to the territories currently controlled by Ukraine

■ Hostilities cease. The West provides Ukraine with serious security guarantees. However, the liberation of the occupied territories is postponed for an indefinite future

■ Hard to say

Ready for certain territorial concessions

Against any territorial concessions

### 7.4.3. Willingness to refuse to join NATO

At the end of February 2022, negotiations between Russia and Ukraine on a ceasefire began. They lasted until mid-August and did not yield positive results. One of the options for achieving peace that was discussed in the media was that Ukraine might refuse or postpone its accession to NATO, but at the same time receive security guarantees from the world's leading powers. In May 2022, we conducted the first survey on the attitude of Ukrainians to such a compromise with certain security guarantees, and in May 2023 we repeated the question. The respondents were asked how acceptable it would be for Ukraine to refuse to join NATO under such conditions. In May 2022, opinions were almost equally divided: 39% insisted on only joining NATO, while 42% considered it acceptable to receive "security guarantees" instead. By May 2023, public opinion had changed significantly: the share of those who insisted on NATO membership had increased to 58%. At the same time, the share of those who would accept "security guarantees" dropped to 29%. It should be noted that in all regions those who insist on joining NATO prevail. See Graph 7.15

**Graph 7.15. Attitudes toward security guarantees instead of NATO, %**

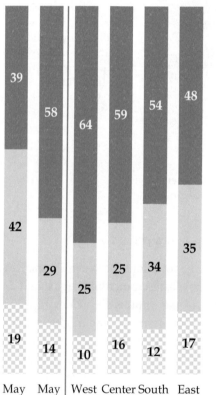

■ Only joining NATO will be able to ensure Ukraine's security, so it cannot be abandoned

▨ This is quite acceptable if, instead of joining NATO, which may be blocked by some NATO members, Ukraine will have security guarantees from countries such as the United States, Great Britain, Germany, France, etc.

▫ Neither or hard to say

According to a KIIS poll for NDI in November 2023, only 19% of Ukrainians considered it acceptable to give up joining NATO in exchange for peace (76% considered it unacceptable). It is important to emphasize once again that it was not Ukrainians' desire to join NATO that "provoked" Russia, but rather Russian aggression that became the catalyst for public support for Euro-Atlantic integration. At the same time, the longer the war lasts, the more Ukrainians insist on full membership in NATO, and "security guarantees" from other states look less convincing. At the same time, we should note that the rhetoric of Ukraine's Western partners regarding "security guarantees" as an alternative to joining NATO (including in the context of "postponing" accession to the future) is perceived skeptically by Ukrainians both in view of historical experience (including the Budapest Memorandum) and the actual scope and speed of Western support for Ukraine after the full-scale invasion. Although the vast majority of Ukrainians view the war against aggressive Russia as a joint one with the Western allies and are grateful for the powerful assistance provided, at the same time, the amount of this assistance is not perceived as sufficient to completely expel the enemy and ensure Ukraine's security. Perhaps the West's provision of convincing, transparent guarantees with specific implementation mechanisms will increase the credibility of "security guarantees." But for now, Ukrainians believe only in full membership.

## 7.5. Level of optimism

One of the components of resilience, and perhaps a factor that influences resilience, is the level of optimism among the population about the prospects for Ukraine's development. In KIIS surveys for NDI, the question of how optimistic Ukrainians are about the future of Ukraine was often asked. KIIS asked this question before the invasion in December 2021, and then again in 2022-2023 after the invasion. Thus, before the invasion, 39% were optimistic about Ukraine's future, and 88% were optimistic immediately after the invasion. The optimism rate remained virtually unchanged a year after the invasion and amounted to 87% in May 2023. However, by the end of 2023, the level of optimism had dropped to 77% and, more notably, the number of those who were very optimistic had decreased from 51% in May 2023 to 31% in November 2023. Thus, optimism among Ukrainians still remains, but it is becoming much more restrained. Ukrainian historian Serhii Hromenko described his feelings at the end of 2023 as "tactical pessimism but strategic optimism." It is possible that he recalled the results of the research of the famous Ukrainian sociologist Yevgen Golovakha, who many years ago found that Ukrainians are always "tactical pessimists but strategic optimists"[64]. In other words, the current circumstances made many people upset, but the majority remained confident that Ukraine would succeed in the long run.

**Graph 7.16. "In general, are you optimistic or pessimistic about the future of Ukraine?"**

*% optimistic*

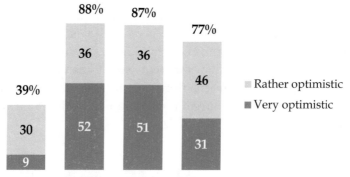

In October 2022 and again in December 2023, KIIS conducted a survey with questions on a related topic. During the interviews, respondents were asked to choose which of the two scenarios of Ukraine's future — optimistic or pessimistic — they agree with more:

---

64   Alla Kotliar, 'Taktichni pesymisty ta stratehichni optymisty: Do 25-richchia KMIS.' *Dzerkalo Tyzhnia*, December 27, 2017, https://zn.ua/ukr/SOCIUM/taktichni-pesimisti-i-strategichni-optimisti-264606_.html.

"In 10 years, Ukraine will be a prosperous country within the European Union" or "In 10 years, Ukraine will be a country with a ruined economy and a large outflow of people." As can be seen in Graph 7.17, in October, 88% of Ukrainians believed that in 10 years Ukraine would be a prosperous country within the EU. Among these optimistic respondents, 96% are ready to endure material hardships for three to five years if Ukraine eventually becomes a prosperous country and a member of the European Union. On the other hand, only 5% of respondents had pessimistic expectations that in ten years Ukraine would be a devastated country with an outflow of people. However, by the end of 2023, there was a slight increase in pessimism: from 5% to 19%, the number of those who believe that in 10 years Ukraine will be a country with a ruined economy and a large outflow of people increased. However, the vast majority of Ukrainians (73%) still believe that in ten years Ukraine will be a prosperous country within the EU. In fact, in all regions, the vast majority were hopeful about Ukraine's future (from 76% in the Center to 67% in the East).

**Graph 7.17."Which of the following statements about the future of Ukraine do you agree with to the greatest extent?", %**

In December 2022, KIIS also conducted a survey commissioned by the Institute of Sociology of the National Academy of Sciences of Ukraine. This is the next wave of the Ukrainian Society monitoring, which was launched in 1994 by E. Golovakha and N. Panina and has been regularly conducted since then. The data obtained were compared with the data of the pre-war survey of November 2021. Analyzing this data, Serhii Dembitskyi noted: Despite all the striking changes in public opinion, the perception of cynicism in society (in the sense of disdain for generally accepted moral norms) has not fundamentally changed. There have been positive changes, but the vast majority of respondents (51.6%) still view others in a cynical light. There are two positive aspects to this. First, the majority of respondents believe in the sincerity of Ukrainians' help to each other, which was not the case before. Secondly, in terms of cynicism, Ukrainian society has reached the level of 1992 (after that, the indicators were steadily worse), when the relevant measurement was first made. There is hope that this upward trend will continue.

Other indicators of the moral and psychological state are quite positive. For example, the number of people who believe that "every person is born with the life they will live" (an indicator of fatalism) has significantly decreased from 59.3% in 2002 to 35.1% in 2022. This indicates an increase in subjectivity in Ukrainian society. The number of those who are confident in their abilities has also increased—from 42% in 2021 to 56.4% in 2022.

Another question asked in this monitoring was as follows:

> The war is causing many problems in people's lives (rising prices for food and goods, problems with electricity and heat supply, job losses). In your opinion, the majority of people in your environment (1) are ready to endure current and future problems as long as it takes until Ukraine wins the war, (2) are ready to endure current and future problems, but only for a limited time, or (3) are not ready to endure these difficulties right now.

The survey showed that 69% are ready to endure as long as necessary, 24% are ready to endure for a limited time, and only 5% are not ready. Even taking into account the possible additional systematic error of 6%, which we discussed in chapter 7.4.1, these results show that during the first year and a half of the war, people have faith in the future of Ukraine and are ready to bear all the burdens of war.

Western media and analysts often ask sociologists about the factors that ensure the resilience of Ukrainian society in the face of

Russia's aggressive policy and the lack of demand for negotiations with the aggressor to end the war. The results of this study partially explain this phenomenon. In particular, Ukrainian society has an established positive vision of Ukraine's future. Significantly, this vision — a successful Ukraine in the European space — is perceived by the majority as realistic and worth the temporary sacrifices. Modern resilience — on the front line and in everyday life — is turning into an investment in one's own well-being and the well-being of future generations. This is one of the factors that contributes to maintaining solidarity and a consistent achievement of a goal (although there is a feedback loop: the level of optimism about Ukraine's future depends on successes at the front, support from the international community and resilience of the population).

# 8. Formation of the Nation and Value Orientations

## 8.1. Ukrainians: an unexpected nation?
### National and civic identification of Ukrainians

September 14, 1994. Ukraine had just declared its independence three years earlier and was undergoing a painful socio-economic and socio-political transformation. On this autumn day, more than 90,000 people gathered at the Olimpiiskyi Stadium in Kyiv to watch the Champions League football match between Dynamo Kyiv and Spartak Moscow. After the first half, Spartak was leading 0-2, but in the second half, Dynamo scored three times and eventually won 3-2 (the Ukrainians scored the decisive goal in the 86th minute!). In addition to the strong-willed victory, the match confused the guests from Russia by the fact that Kyiv fans chanted in pure Russian "Beat, beat the Muscovites!"

One might attribute this to the historically passionate rivalry between Dynamo and Spartak, and this is partly true. It is hard to deny the emotionality of loyal football fans. It is important that this chant did not imply a xenophobic attitude toward Russians. Earlier in this book, inter-ethnic prejudice and social distance were discussed along with attitudes toward Russia and Russians. It is worth recalling once again that historically, Ukraine had a very warm attitude toward Russians. Before 1994 and the strong-willed victory of Dynamo over Spartak, Russians were right behind Ukrainian and Russian-speaking Ukrainians on the Bogardus social distance scale (for the first two groups, the index on the 1-7 scale was 1.7 and 1.76, respectively, and for Russians it was 1.95). Even after the occupation of Crimea and Russia's aggression in Donbas and on the eve of the full-scale invasion in November 2021, 75% of Ukrainians had a good attitude toward "ordinary" Russians.

Such seemingly simple sporting events were in fact grassroots indicators that a rapid process of crystallization of national identity was underway among the country's ordinary population. Kyiv residents, who were predominantly Russian-speaking at the time, were demonstrating their Ukrainian identity and differentiating themselves from Russians and Russia.

It was not the first time that Kyiv residents were destroying Russian myths about Ukraine and Ukrainians. It is less often mentioned now, but in 1991, in March, an all-Union referendum was held "on the preservation of the Soviet Union." The wording of the referendum was openly manipulative and non-transparent, so Ukraine managed to get 70% of the answers "yes" (while with the unambiguously correct wording in the referendum on December 1, 1991, 90% voted for independence). However, the remarkable thing was that only three regions of Galicia and the city of Kyiv voted against the preservation of the USSR. The Russians sincerely considered Kyiv and Kyivans to be part of the "Russian world," but Kyivans themselves, despite centuries of Russification and the destruction of national consciousness (in the 1991/1992 school year, only 31% of students in Kyiv attended Ukrainian-language schools), felt that they were primarily Ukrainians.

As sociologists, we understand that emotionally exciting moments or events cannot always be extrapolated to the entire society. They can perfectly illustrate public sentiment, but only if there is representative data available. Since the early 1990s, KIIS colleagues and partners from the Institute of Sociology of the National Academy of Sciences of Ukraine have been adding the question "Who do you primarily consider yourself to be?" to all-Ukrainian monitoring surveys and asking the respondent to choose one of the territorial and political options (see Table 8.1. below).

**Table 8.1.** "Who do you consider yourself to be in the first place?", %

| | 1992 - 1993 | 2000 - 2004 | 2005 - 2013 | 2014 - 2021 | 2022 - 2023 |
|---|---|---|---|---|---|
| A resident of the village, district or city where you live | 25 | 31 | 27 | 22 | 7 |
| Resident of the region (oblast or several oblasts) where you live | 8 | 7 | 7 | 6 | 2 |
| **Citizen of Ukraine** | **42** | **40** | **51** | **60** | **81** |
| A representative of one's ethnicity, nation | --- | 3 | 2 | 3 | 3 |
| A citizen of the former Soviet Union | 14 | 13 | 8 | 4 | 1 |
| European citizen | 3 | 2 | 1 | 1 | 2 |
| A citizen of the world | 5 | 4 | 3 | 3 | 3 |
| Other | 2 | 1 | 1 | 1 | 1 |
| Not answered | 1 | 0 | 0 | 0 | 1 |
| Total | 100 | 100 | 100 | 100 | 100 |

In 2022, KIIS included this question in its own survey, and in 2022 and 2023, KIIS collected data for the Institute of Sociology for the next waves. We can see a trend that since the declaration of independence, the share of those who primarily identify themselves as citizens of Ukraine has been growing. In 1992-1993, this number was 42%, while 33% had a local or regional identity, and 14% continued to identify themselves with the USSR. Given the heavy legacy of centuries of eradication of Ukrainian identity and the difficult socio-economic situation, the figure of 42% of those who primarily considered themselves Ukrainian citizens reflected a very tangible national identity.

The situation did not change significantly between the declaration of independence in 1991 and the Orange Revolution in 2004. In 2000-2004, there were slightly more people with local and regional identities (38%), and the share of those who primarily considered themselves citizens of Ukraine was approximately the same 40%. In waves since the early 2000s, the option "representative of their ethnicity, nationality" was added, so it is very possible that 3% of those who chose this option had previously chosen "citizen of

Ukraine". The number of those who continued to consider themselves citizens of the USSR was 13%. More significant shifts occurred after the Orange Revolution. In the period 2005-2013 (before the Revolution of Dignity), 51% of people considered themselves primarily citizens of Ukraine, while the share of local/regional identity decreased to 34% and the share of Soviet identity to 8%. Already on the eve of the occupation of Crimea and Russia's unleashing of the war in Donbas, Ukrainians felt the crystallization and strengthening of national identity. This determined the preservation of statehood and the rebuff to Russian aggression in early 2014. The subsequent Russian aggression certainly accelerated the process, but it is a mistake to consider Russia's actions as the primary cause of the formation of the Ukrainian political nation.

In 2014-2021, during the period of occupation of Crimea and parts of Donbas and before the full-scale invasion, the share of those who considered themselves primarily Ukrainian citizens increased to 60%. Local and regional identity continued to decline to 28%, and the share of those who considered themselves citizens of the former USSR dropped to 4%. At the same time, for the sake of objectivity, it should be noted that since 2014, the surveys have not included the temporarily occupied territories, so the increase in indicators is partly a result of the population of the occupied territories not being included in the sample, which had slightly lower indicators of Ukrainian identity before the Russian aggression in 2014. However, even taking this fact into account, there was indeed a further increase in the national identity of the population.

In the end, the Russian full-scale invasion "dotted the I's and crossed the t's" for ordinary Ukrainians, and in 2022-2023 we have 81% of Ukrainians who primarily consider themselves citizens of Ukraine. Local or regional identity is held by 9%, and the share of those who consider themselves citizens of the former USSR is only 1%. We certainly agree that national identification is a complex social phenomenon that has different dimensions and manifests itself in different circumstances. It is impossible to exhaustively study the process of national self-identification with a single question, but the question discussed in this section is a reliable measure of general trends in Ukrainian society. Another important aspect that is important to illustrate with the available data is national self-identification among certain population groups.

Even pro-Ukrainian academics in the West often have a misconception of Ukrainians as a "split nation" based on region and language. Russia has invested heavily in poisoning Western public opinion and academics, particularly with narratives about Ukraine's divide and that residents of the South and East or Russian-speaking Ukrainians actually identify with Russia and Russians. It is unfortunate that Western experts and journalists have ignored the numerous polls in Ukraine that easily refute Russian propaganda myths. The author of the current work met with some journalists from the world's leading publications on the eve of the invasion. Despite their status and alleged expertise, one could often hear generalizations such as "Kharkiv is a Russian-speaking city and therefore has a Russian identity." Similar arguments could also be heard following the results of national elections because of the different voting patterns of the West and Center compared to the South and East. The first time a clear regional difference was manifested was in the 1994 presidential election, and the already famous S. Huntington used this fact in his early 1990s work "The Clash of Civilizations" to present Ukraine as a country with an internal split.

We cannot and do not deny the fact of different linguistic composition in different regions of Ukraine, nor do we deny the fact of different regional domestic political orientations (though the differences have greatly diminished since the invasion of 2022). However, the fundamental question is how this affects the perception of Ukraine as one's homeland and the perception of oneself as part of the Ukrainian political nation. Reading some of the "expert" opinions about Ukraine from abroad leaves a bitter taste of hypocrisy. Almost every presidential election in the United States, a country that is often considered almost a model democracy, is characterized by a fierce struggle, where representatives of the two main parties have very close support (and due to the peculiarities of the electoral system, a candidate can also receive more votes but still lose the election). At the same time, there is a historically established division between states that predominantly vote for a representative of one party and states that predominantly vote for a representative of another party. Doesn't this also raise analogies with Ukrainian realities? Another point is language as the basis of identification. The United States is a country with a predominant use of the English language, but this did not prevent it from gaining independence from the British crown in a selfless struggle in the eighteenth century. A number of successful countries have different linguistic compositions, which does not prevent them from existing as a united nation. It is a mistake to assume by default (without additional facts, such as survey results) that the use of the Russian language in Ukraine is equivalent to the presence of a Russian identity. And it is also wrong to assume by default that the presence of a significant share of the Russian-speaking population is a sign of a split in the country.

While such population characteristics can indeed provoke tensions in society, it is how society deals with them that is more important. If a common core of values and a common sense of belonging to Ukraine is maintained regardless of the region of residence or language of communication, if there is a commitment to peaceful and fair dialogue (including through a peaceful transfer of power in elections), then conflict issues will be channeled and resolved over time. In April 2014, after the almost bloodless occupation of Crimea, but before the active hostilities in Donbas, KIIS conducted a representative survey for the Dzerkalo Tyzhnia weekly in each of the eight regions of the South and East (except Crimea), including the entire territory of Donetsk and Luhansk oblasts. Although many people in the South and East had a negative attitude toward the Revolution of Dignity, the vast majority (and the majority in Donbas) were against secession from Ukraine. That is, again, dissatisfaction with domestic political issues did not lead to the delegitimization of Ukraine as a state, even in such a difficult period (and against the backdrop of decades of aggressive Russian propaganda). Only Russian military intervention since 2014 is responsible for the outbreak of war.

But back to the "dry sociological facts". The graph below shows the share of residents of certain regions and linguistic and ethnic groups who primarily identify themselves as "citizens of

Ukraine" (as of 2022, after the invasion[65]). In Ukraine as a whole, 85% identified themselves as citizens of Ukraine in July 2022. As can be seen, in the South and East, respectively, 86% and 81% identified themselves primarily as citizens of Ukraine. Among Russian-speaking Ukrainians, 81% identified themselves primarily as citizens of Ukraine, and even among Russian-speaking Russians, 78% considered themselves primarily citizens of Ukraine.

**Graph 8.1. National and civic identification among residents of certain regions and among certain linguistic and ethnic groups (July 2022), % who consider themselves primarily „citizens of Ukraine"**

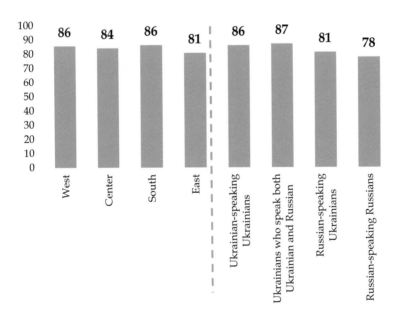

British historian E. Wilson called Ukraine an "unexpected nation" in his long-standing work[66]. Ukraine surprised Western observers in 2022, when it was able to repel the Russian aggressor, and its

65    S. Dembitskyi, "Pokaznyky natsionalno-hromadianskoi identychnosti," *KIIS*, 2022, https://kiis.com.ua/?lang=ukr&cat=reports&id=1131&page=4&y=2022.
66    Andrew Wilson, *The Ukrainians: Unexpected Nation* (New Haven, CT: Yale University Press, 2000).

population, regardless of region and language of communication, showed patriotism and selfless defense of the Motherland. We hope that the data discussed here will put an end to the image of Ukraine as a failed state with a strong internal split and take its rightful place as a legitimate European nation.

## 8.2. Attitudes toward Russian language learning in Ukrainian schools

Continuing with the previous discussion, we cannot ignore the attitude toward the Russian language in Ukraine. We have already seen that Russian-speaking Ukrainians consider themselves citizens of Ukraine and have a Ukrainian identity. However, the question of the perception of the Russian language in general remains open. Since the 1990s, there have been numerous surveys on the perception and status of the Russian language in Ukraine. The results of the surveys strongly depended on the wording of the question and the emphasis. Until 2014, the majority of Ukrainians were not against raising the status of the Russian language, but the modalities of raising the status determined greater or lesser support. In particular, since the 1990s, there has been a tendency to reduce support for granting Russian state status at the expense of more moderate options, such as official status in certain regions where the majority of the population wants it, provided that the Ukrainian language is adequately supported. The sensitive issue of language was the subject of political speculation within the country and was subject to strong pressure from Russia, which was interested not so much in finding comfortable conditions for the functioning of the Russian language as in artificially fomenting conflict among citizens. At the same time, the citizens of Ukraine themselves recognized and admit in polls that there are no particular problems with the use of the Russian language: according to the latest data, in 2023, 84% of Ukrainians in general and 81% of Russian-speaking Ukrainians in particular say that there is no systematic harassment or persecution of Russian-speaking citizens.

In order to understand the shifts in the attitudes of Ukrainians, we propose to look at how attitudes toward the teaching of Russian in Ukrainian-language schools have changed. The Constitution of

1996 defined Ukrainian as the only state language, but guaranteed the protection of national minority languages, specifically mentioning Russian. In the field of school education, Ukrainianization and the transition to the Ukrainian language of instruction did indeed take place, but Russian-language schools and the study of Russian language and literature were preserved. In addition, a strong informal aspect remained, when teachers still taught in Russian or communicated in Russian with students during extracurricular time. Attitudes toward the teaching of Russian in schools also signal how Ukrainians see the future of the language in Ukraine. The graph below shows how much time should be allocated to Russian language instruction in schools according to the results of surveys conducted in 1998, 2019, and 2023.

Ukrainians demonstrated surprising tolerance for the Russian language. In 1998, it was also possible to chant "Beat, beat the Muscovites" in the stands, but almost all Ukrainians did not mind Russian being taught in schools, and 46% generally believed that Russian should be taught to the same extent as Ukrainian. Another 32% believed that it should be taught to a lesser extent than Ukrainian, but to a greater extent than foreign languages such as English or German. That is, for 78% of Ukrainians in 1998, Russian was a very important language.

In 2019, despite the occupation of Crimea and Russia's war in Donbas, 81% of Ukrainians still believed that Russian should be taught in schools. Moreover, 30% spoke of the same amount as the Ukrainian language, and 26% would like to study it at a higher level than foreign languages. In other words, for almost two decades, the status of the Russian language in the eyes of the population has been shaken, but its legitimacy in the public space and in the institution that forms the next generations has remained very tangible. One can, of course, assume that part of the population sought to learn Russian to "understand the aggressor," but still, a significant part of the population maintained a warm attitude toward ordinary Russians and Russian culture and differentiated attitudes toward the Russian government, which was blamed for the outbreak of the war. In another 2020 poll, respondents were offered two statements about the Russian language, and 50% chose the option that "the Russian language is a historical heritage of Ukraine that needs to be developed" and only 30% believed that "the Russian language threatens Ukraine's independence" (the remaining 20% were undecided).

Already in 2023, 52% of Ukrainians in the survey said that Russian should not be taught at school at all. Only 3% believe that it should be taught to the same extent as Ukrainian, and only 6% believe that it should be taught at a level higher than foreign languages. Another 33% said that Russian should be taught at a level lower than foreign languages.

**Graph 8.2. "Do you think that the study of Russian in Ukrainian-language schools should be given ...", %**

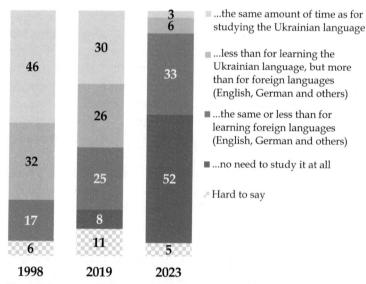

* *The 1998 survey did not include the option "do not study it at all", but did include the option "other" (0.4%, added to "hard to say" in the graph). Also, the 1998 survey covered the entire Donbas and Crimea. However, taking this factor into account would not significantly affect the meaningful results and understanding of key trends.*

The change in attitudes in the South and East of Ukraine between 2019 and 2023 is particularly noteworthy. Back in 2019, more than half of the population in these regions were in favor of teaching

Russian to the same extent as Ukrainian. In 2023, only 4% of them were left. While in 2019, almost no one in the South and East said that Russian should not be taught in schools at all, in 2023, the number of such people was already 49% in the South and 30% in the East.

**Graph 8.3. Russian language teaching in Ukrainian-language schools by regions, %**

▪ ...the same amount of time as for studying the Ukrainian

▪ ...less than for learning the Ukrainian language, but more than for foreign languages
▪ ...the same or less than for learning foreign languages

▪ ...no need to study it at all

▫ Hard to say

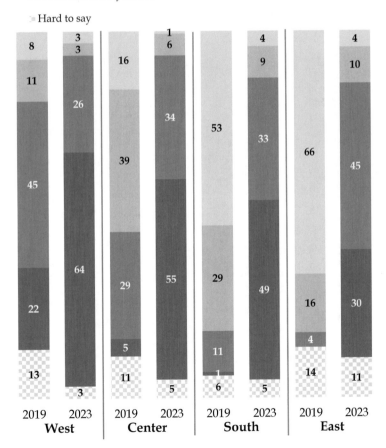

In the 2023 survey, there was no question about the language spoken at home, only a question about the language preferred for interviews. Nowadays, many of those who speak Russian at home choose Ukrainian for interviews as a political indicator of their pro-Ukrainian position. That is, those who chose Russian for interviews represent only a narrower part of the Russian-speaking population, and often those with more politically divergent positions. However, even among them, only 7% believe that Russian should be taught to the same extent as Ukrainian, and only 23% believe that it should be taught to a greater extent than foreign languages.

**Graph 8.4. Russian language learning in Ukrainian-language schools by the language chosen for interview, % (February 2023)**

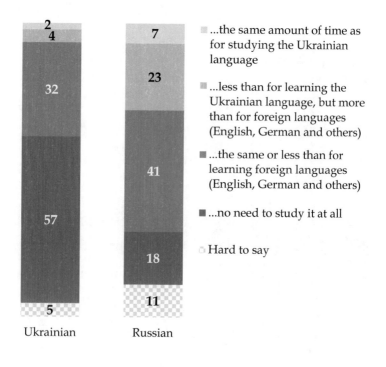

## 8.3. The complicated relationship between Ukrainians and democracy

In addition to the processes of national self-awareness and socio-economic restructuring, Ukraine and Ukrainians are also undergoing a rethinking and transformation of values. There are various studies of values and various projects have been implemented in Ukraine. For example, as we write this, KIIS is preparing to conduct fieldwork and collect data as part of the European Social Survey. We are certainly fascinated by large-scale cross-cultural comparisons based on a standardized methodology, which allow us to identify interesting dependencies and understand the place of our country on the world's value map. However, Ukraine is often, unfortunately, a "victim" of such studies as ESS or WVS (World Values Survey) and experiences the "political" consequences of the supposedly neutral methodology. For example, the results of such surveys usually result in a map that places different countries based on the results. The closer the countries are to each other, the closer their values are. And Ukraine turns out to be very close to, for example, Russia and Belarus, which signals to many interpreters that the societies are "significantly close in values."

While this question may seem purely scientific, it has real "political" implications. For example, few people think about whether the ESS or WVS methodology is an exhaustive tool for studying all important values and has sufficient sensitivity to distinguish between neighboring countries. Despite covering a large part of the important values, it is safe to say that these schemes are not sensitive enough to the obvious differences in the political cultures of Ukraine and Russia. The very history of the last thirty years, which has been unfolding in real time in Ukraine and Russia, shows that despite the similar value profiles of Ukraine and Russia from the point of view of some studies, political processes and the formation of political cultures have been different. However, an outside observer may not understand this based on the results of such studies alone, and may draw erroneous conclusions and make false recommendations. In particular, the subjectivization of Ukraine will drown in these allegedly scientific arguments about the value proximity, and thus the practical identity, of both countries. Hence, it is quite close to Putin's false and manipulative argument about the "single nation" and that Russia is not at war, but is engaged in a "civil war within a single nation."

KIIS has touched upon certain value issues in various surveys, and we would like to touch upon the issue of Ukrainians' attitudes toward democracy, which is important for understanding political culture. KIIS has long been cooperating with the National Democratic Institute (USA), and one of the monitoring questions is whether Ukrainians want Ukraine to become a fully functioning democracy. On the eve of the invasion, 76% of Ukrainians wanted this, and in 2023, 95% desired this outcome. When asked an additional question about the main criteria of democracy, among the seven proposed criteria (among which up to three could be chosen), most respondents mentioned fair justice for all (64%), freedom of speech (59%), and free and fair elections (44%). Slightly fewer respondents mentioned the protection of human rights (31%) and government transparency (27%). Relatively fewer respondents chose such options as accountability of the Government (13%) and representation of citizens' interests by political parties (3%).

In other words, the demand for a stable democratic regime in which free expression and, especially, justice are ensured remains and is even growing among Ukrainians. Justice is one of the most important focuses because, as will be shown in the following sections, there is a critically low level of trust in justice institutions in Ukraine, such as courts and prosecutors. According to a KIIS survey for the European Union Advisory Mission conducted in 2023, 68% of Ukrainians believe that in order to get justice, they need to bribe someone.

**Graph 8.5. "How important is it for you that Ukraine becomes a fully functioning democracy?" % who answered "important" or "very important"**

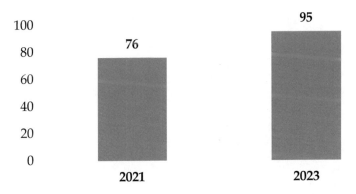

At the same time, it is fair to say that Ukrainians still tend to trust "strong leaders." In particular, this is why there are virtually no real ideological parties in the political system, and all major political forces are leadership projects around a particular leader. Against the backdrop of a poor understanding of the areas of constitutional responsibility, Ukrainians also tend to personalize responsibility on one top-level leader (for example, to believe that the President is responsible for everything that happens in the country).

In July 2022, a few months after the full-scale invasion, KIIS conducted a survey for an influential NGO (Opora), asking what was more important for Ukraine right now: a strong leader or a democratic system. Although the vast majority of people want to see Ukraine as a fully functioning democracy, in the choice between a strong leader and a democratic system, 58% of respondents found a strong leader more important. The democratic system was preferred by 27%.

**Graph 8.6. "Which statement do you agree with to the greatest extent?", % (July 2022)**

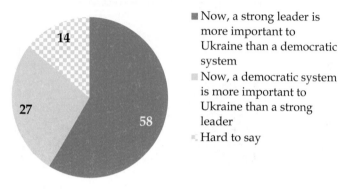

- Now, a strong leader is more important to Ukraine than a democratic system
- Now, a democratic system is more important to Ukraine than a strong leader
- Hard to say

The results of the survey, where the majority of the population spoke about the greater importance of a strong leader now, caused a certain public outcry in the country's intellectual circles, as they were at odds with a rather "rosy" view of the Ukrainian public, which was supposedly unconditionally committed to the fight for democracy. At the end of 2023, we decided to repeat this question, but in the verbatim wording that we used earlier in 2020. In this wording, we are not talking about the need now, but what is more important for Ukraine in general. In 2020, only 31% of respondents in general preferred a democratic system, while at the end of 2023, the figure was 59%. At the same time, the number of those who prefer a strong leader has decreased from 54% to 32%.

**Graph 8.7. "Which statement do you agree with the most?", %**

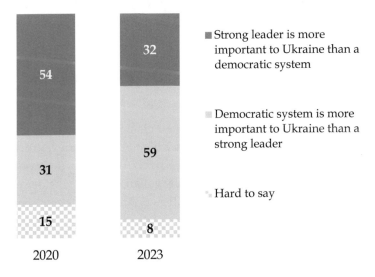

Could this be a sign of the democratization of citizens' consciousness? We should be very careful to assert this. Perhaps if we were to ask about the need now, again more people would talk about a strong leader, given the very difficult situation due to the full-scale invasion (while still maintaining the view that in the long run Ukraine should build a fully functioning democracy). Or, indeed, amid growing criticism of national leaders, more and more Ukrainians are beginning to realize the benefits of well-functioning democratic institutions.

Ukrainians still have a lot of work to do, including building their own political culture and stable institutions. There are also tangible risks. The difficult environment leaves room for populists to stir up the people especially in the context of the power of populists globally. In particular, on the sensitive issue of corruption, at the end of 2023, 55% of respondents agreed to extrajudicial punishment of corrupt officials so the latter would feel the responsibility and anger of the citizens. However, this obviously contradicts the focus on strict adherence to the law. Our observations nevertheless give us a sense that Ukrainians are becoming more democratic in their views. In any case, the 95% who think it is important for

Ukraine to be a fully functioning democracy show that this idea is not perceived as alien or imposed on Ukrainians, but is accepted as an organic component to which Ukraine is returning, just as Ukraine's return to Europe is.

## 8.4. Which public holidays do Ukrainians like the most?

The values of the population and their changes can manifest themselves in unexpected places, such as which public holidays are most honored by the population. One of KIIS's own monitoring questions asks which public holidays Ukrainians like or consider most important. Below, we compare 2021 and 2023 to illustrate the impact of a full-scale invasion.

Table 8.2. "Which of the following Ukrainian national holidays are the most important or favorite for you? Please indicate no more than 5 holidays", %

|  | 2021 | 2023 |
|---|---|---|
| Easter | 72 | 70 |
| Christmas | 63 | 69 |
| Independence Day of Ukraine | 37 | 63 |
| Day of Defenders of Ukraine | 29 | 54 |
| New Year | 55 | 52 |
| Constitution Day of Ukraine | 14 | 29 |
| International Women's Day | 34 | 25 |
| Trinity | 17 | 22 |
| Victory Day | 30 | 13 |
| Labor Day (May 1) | 12 | 5 |
| Total | 100 | 100 |

The most popular religious holidays remain Easter (70% in 2023 vs. 72% in 2021) and Christmas (69% in 2023 vs. 63% in 2021) (only 22% chose another religious holiday, Trinity). However, the dominance of these religious holidays is not so clear. As will be shown below, trust in the Church as an institution is steadily declining in Ukraine, so when Ukrainians talk about Easter or Christmas, they are more likely to perceive them as family holidays, rather than manifestations of religiosity. That is, these Christian holidays are the leaders, but its meaning is changing. Another neutral holiday, more related to private affairs, also retains its importance: New Year's Eve (in 2023, 52% ranked it as the most important, in 2021, 55% ranked it as the most important).

At the same time, we can see the rapid growth of secular public holidays. In 2021, only 37% honored Independence Day the most (in 2013, before the occupation of Crimea and Russia's war in Donbas, only 12% honored it), and in 2023, 63% did. Those who selected The Day of Defenders of Ukraine as one of their five preferred holidays increased from 29% to 54%, and even Constitution Day shows an increase from 14% to 29%.

In addition, there are three other holidays that have a strong association with the Soviet past and for which the continuation of "decommunization of consciousness" is evident. There are fewer people who like International Women's Day (from 34% to 25%), and fewer people who like Victory Day (from 30% to 13%), while Labor Day has also declined (from 12% to 5%). In the long run, these holidays were naturally losing support, but the Russian invasion accelerated this process.

Earlier in this chapter, we discussed the processes of national self-identification and the development of national consciousness. The sharp increase in respect for state holidays is precisely a reflection of the nation-building processes that Ukraine is currently undergoing.

## 8.5. Gender balance and attitudes towards the LGBT+ community

Achieving gender equality and ensuring the rights of the LGBT+ community is increasingly becoming a topic of discussion in Ukrainian society, especially as European integration processes accelerate. The adoption of the Istanbul Convention in 2022 and its further practical implementation, as well as the approval of the draft law on registered partnerships for gay and lesbian couples in the future will be a test for Ukrainian society. Some public actors in

Ukraine are already trying to form an image of defenders of "traditional Ukrainian values." However, this is not really very easy, because too much conservatism evokes analogies with Russian "spiritual bonds" and Russian traditionalists. Few people in today's Ukraine want to be seen as similar to Russia.

At the same time, as with many issues, few people engage in civilized, reasoned discussions, and instead we are talking about emotionally charged communication and polarization of communities depending on their views. Even the terminology used in the questions affects the results of the surveys. The equality of men and women will not be objected to by the vast majority of Ukrainians, but the word "gender" is perceived by many with caution. The use of the term "LGBT+" is perceived better by respondents than, for example, the term "homosexuals." Accordingly, there are many ways to phrase questions in such a way to get the desired answers. Below we will focus on the results of KIIS surveys.

To begin with, it is worth noting for the sake of objectivity that neither the issue of gender equality nor the issue of ensuring the rights of the LGBT+ community is relevant to the general population. Perhaps, when Ukrainians finally satisfy their basic needs in their "pyramid of needs" (including victory, socio-economic changes, and overcoming corruption), ordinary citizens will more tangibly raise the issue of justice for certain disadvantaged groups. In 2023, in a survey for the European Union Advisory Mission, KIIS asked which of nine tasks were the highest priority. Among the tasks was ensuring equality between men and women, and only 4% (the last place out of nine) included it among the three most important for Ukraine now. In particular, few women ranked this task as a top priority.

In fact, many Ukrainians already hold the view that equality between women and men is sufficiently ensured in Ukraine. In addition, many are indeed free of a number of harmful stereotypes. For example, in a KIIS survey for the Council of Europe Office conducted in 2022, 85% of respondents said that the gender of the head of a community such as those in local government is not related to the quality of performance of duties under martial law. Only 11% believe that gender has an impact, with 5% of them saying that women are more effective and 6% saying that men are more effective. In the aforementioned EUAM survey, 85% believe that women are as qualified and capable as men to work and/or hold positions in the security sector. Certainly, a number of stereotypes continue to exist and influence Ukrainians, but many positive changes can already be seen.

In KIIS surveys for the National Democratic Institute (USA), the question of the participation of men and women in politics is often asked. While on the eve of the invasion, 66% of Ukrainians wanted to see a better balance of men and women in political life, in 2023, the figure was 74%. For the majority of Ukrainians, women's participation in politics is quite natural. It is unfortunate that the share of women in top-level government and in more senior positions is still far from fair. In addition, horizontal segregation persists, with women occupying more positions in certain sectors. However, legally, Ukraine is indeed making efforts to increase equality and improve legislation (and the issue of fair and effective implementation will remain important), and at the level of stereotypes, many have already been overcome and we are witnessing a process of strengthening the worldview of equality.

**Graph 8.8.** "Who do you think should be more involved in political life — men or women?", % who answered "approximately equally men and women"

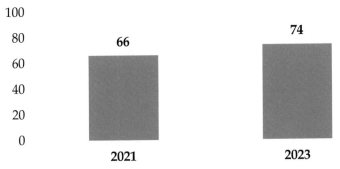

The situation with the LGBT+ community is more complicated, as equality between women and men is easier to accept for the general population than the issues discussed by representatives of the

LGBT+ community. In Ukraine, unfortunately, homophobic rhetoric is still present in public life. However, public opinion is now becoming warmer towards the LGBT+ community. In the KIIS survey for NDI in 2023, as seen in the graph below, more than half of the respondents agreed that members of the LGBT+ community should have the same rights as all other communities, that they have the right to civil partnerships, and that they have the right to demonstrate to defend their rights. No more than a quarter of respondents disagreed with these ideas. The issue of adoption of children remains more sensitive, with a higher number of those who do not support the right of the LGBT+ community to adopt. It is also worth adding that among those respondents who personally know someone from the LGBT+ community, the rate of support for equal rights is twice as high as among those who do not know anyone from the LGBT+ community.

Also in 2023, KIIS conducted a survey for one of the NGOs "Nash mir" fighting for the rights of the LGBT+ community. One of the questions was "Do you support the introduction of a registered partnership for same-sex couples, similar to a regular marriage, but without the right to jointly adopt children?" In this case, a different term than LGBT+ was used, and the question was more expansive to explain civil partnerships. By 2023, 28% of respondents answered "yes," 39% answered "no," and 33% answered "I don't care" or "hard to say." Although the share of "no" answers outweighs the share of "yes" answers, in fact, the majority of the population either supports or does not care, which creates potential space for the eventual approval of the long-overdue decision on registered partnerships for the LGBT+ community.

**Graph 8.9. "Please tell me to what extent, if at all, do you agree or disagree with the following statements?", % (November 2023)**

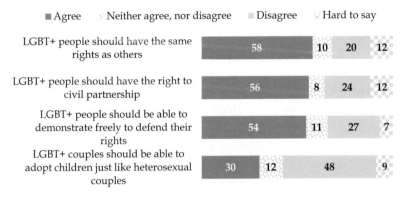

■ Agree    Neither agree, nor disagree    ■ Disagree    Hard to say

| | Agree | Neither agree, nor disagree | Disagree | Hard to say |
|---|---|---|---|---|
| LGBT+ people should have the same rights as others | 58 | 10 | 20 | 12 |
| LGBT+ people should have the right to civil partnership | 56 | 8 | 24 | 12 |
| LGBT+ people should be able to demonstrate freely to defend their rights | 54 | 11 | 27 | 7 |
| LGBT+ couples should be able to adopt children just like heterosexual couples | 30 | 12 | 48 | 9 |

Finally, in terms of gender balance and attitudes toward the LGBT+ community, it is important to understand the potential impact of the context of a full-scale invasion. A full-scale invasion creates both the conditions for achieving a better situation in these areas and the risks of a rollback. The proportion of women in the Ukrainian Defense Forces is one of the highest in the world, and women in general are actively involved in the defense of Ukraine, which certainly further legitimizes women in public space and helps to overcome stereotypes about "female" types of employment. The same applies to members of the LGBT+ community who also participate in the defense of the country, and 68% of Ukrainians have a positive attitude towards their service in the Defense Forces. In other words, strengthening the association between these groups and Ukraine's defense forces improves their image among the population and increases understanding of the importance of equality (and in the case of the LGBT+ community, the sense of justice is heightened, as under current legislation, partners have limited rights to, for example, hospital visits, benefits, etc.)

At the same time, there are tangible risks. In the public space, organizations that fight for the rights of these groups are often accused of being "leftist" and allegedly engaged in latent (or even open) pro-Russian activities to undermine Ukraine's defense capabilities. Another cluster of accusations relates to focusing on their own activities and not taking into account national interests in the priority of repelling the aggressor immediately. In addition, there is a wide category of people with conservative views in Ukraine who do not support legislative changes for these value reasons. Moreover, when hundreds of thousands of citizens are in a rigid military hierarchy or in an environment that requires strict discipline and order, this stimulates the development of more traditionally authoritarian values.

KIIS has been researching public attitudes and values for over 30 years. From the early 1990s to the present day, the values of Ukrainians have undergone significant changes. These changes have been in favor of more modern European values. In terms of gender balance and attitudes toward the LGBT+ community, Ukraine may not be moving so fast, but it is steadily moving toward greater equity.

## 8.6. Ukrainians' changing commitment to traditional Ukrainian values

When discussing the issue of values, and especially "traditional" values, it is important to realize that Ukrainians themselves do not fully understand what exactly is meant. Moreover, attitudes toward "traditional" values can change dramatically depending on the context. In 2022, KIIS conducted an experiment. Respondents were asked the same simple question about which values they preferred: modern European and Western values or traditional values. Only half of the respondents were asked about "traditional Ukrainian values" and the other half about "values that are traditional for Eastern Slavs: Ukrainians, Russians, Belarusians". In the first case, 78% gave preference to traditional Ukrainian values and only 12% preferred modern European and Western values. However, when we "remembered" the values common to Ukrainians, Russians and Belarusians, 51% chose modern European and Western values and only 33% chose traditional values!

In other words, an average Ukrainian may be a supporter of traditional Ukrainian values, but he or she will easily become a modern European if these values are associated with Russian "staples."

**Graph 8.10. "Do you think that Ukraine should encourage the spread and strengthening of ... ?", % (July 2022)**

■ Modern European / Western values

▨ Values that are traditional for Eastern Slavs - Ukrainians, Russians, Belarusians

▨ Hard to say

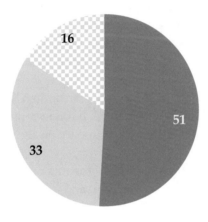

■ Modern European / Western values
▨ Traditional Ukrainian values
▨ Hard to say

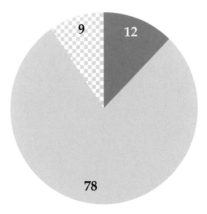

## 8.7. Religious self-identification of the population

When discussing values, it is impossible to avoid the issue of religion among the Ukrainian population. Moreover, although the Orthodox Church of Ukraine (created after the Unification Council in 2019), avoids overtly political activities, it does demonstrates a public conservative position: For example, in 2022, the OCU issued a warning against the approval of the Istanbul Convention. In addition, in recent years, trust in the Church as an institution (regardless of a particular denomination, in general) has been steadily declining in Ukraine. While in 2021, on the eve of the invasion, 51% trusted the Church, in 2023 it was 38%. The Church used to be a leader of trust among institutions, but now trust in it has been severely eroded, and with it the influence on the views of the population.

Table 8.3. below shows the dynamics of religious self-identification in 2021 (before the invasion) and in 2022 (after the invasion).

**Table 8.3.** "To which denomination or religion, if any, do you belong? And to which Orthodox Church do you belong?", %

| 100% in the column | 2021 | 2022 |
|---|---|---|
| Orthodox Church of Ukraine | 42 | 54 |
| The Orthodox Church without specification | 12 | 14 |
| I consider myself an atheist | 7 | 10 |
| Greek Catholic Church | 9 | 8 |
| Ukrainian Orthodox Church (Moscow Patriarchate) | 18 | 4 |
| Protestant Church | 2 | 2 |
| Other Christian churches (e.g., Jehovah's Witnesses, etc.) | 2 | 2 |
| Roman Catholic Church | 1 | 1 |
| Judaism | 0 | 0 |
| Islam | 0 | 0 |
| Other | 4 | 3 |
| It's hard to say | 2 | 2 |
| Total | 100 | 100 |

First, the overwhelming majority of respondents continue to identify themselves as Orthodox. Currently, 72% of respondents identify themselves as Orthodox (and 85% generally consider themselves Christians). Secondly, the Orthodox Church of Ukraine is by far the "leader" among the Orthodox Churches. In general, 54% of all respondents identify themselves as belonging to the Orthodox Church of Ukraine (an increase from 42% in 2021). Only 4% now identify themselves with the Ukrainian Orthodox Church (formerly the Moscow Patriarchate, now the question of how to properly call the Church is debatable), although this Church retains a significant lead in the number of parishes (in 2021 it was 18%). Another 14% consider themselves simply Orthodox, without specifying the Patriarchate. Among other results: after Orthodoxy, most respondents identified themselves as either atheists (at 10%, with the share of atheists among young people aged 18-29 being 22%), or Greek Catholics (at 8%, mostly concentrated in western Ukraine). Other religions or denominations were mentioned less frequently.

In Ukraine, there is a long-term trend toward a decline in the influence of the Church in society. Already, almost a quarter of young people consider themselves atheists, and trust in the Church as an institution continues to decline. For a long time in Ukraine, the Church has been a participant in political processes and part of national identification. In the period before the creation of the Orthodox Church of Ukraine, there was the Ukrainian Orthodox Church of the Kyiv Patriarchate, which was not officially recognized by world Orthodoxy, and there was a joke that went around: "I am an atheist, but an atheist of the Kyiv Patriarchate." That is, a significant number of people were actually indifferent to religious issues, but associated the UOC (formerly the Moscow Patriarchate) with a pro-Russian vector, and the UOC-KP with a pro-Ukrainian or pro-Western vector. Accordingly, in surveys, people identified themselves with a particular denomination rather for political reasons. At the moment, it can be stated that the UOC (formerly the Moscow Patriarchate) has done a "titanic" job of strengthening its negative and pro-Russian image, even against the backdrop of a full-scale invasion. The sluggish position on the invasion, the inability to unequivocally break ties with Russia, and numerous cases of cooperation of UOC representatives (especially senior hierarchs) with the occupiers or sympathy for them led to the fact that in 2023, 66% of Ukrainians were in favor of a complete ban on the UOC, and another 19% were in favor of establishing state supervision over it. Although the UOC retains control over the largest number of parishes in Ukraine, it has only very low legitimacy among the population.

## 8.8. Dynamics of Attitudes Toward Stalin and Perceptions of the OUN-UPA Activities during the Second World War

History in Ukraine is a special battlefield. Putin's misconceptions about history have become the foundation of his aggressive policy. Putin's misconceptions about history have become one of the foundations of his aggressive policy. In addition to Russians studying anything but true history, Russia is taking powerful steps to influence historical scholarship in the West and in Ukraine. Ukrainian historians are constantly faced with the fact that Western scholars look at the history of Ukraine through "Russian glasses." Ukraine still has a long way to go before the Western community reconsiders its views on Ukraine's history based on real facts, not falsified delusions of the Russian tsarist, Soviet and post-Soviet periods. Both before and after the full-scale invasion, KIIS conducted large-scale surveys on attitudes toward various historical events and figures. Here, we propose to focus on two marker points: attitudes toward Stalin and attitudes toward the OUN-UPA (Organization of Ukrainian nationalists-Ukrainian insurgent army).

In Ukraine, at the time of independence, only 27% considered Stalin a great leader. Although this proportion increased slightly by the early 2000s, it continued to decline, and in 2023 only 9% of Ukrainians considered Stalin a great leader. Often, in order to understand a certain value dimension, we have to compare the current results with something. If everyone around the world knows that Stalin was a bloodthirsty tyrant who deserves to be cursed by his successors, then the current results for Ukraine are nothing special. For Ukraine, Russia is an illustrative comparison. Earlier, we noted that in terms of many value surveys, Ukraine and Russia are close together. However, it is worth looking at the graph below to see once again that these studies apparently "overlook" many of the features that distinguish the two societies. As we can see, in 1991-1992 there was practically no difference in the number of those who considered Stalin a great leader, in 2016 the difference was already statistically significant, but not very large. We do not have data for 2017-2020, but we can assume that the difference grew rapidly thereafter. In 2021, the difference was already 40%, and in 2023 it was 45%. The proportion of Russians who somehow agree that Stalin was a great leader has remained virtually unchanged since 2021. In 2023, 54% of respondents think he was a great leader and in May 2021 this figure was at 56%, but the share of those who disagree with this judgment has decreased, it amounted to 12% in 2023 and in May 2021 it was 14%.

**Graph 8.11. "Do you agree or disagree with the statement: 'Stalin was a great leader'?", %**

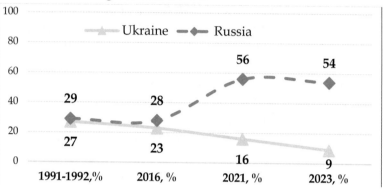

The difference in the dynamics of Ukrainians' and Russians' personal attitudes toward Stalin is even more striking. The graph below shows the percentage of those who have a positive attitude toward Stalin. While in 2012 the share of the population with a positive attitude toward Stalin was only 5 percentage points higher in Russia, in Ukraine there were fewer sympathizers of the Soviet dictator in general, and in Russia, on the contrary, the favorable attitude toward him grew rapidly and now the majority of the population has a positive attitude. In Russia, between 2012 and 2023, the share of those who have a positive perception of Stalin increased from 28% to 63%.

**Graph 8.12. Comparison of positive attitudes toward Stalin in Ukraine and Russia, %**

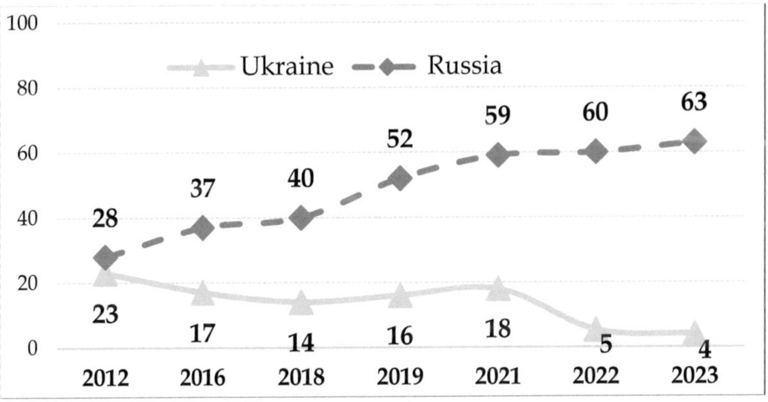

*Data for 2022 are not available for Russia, so the modeled results are illustrative.*

Another painful page of history is the activities of the OUN-UPA. The Soviet authorities, and later the Russian authorities, made a powerful effort to falsify many facts related to the OUN-UPA. Western scholars also did not always make the necessary efforts to objectively study the activities of the OUN-UPA and often broadcast very simplified, very stereotypical narratives.

During the period of Ukrainian independence, attitudes toward the OUN-UPA have been studied in various polls and with the help of various questions. In 2012, long before the Revolution of Dignity and before the occupation of Crimea and the war in Donbas, we asked how Ukrainians assessed the activities of the OUN-UPA during World War II. At that time, 47% of Ukrainians had a negative assessment of the OUN-UPA, and 20% had a positive one. The rest were undecided. By 2022, after the full-scale invasion, 43% of Ukrainians had a positive assessment of the OUN-UPA, and only 8% had a negative one. At the same time, a significant proportion maintained an undecided attitude, which is obviously a consequence of the lack of reliable objective information (and Russia's invasion made many people realize that Russia had been imposing lies about World War II for decades).

In 2023, KIIS conducted a survey for the Center for the Study of the Liberation Movement (Ukraine) on attitudes toward the UPA. In fact, 72% knew something about the "Ukrainian Insurgent Army". Among them, 77% believed that the UPA primarily fought for an independent Ukraine, and 90% had a positive attitude toward the recognition of UPA soldiers as fighters for independence. In other words, after the invasion, the emotional feeling that the UPA fought for Ukraine with the main goal of gaining independence still crystallized, but the lack of information still remains significant.

**Graph 8.13.** "In general, how do you assess the activities of the Organization of Ukrainian Nationalists—Ukrainian Insurgent Army (OUN-UPA) during World War II?", %

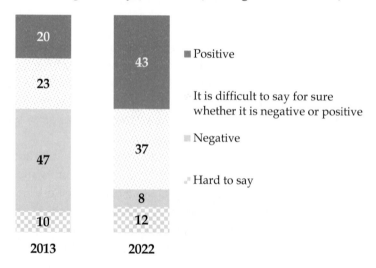

Like the history of any other national liberation movements, the history of the OUN-UPA is not black and white. It is impossible to deny the tragic events that accompanied it. At the same time, it would be wrong and hypocritical to reduce their position to a comprehensive assessment as "Nazi collaborators." There are many unequivocal events and figures in history, for example, Hitler, Stalin, and Putin are undoubtedly villains and world criminals who must be condemned for eternity. However, most historical figures and historical events are probably too multidimensional for us to have a clear positive or clear negative assessment, especially since the current assessment is highly dependent on the current context.

The heroes of one nation can (and will) be perceived as enemies by other nations. Unfortunately, it is impossible to find a common denominator that will satisfy everyone. The only possible civilized way is to take historical discussions out of politics and focus on the most impartial work of professional historians. In addition, it is important to recognize that residents of different countries may have different views on the same figures or events. According to the results of the previously mentioned poll for the EDC, 55% of Ukrainians believe that Ukraine should not coordinate its historical policy with neighboring European states. At the same time, 60% recognize that neighboring European states should not coordinate their policies on their past heroes with Ukraine.

# 9. Attitudes Towards the State, Social Institutions and Political Forces

## 9.1. Dynamics of attitudes towards the state and social institutions in 1991-2022 (before the invasion)

From the day Ukraine declared its independence in 1991 to the outbreak of the conflict with Russia, state policy and social dynamics underwent numerous changes. This period is so eventful that it could be explored in a book of its own, but there are a few key aspects that help to understand the context.

Ukraine has had a minimalist form of democracy in which the government was changed by election. At the same time, Ukrainians have often been highly critical of their government. This feature can be studied through a historical lens, as the government in modern Ukraine has long been an alien power, the power of invaders. This legacy may reflect a deep distrust of any form of government, which has led to resistance, maidans, and mass protests.

Unlike the situation in Russia, where Vladimir Putin has been in power for a long period of time (and apparently not by democratically persuading people, but by increasing authoritarianism), in Ukraine it is common for an elected government to lose the support of citizens within a few months of the election. This dynamic often leads to the election of another political force or another president for the next term. This difficult path of statehood formation, with its turbulent elections, mass protests, and interaction between the government and citizens, reflects the unique nature of Ukrainians' attitudes toward their state and social institutions.

The dynamics of attitudes toward the Presidents of Ukraine is very characteristic. Graph 9.1 shows the balance of trust and distrust in the Presidents of Ukraine (i.e., the percentage of those who trust minus the percentage of those who distrust the President). We did not find any data on trust in L. Kravchuk (the first sociological surveys representative of the Ukrainian population began only in 1991, and in the early years there were few studies, we found only electoral ratings). Therefore, the graph begins with Kuchma's second term (although given the results of the 1991 and 1994 presidential elections, the trends were similar). For each president, we took as the first point the results of the survey close to the beginning of his or her term, and the second point close to the end of his or her term. For Zelenskyi, we took three points: at the beginning of his term; before the start of the full-scale war in 2022; and after the war. As you can see, all presidents started with a trust-distrust balance of +40-44% (Kuchma had +5%, because it was his second term, he was the only one who was able to win his second election and stay for a second term, we think that at the beginning of his first term his balance was also about +40%). All of them ended their term with a negative balance of less than -40% (V. Zelenskyi's was -23%, but it was not at the end of his term, but only 2 years after it began).

**Graph 9.1. Zigzag of trust in Ukrainian presidents, balance of trust and distrust, %***

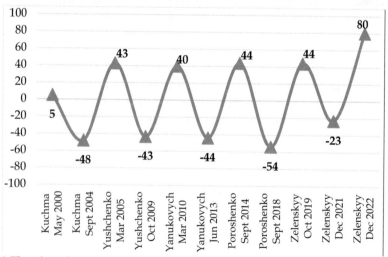

* The idea of such a graph belongs to the Director General of KIIS Natalia Kharchenko.

Perhaps this type of schedule is typical for any country with a democratic system. For comparison, here is a similar graph for the Russian presidential election, only we provide data not on the balance of trust in Putin, but on the approval of his activities[67] (he has been in power for 24 years, if we do not take into account the "rollover" with D. Medvedev, which was not perceived by the population as a real change of power). Just as for the Ukrainian presidential election, we took points at the beginning of the term (the year of the "election", if it can be called an election at all) and at the end of the next term, the year before the next "election".

**Graph 9.2. Russians' approval of V. Putin's activities (by election cycles), %**

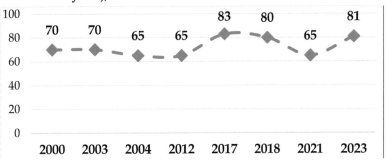

As we can see, there is no such pattern here at all; approval does not decrease at the end of a term and does not increase at the beginning. In fact, there has been no change of power in Russia since 2000.

One of the key features of Putin's rule is the establishment of an authoritarian system of government in which the opposition faces numerous restrictions, the ordinary population is depoliticized with the exchange of material goods and non-interference in politics, and where loyalists hold important government positions. This creates a structure where control of power is concentrated in the hands of a small group of loyalists. Putin has managed to secure

67    Levada Center, 'Pokazateli: Odobreniye deystviy Vladimira Putina.' *Levada Center*. Accessed December 1, 2023, https://www.levada.ru/indikatory/.

control over most of the important media in the country, which allows him to manipulate information, shaping a positive image of
the government and hiding or distorting the negative aspects of its
activities. It turned out that, unlike the Soviet Union with total control over the media, which is difficult to achieve today, it is enough
to have control over most of the most popular media and partial
control over the Internet and social networks. In addition, in the
value dimension, ordinary Russians remained "traumatized" by
the loss of their former "greatness" and retained (depending on the
period, in a more latent or open form) a tendency to an imperialist
worldview that generated resentment. This allowed the authorities
to use sensitive topics (e.g., longing for the collapse of the Soviet
Union) to manipulate the population, divert attention from real internal problems, and focus the population on things like creating a
hostile image of Ukraine. Further, the patterns of media consumption lead to the spread of the dominant point of view formed by the
authorities. In particular, as S. Hromenko aptly notes, during
Putin's rule, public attitudes toward Ukraine have moved to the
concept of not even "fraternal" but already "one people," which
justifies the need to "denazify" Ukraine, which "dared to separate
from Russia"[68]. Accusations of manipulation during the electoral
process are a constant phenomenon in Russia, from restrictions on
candidate registration to accusations of vote fraud, these methods
help ensure the desired result for the authorities. Putin also uses the
legislative process to secure his power; changes to the Russian Constitution and other laws have helped him find ways to stay in
power even after his official presidential term ends. Overt or covert
repression of opposition leaders, activists, and journalists is another
means of maintaining power. Detentions, prosecutions, violence
and assassinations are used as a means of pressure and intimida-
tion. For example, a talented opposition leader, former Deputy
Prime Minister Boris Nemtsov, Anna Politkovskaya, who investigated government crimes and was killed on Putin's birthday, and

---

68   S. Hromenko, 'Stavlennia Putina do ukraintsiv ne zminylosia, prosto vin peres-
tav prykydatysia.' *Gazeta.ua*, January 23, 2023, https://gazeta.ua/articles/pog
lyad/_stavlennya-putina-do-ukrayinciv-ne-zminilosya-prosto-vin-perestav-pr
ikidatisya/1129967.

Galina Starovoitova, a prominent politician and State Duma member, were murdered. In 2020, opposition leader Alexei Navalny was openly poisoned with the Novichok nerve agent, and in 2023 he was sentenced to 19 years in prison; Vladimir Kara-Murza, who was twice in a coma as a result of suspected poisoning, was sentenced to 25 years in prison. It is contextually important that the egregiousness of these cases did not find strong condemnation and protest among Russians. Ordinary Russians remained committed to the social contract of material benefits in exchange for depoliticization and mostly silently watched the rise of authoritarianism, which actually turned into outright fascism (some protests took place, but given the size of Russia and the population, they were obviously not particularly large-scale). By the way, it is worth drawing parallels with Ukraine, where the murder of journalist Gongadze in 2000 initially led to mass protests against the government, and in 2004 led to the Orange Revolution. All these methods together create a complex system of control and manipulation that allows Putin to remain in power for a long period of time, minimizing the possibility of challenges and changes from the opposition or the dissatisfied population.

**Graph 9.3. Approval of V. Putin's performance in 1999-2022, %.**

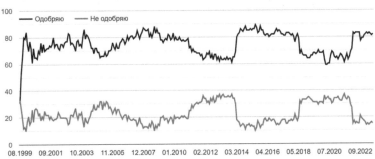

As for the fluctuations in the approval of Putin's activities, they are not related to the elections, but to Russia's military aggression. Let's look at a more complete graph (Figure 9.3) of the same Levada Center data[69] that we used for the previous graph. After a peak of 86%

---

69   Levada Center, 'Pokazateli.'

during Russia's attack on Georgia in 2008, approval of Putin's performance gradually decreased and in November 2013 it dropped to 61% (i.e., minus 25%), but after Russia's seizure of Crimea and the war in Donbas it rose to 88%, after a while the potential of the "Crimean euphoria" was exhausted and approval of his performance dropped to about 60%, but after the outbreak of war on February 24, 2022, it jumped again to 83%. Putin's regime deliberately promotes the "revival of national pride" and Russia's great-power ambitions. To exemplify the effects of this, 63% of Russians have a positive attitude toward Stalin, one of the greatest tyrants of mankind. One can argue about the real reasons for the war (the ones Putin gives do not stand up to any criticism), but one of the most important reasons is his desire to stay in power.

Changes in attitudes towards social institutions in Ukraine can be divided into 3 periods: before 2014 (before the Russian aggression, annexation of Crimea and the war in Donbas); from 2014 to February 24, 2022 (the beginning of the war); and after the war. The structure of trust in social institutions as outlined in Table 9.1 is typical for the first period.

**Table 9.1. Trust in the social institutions, % (February 2012)**

|  | Trust | Do not trust | The balance of trust and distrust |
|---|---|---|---|
| Church | +62 | +17 | +45 |
| Media | +41 | +28 | +12 |
| For non-governmental organizations | +27 | +29 | -2 |
| To the Armed Forces | +34 | +37 | -2 |
| Opposition | +24 | +53 | -29 |
| To the President | +22 | +66 | -44 |
| Militia or police | +16 | +63 | -47 |
| Government | +16 | +69 | -53 |
| Verkhovna Rada (Parliament) | +12 | +73 | -61 |

As we can see, the positive balance of trust and distrust is only in the church (+45%) (the first place with a margin over other institutions) and the media (+12%), with approximately zero balance in public organizations and the Armed Forces of Ukraine, and negative balance in all others.

Changes in the second period compared to the first are shown in Table 9.2. We report only the percentage of those who trust in social institutions.

**Table 9.2.   Trust in the social institutions, % who trust**

|  | 2012 | 2015 | The difference 2015 i 2012 |
|---|---|---|---|
| Church | 62 | 59 | -3 |
| Media | 41 | 32 | -9 |
| For non-governmental organiza-tions | 27 | 35 | +8 |
| To the Armed Forces | 34 | 45 | +11 |
| Opposition | 24 | 9 | -15 |
| To the President | 22 | 17 | -5 |
| Militia or police | 16 | 18 | 2 |
| Government | 16 | 9 | -7 |
| Verkhovna Rada (Parliament) | 12 | 6 | -6 |

As we can see, the biggest changes occurred in attitudes toward the opposition and the Armed Forces of Ukraine. Trust in the Armed Forces has increased from 34% to 45% and they are now second only to the Church (the Church remained in first place). Obviously, this is a consequence of the Russian aggression and the Armed Forces' fight against the enemy. It should be noted that as tensions in the relationship grew and Russia brought troops to the border with Ukraine, trust in the Armed Forces increased.

Confidence in the opposition has decreased, but earlier in 2012 it was a pro-European opposition that opposed fugitive President Viktor Yanukovych, and in 2015 it was mostly a pro-Russian opposition. One of the most significant changes is the decline in trust in the media. This phenomenon is somewhat paradoxical. In 2012, all major media outlets, especially television channels, which were the main source of political information for the population, were controlled by Viktor Yanukovych and his Party of Regions, except for two small channels with a share of about 1% (Channel 5 and TVI). After 2014, with the change of government, the media became freer, almost all channels became opposition channels, criticism of the government and other media increased significantly, and attitudes toward the media deteriorated. Trust in the President, the Government and the Parliament decreased due to the intensification of political struggle on television and more critical media coverage.

## 9.2. Changes in attitudes toward the state and social institutions after the outbreak of war

After the outbreak of full-scale war in 2022, there were more radical changes in the attitudes of Ukrainians toward the state and social institutions. We have already mentioned the survey conducted by KIIS in December 2022 at the request of the Institute of Sociology of the National Academy of Sciences of Ukraine. This is the next wave of Ukrainian Society monitoring, which was launched in 1994 by Ye. Golovakha and N. Panina and has been regularly conducted since then[70]. The project is now managed by S. Dembitskyi. The authors have developed an Index of General Attitudes Toward the State, which consists of 5 indicators. Below are the results for 3 of those indicators, which are interesting separately, as well as the results for this Index.

---

70   S. Dembitskyi, 'Hromadska dumka v Ukraini pislia 10 misiatsiv viiny.' *KIIS Press Releases.* Accessed December 1, 2023, https://kiis.com.ua/?lang=eng&cat =reports&id=1175&page=1.

**Graph 9.4.** "How do you assess the effectiveness of the Ukrainian state at this stage?", %

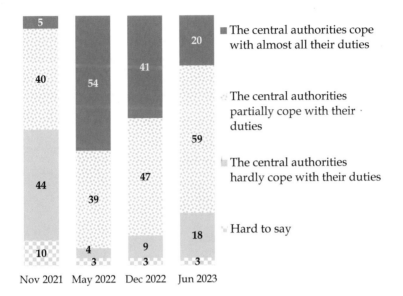

As we can see (Figure 9.4), two months before the war in November 2021, only 5% believed that the central government was coping with almost all of its responsibilities, and 44% believed that it was almost not coping. And after 8 months of war, in December 2022, the assessments were almost reversed: 41% believed that they were coping and 9% that they were not. However, by June 2023, assessments had deteriorated somewhat, although they remained significantly better than they had been before the invasion.

In its own survey in December 2023, KIIS asked whether Ukrainians generally perceive the Government as an employee or a parent. Of those surveyed, 66% of Ukrainians answered that the Government is an employee, and people should be the managers who control its actions. Over the past three years (since 2020), the share of people who share this view has increased from 55% to 66%. At the same time, the number of people who believe that the Government is like a parent who should take care of people like children has decreased from 36% to 30%.

A significant change in assessments also applies to the future of Ukraine. Before the war, Ukrainians were quite pessimistic in their assessments: 35% believed that the situation was likely to deteriorate and only 13% thought it would improve. In December 2022, the number of pessimists decreased from 35% to 8%, while the number of optimists increased dramatically to 76% (see Section 7 for more details). No less paradoxical are the results of the survey on the assessment of living conditions in Ukraine for the majority of the population (see Graph 9.5).

**Graph 9.5. "In your opinion, what are the living conditions in Ukraine for the majority of population", %**

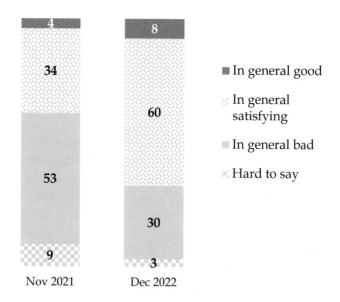

Objectively, the living conditions of Ukrainians have deteriorated significantly (see Chapter 3. Socioeconomic changes). On the contrary, people's assessments have changed from critical (overall poor 53%, overall satisfactory 34%) to positive (overall poor 30%, overall satisfactory 60%).

## Graph 9.6. General attitudes toward the state, %

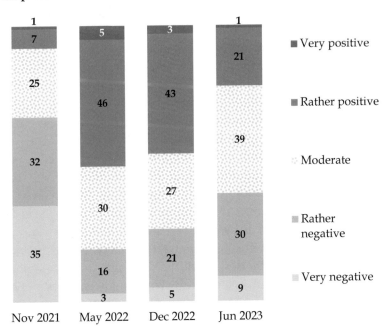

Finally, Graph 9.6 summarizes the information obtained using the General Public Attitudes Index. Strongly positive attitudes remained at 3%, while moderately positive attitudes increased from 4% to 43% by December 2022 (i.e., the number of positive assessments, both strong and moderate, increased from 7% to 47%), but then decreased to 21% by June. The total number of positive assessments in June 2023 was 22%. The number of negative ratings decreased from 55% to 40%, especially for strongly negative ratings, which decreased from 35% to 9%.

During the war with neighboring Russia, the situation in Ukraine turned out to be paradoxical: **although the situation in the country deteriorated dramatically, assessments of its condition and positive attitudes toward the state increased.** This feedback can be explained by several key factors:

**Reassessment of values due to the threat of loss:** The possibility of losing their statehood made Ukrainians reassess their prewar views. Ukrainians began to value their state much more,

**Comparative analysis:** Comparing democratic Ukraine to totalitarian Russia has made us appreciate our own sovereignty, freedom, and citizens' rights more.

**Community and unity:** War helps unite a nation against a common enemy. This sense of unity and common purpose leads to an increase in patriotism and pride in one's country and state. The main emotion that respondents feel when thinking about Ukraine after the war started is pride, according to the sociological group "Rating", 75% feel this way compared to 34% before the war[71].

**The pre-war situation as attractive:** What may have seemed like disadvantages, uninteresting or unsatisfactory before, may now look attractive in comparison to the war, and be perceived as valuable and important. A return to stability and peaceful life is desirable even in a form that was not satisfactory before the war.

**The ability to withstand a powerful enemy:** Successful confrontation with Russia, despite all the difficulties, can strengthen national pride and faith in the state's own strength and capabilities.

In general, the growth of optimism and positive attitudes toward the state during the war can be attributed to these factors, which are evidence of deep national self-knowledge and reflection in times of crisis.

We also consider the results of a survey on trust in social institutions conducted by KIIS in December 2022. Below is information on the dynamics of trust (Graph 9.7) and the balance of trust and distrust in social institutions (Graph 9.8) from December 2021 to December 2022. The question in the questionnaire read as follows: "Now I am going to name some social institutions. Please tell me how much you trust those I will name?". The scale of answers was: Fully trusted / Rather trusted / Hard to say / Rather distrusted / Not at all trusted / Refused to answer.

---

71  Rating Group, 'Rik viiny: yak zminyvsia portret ukraintsiv ta Ukrainy.' *Ukrainska Pravda*, February 22, 2023, https://www.pravda.com.ua/columns/2023/02/22/7390482/.

**Graph 9.7. Dynamics of trust in the social institutions***

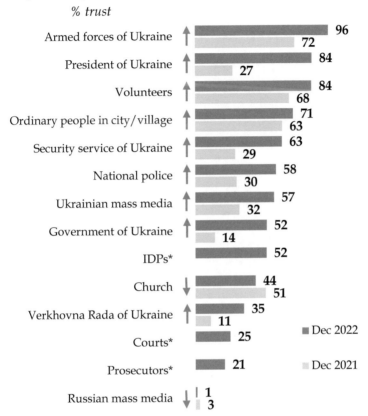

% trust

| Institution | Dec 2022 | Dec 2021 |
|---|---|---|
| Armed forces of Ukraine ↑ | 96 | 72 |
| President of Ukraine ↑ | 84 | 27 |
| Volunteers ↑ | 84 | 68 |
| Ordinary people in city/village ↑ | 71 | 63 |
| Security service of Ukraine ↑ | 63 | 29 |
| National police ↑ | 58 | 30 |
| Ukrainian mass media ↑ | 57 | 32 |
| Government of Ukraine ↑ | 52 | 14 |
| IDPs* | 52 | |
| Church ↓ | 44 | 51 |
| Verkhovna Rada of Ukraine ↑ | 35 | 11 |
| Courts* | 25 | |
| Prosecutors* | 21 | |
| Russian mass media ↓ | 1 | 3 |

\* In 2021, the question was not asked for these institutions.

In the diagrams, arrows indicate cases where the difference compared to December 2021 is statistically significant. An upward arrow indicates an increase in trust, while a downward arrow indicates a decrease. As you can see, trust in almost all social institutions has increased. Only the church and Russian media have decreased in trust (but it was close to zero anyway).

## Graph 9.8. Dynamics of trust in social institutions*

*% balance of trust-distrust*

| Institution | Dec 2022 | Dec 2021 |
|---|---|---|
| Armed forces of Ukraine | 96 | 60 |
| President of Ukraine | 80 | -23 |
| Volunteers | 81 | 57 |
| Ordinary people in city/village | 62 | 52 |
| Security service of Ukraine | 54 | -7 |
| National police | 45 | -14 |
| Ukrainian mass media | 43 | -7 |
| Government of Ukraine | 33 | -46 |
| IDPs* | 41 | |
| Church | 22 | 27 |
| Verkhovna Rada of Ukraine | 2 | -56 |
| Courts* | -9 | |
| Prosecutors* | -11 | |
| Russian mass media | -92 | -76 |

*legend:* ■ Dec 2022   ■ Dec 2021

* In 2021, the question was not asked for these institutions.

In December 2022, **the Armed Forces** continue to enjoy the highest level of trust in Ukraine, and over the past year (between December 2021 and December 2022), the level of trust has increased from 72% to 96%. The balance of trust and distrust in the Armed Forces (i.e., the difference between the share of those who trust and the share of those who distrust) was +96% (in December 2021 it was +60%). This was followed by trust in the **President of Ukraine** and trust in volunteers. In December 2021, 27% trusted the President (and the balance was negative -23%, i.e. there were more people who did not trust than trusted), but over the year, the figure increased to 84%, and the balance is now +80%.

There was another interesting study on the change in attitudes toward V. Zelenskyi as president. The fact is that before the war started, political opponents and some media, as well as social networks, wrote that Zelenskyi would not be able to work effectively as the Supreme Commander-in-Chief. Before the full-scale Russian invasion in November 2021 and January 2022, KIIS asked respondents whether they thought Zelenskyi could effectively work as the Supreme Commander-in-Chief and organize the country's defense. In May 2023, KIIS repeated the question to track how much Ukrainians' views on this issue have changed. Before the full-scale invasion in January 2022, only a third of Ukrainians (32%) believed that V. Zelenskyi was able to work effectively as the Supreme Commander-in-Chief, while the majority (53%) did not. Moreover, between November 2021 and January 2022, confidence in V. Zelenskyi's ability to be the Supreme Commander-in-Chief even slightly decreased (from 36% to 32%). However, after the full-scale invasion, Ukrainians changed their views dramatically, and in May 2023, 86% believed that V. Zelenskyi was working effectively as the Supreme Commander-in-Chief. The perception of V. Zelenskyi's ability to work effectively as the Supreme Commander-in-Chief demonstrates several important trends in public attitudes.

First, it confirms the concept of "rally around the flag". This is the rallying of the population around a leader in very difficult situations, especially in times of war. This concept was proposed in 1970 by the American sociologist John Mueller and has been observed in various countries. Until mid-February 2022, there was a steady downward trend in trust and approval of V. Zelenskyi's activities, but after the invasion, the indicators increased sharply. V. Zelenskyi is now perceived by Ukrainians as "in his place" and has become one of the symbols of resistance to the occupiers.

Secondly, in May 2023, V. Zelenskyi and the then Commander-in-Chief of the Armed Forces of Ukraine V. Zaluzhnyi had the highest levels of trust and approval among the population. At the same time, despite Russian propaganda and the short-sighted position of some Ukrainian actors, the vast majority of Ukrainians believed that the political and military leadership were acting in concert as a team. Ukrainians believed that we were finally moving away from the principle "where there are two Ukrainians, there are three hetmans," which was one of the stereotypes used to describe the characteristics of Ukrainians.

Third, although public opinion is important, people can be wrong about many expert issues. Very often, politicians even put to referendums issues that are debated among experts ("should Ukraine be a presidential-parliamentary or parliamentary-presidential system", "which parliament is better for the country – a unicameral or bicameral", etc.) In this case, Ukrainians initially largely did not believe in V. Zelenskyi as the Supreme Commander-in-Chief, but after the full-scale invasion, they radically changed their views and now, after almost a year and a half of war, they remain confident in him.

**Volunteers.** Trust in volunteers increased from 68% to 84%, and the balance improved from +57% to +81%. The active work of volunteers during the war plays an important role in the development of civil society in Ukraine. Volunteers bring together diverse groups of citizens to help at the front and on the home front, creating a strong sense of unity and cooperation between different parts of society. Through fundraising, medical services, information support, and other assistance, volunteers have demonstrated the importance of social responsibility and mutual aid. The growth of trust in volunteers reflects the strengthening of mutual respect and trust in society, which encourages more people to participate in civic initiatives. The response to the needs of those affected by the war shows the strength of empathy and solidarity in Ukrainian society. The activism of volunteers emphasizes the importance of civic participation and democratic values, reinforcing the idea that every citizen can contribute to victory and to improving life in their country. They also played a role in shaping a positive image of Ukraine, showing the strength, determination and compassion of the Ukrainian people. Overall, the volunteers' work has become a symbol of unity, strength and kindness in a difficult period for Ukraine.

There has been a significant improvement in trust in the other two law enforcement **agencies** on the list: trust in the SBU increased from 29% to 63% (the balance increased from -7% to +54%), and in the National Police: from 30% to 58% (the balance increased from -14% to +45%).

Perceptions of the **Government and the Parliament (Verkhovna Rada) have** also improved significantly. Trust in the Government increased from 14% to 52% (the balance increased from -46% to +33%). In the case of the parliament, although the overall trust scores are not high, there has also been a significant increase in trust: from 11% to 35%, and the balance has increased from -56% to +2%.

This year, we added two institutions to the list that are more associated with ensuring the rule of law in the country: **prosecutors and courts**. As it turned out, these are the only Ukrainian institutions that have a negative balance of trust and distrust and are the most critically viewed by Ukrainians. Thus, courts are trusted by 25%, distrusted by 34% (the rest have no definite attitude) (the balance is -9%). Prosecutors are trusted by 21%, distrusted by 32% (the balance is -11%). In 2021, we did not have similar institutions on our list, so we cannot speak directly about the dynamics. However, in 2018, in another KIIS survey, 12% trusted the judiciary, and 78.5% did not. Most likely, compared to 2021, there have also been noticeable improvements in attitudes toward courts and prosecutors, although significant skepticism still remains.

In another survey, we asked: "In your opinion, after the victory in the war, is it necessary or not necessary to reboot and replace the central government—the President, the Government, the Verkhovna Rada—to restore the country?" The overwhelming majority of Ukrainians (73%) support the renewal of the central government at one level or another. At the same time, the biggest request for renewal concerns the Verkhovna Rada: 69% of respondents would like to change the parliament after the Victory. Next comes the Government: 47% of respondents would like to change it. The least number of respondents, at 23%, would like to change the President after the President's victory. The high level of trust in the government does not remove the existing desire of Ukrainians to renew the government, to have more honest and competent managers at various levels. In addition to President Zelenskyy, the demand for renewal of the parliament and the government is tangible.

Ukrainians have united to repel the enemy, but this does not mean turning a blind eye to the abuses or incompetence of certain politicians or government officials. Although we did not ask this question in this survey, there is an even greater demand for renewal of the judicial and prosecutorial systems, which have the lowest trust scores.

Trust in the **Ukrainian media has** increased from 32% to 57% over the year (the balance has increased from -7% to +43%). Trust in the Russian media was absent before, and now this absence has become even more pronounced: from 3% to 1%, there are even fewer trusters, and the balance has decreased from -76% to -92%. Changes in the consumption of Ukrainian media will be discussed in Chapter 10.

There is a slight deterioration in attitudes toward the **Church**: the share of those who trust the Church has decreased from 51% to 44%, and the balance has decreased from +27% to +22%. It is possible that this is due to the following. After Russia's full-scale invasion, one of the most pressing issues for Ukrainian society was the functioning of the UOC-MP (the Ukrainian Orthodox Church of the Moscow Patriarchate)[72]. Since 2022, the Security Service of Ukraine (SBU) has opened more than 60 criminal cases against clergy of the Ukrainian Orthodox Church of the Moscow Patriarchate[73]. Although the church itself has denied these accusations, it could affect the credibility of the church. At the end of 2022, after a number of high-profile cases against representatives of this church, KIIS raised questions about the appropriate policy of the authorities. In the period up to May 2023, the situation around the UOC (MP) remained highly tense (especially in the context of the Kyiv Pechersk Lavra), so KIIS again asked a similar question.

According to the survey, from 78% in December 2022 to 85% in May 2023, the number of Ukrainians who believe that the state

---

72   O. Yanevskyi, 'Voina postavila pod vopros loyalnost UPTs Moskovskoho patriarkhata v Ukraine.' *Voice of America*, April 1, 2022, https://www.golosameri ki.com/a/ukraine-orthodox-church-russia/6511546.html.
73   'SBU nazvalo chislo ugolovnykh del protiv dykhovenstva UPTs s 2022 goda.' *RBC.ru*, accessed December 1, 2023, https://www.rbc.ru/politics/01/04/2023 /642844d59a7947b8add3f546.

should intervene in the activities of the UOC (MP) to some extent has increased. In particular, the number of those who believe that this Church should be completely banned in Ukraine has increased from 54% to 66%. Another 19% stand for a somewhat "softer" approach that does not imply a complete ban, but provides for the establishment of state control and supervision (in December 2022 this was at 24% of respondents). At the same time, the number of respondents who believe that nothing should be done and that it is not necessary to interfere in the affairs of the UOC (MP) and that only certain possible cases of offenses should be investigated has decreased from 12% to 6%.

Also, according to the survey, Ukrainians have become more trusting of **ordinary people** in their localities. The trust rate has increased from 63% to 71%, and the balance has improved from 52% to 62%. This year, we also asked about attitudes toward **IDPs**: overall, 52% of respondents trust them and only 10% do not (the rest have an undecided/indifferent attitude), and the balance is +41%.

The growth of trust in the political leadership and law enforcement agencies during the war is another indication of the unity of citizens in critical circumstances. Social cohesion is one of the key factors in successful resistance to the enemy. It is important that Ukrainians have more trust not only in the Armed Forces, but also in the Security Service of Ukraine and the National Police, which also perform very important functions. It is vital not only to improve the attitude towards the President, but also to improve the perception of the Government and Parliament, as these institutions play an important role in organizing the country's life during the war and are responsible for reforming the country according to European standards. At the same time, it is necessary to pay attention to the significant "lag" of prosecutors and courts, which are critical elements of the rule of law. If the political leadership and law enforcement agencies respond to the demand for citizens' security (in the minds of citizens themselves), then prosecutors and courts should respond to the demand for the rule of law and justice. Many Ukrainians remain distinctly skeptical of them, and, accordingly, of justice in the country, and now there is a significant question for prosecutors and courts themselves to be the engine of positive change and not to claim that negative attitudes toward them are the results of unfounded "black" PR. This is also a question for Ukrainian lawmakers and government officials to understand that after the victory, the demand for the rule of law and justice will only become more urgent, so we need to act proactively and solve problems now. Moreover, attitudes toward prosecutors and courts have softened considerably, as evidenced by the increase in the number of those with an "uncertain" attitude and the decrease in those with a strongly negative attitude towards prosecutors and courts. This creates a window of opportunity to implement the necessary changes.

By the end of 2023, the situation had changed somewhat, the level of "rallying around the flag" had decreased, and trust in social institutions had also declined.

**Graph 9.9. Dynamics of trust in the social institutions in 2021, 2022, and 2023**

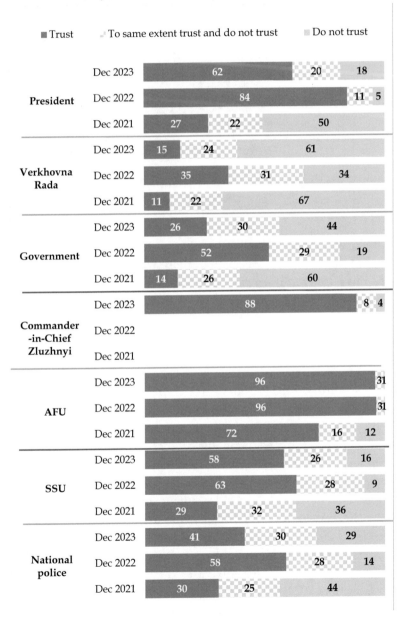

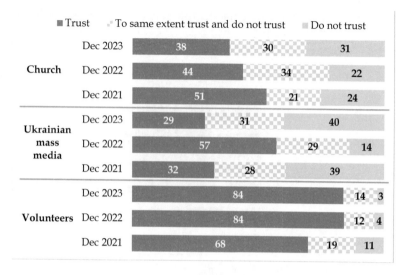

Compared to December 2022, criticism of the authorities has increased. In particular, the share of those who trust the Verkhovna Rada has dropped from 35% to 15%, but this is higher than it was before the war when the figure was only 11%. Trust in the Government has dropped from 52% to 26% (and in 2021 it was only 14%). Although there is also a downward trend in the case of the President, he retains overwhelming trust among the Ukrainian public. Thus, in December 2023, 62% trusted the President. In December 2022, 84% trusted the President and 5% did not. Accordingly, if the balance of trust and distrust in December 2022 for the President was +80%, now it is +42%. That is, on the one hand, we see a significant decline, but on the other hand, the balance remains clearly positive with a significant predominance of those who trust the President compared to those who do not. The level of trust at 62% is much higher than the 27% he had in December 2021.

The Armed Forces retain absolute trust in society. Just as in December 2022, 96% trust the Armed Forces now.

Trust in the SBU has slightly decreased, but in December 2023, the majority of Ukrainians still trusted it: 58% vs. 16% who did not (in December 2022, 63% trusted the SBU, 9% did not). At the same time, trust in the police decreased more significantly—from 58% in

December 2022 to 41% in December 2023. Again, this figure is higher than the pre-war 30%.

Trust in volunteers remained high in Ukraine, with 84% trusting them in December 2023 (in December 2022, the figures were almost identical).

The Ukrainian media have significantly lost trust, with trust scores returning to the level of December 2021. Thus, over the past year, the number of those who trust the Ukrainian media has decreased from 57% to 29%.

In addition, the Church is steadily losing public trust. Between December 2021 and December 2022, trust in the Church decreased from 51% to 44%, and between December 2022 and December 2023, from 44% to 38%.

Thus, in December 2023, the indicators of trust in the Armed Forces and law enforcement agencies remained almost at the same level, while the indicators of trust in the government declined, but still remained above the pre-war level. What could this be due to? Since the beginning of 2023, Western and Ukrainian media and statements by government officials in Ukraine and the West have made many statements about the next counteroffensive. In particular, the head of Ukraine's Main Intelligence Directorate, Kyrylo Budanov, said that Ukraine could regain control of Crimea by the end of spring 2023. Western officials claimed that they had provided enough weapons for successful action. Such statements raised high expectations among the Ukrainian population, as many hoped for a repeat of the successes of 2022. The Armed Forces counteroffensive began in early summer 2023, with the main goal of making a strategic breakthrough on the front, especially in Donetsk and Zaporizhzhia regions. Despite plans for a rapid offensive, the counteroffensive was delayed due to unfavorable weather conditions and delays in the supply of weapons from abroad, which forced it to wait until the summer. Ukraine's military faced elaborate enemy defenses, including deep defensive lines with trenches and minefields, which made their advance difficult (which Russia had been preparing since the fall of 2022, while Ukraine was forced to wait for sufficient weapons from the West and overcome resistance to provide, for example, modern tanks). Despite some successes (14 settlements were liberated during the counteroffensive, and about 370 square kilometers were liberated), the progress became less visible, and by November, the effectiveness of the counteroffensive began to raise doubts among the top military leadership. Subsequently, the Ukrainian leadership, in particular General Zaluzhnyi and President Zelenskyi, emphasized that the conflict was entering a new phase, as the original objectives had not been met. At the end of the year, the achievement of the counteroffensive goals was assessed as limited. As a result, a significant number of Ukrainians were disappointed (but not despondent or willing to surrender).

Another factor may be the realization that the war is dragging on, its outcome is becoming uncertain, there is a need for increased mobilization and the need to distribute their life resources and those of their families over a long distance. The level of optimism of the population has somewhat decreased (although it has remained at a fairly high level, as shown earlier in the book). Finally, V. Zelenskyi's political opponents could not stand the long moratorium on ending the political struggle to increase social unity and resistance to Russia and began to criticize the government more actively on social media and their television channels.

# 10. Changes in Media and Internet Consumption

## 10.1. Changes in media consumption

Since the outbreak of war on February 24, 2022, Ukraine's media space has undergone significant changes. One of the most important was the creation of United News ("Yedyni Novyny"), a joint project of public and private TV channels aimed at informing citizens about the situation at the front and in the country. In fact, the channels stopped working independently, and each channel has several hours to broadcast its content as part of a single project called "United News." As of today, writing at the end of 2023, nine national channels (Suspilne, Rada, 1+1, ICTV, Inter, UNIAN, We Are Ukraine, K2, and Zoom) are united in the United News project[74]. Other channels (e.g., former President Poroshenko's channels "Pryamyi" and "Channel 5"[75]) were disconnected from digital broadcasting and could only broadcast their programs online.

On the one hand, this contributed to the consolidation of society, reduced criticism of the authorities and the diversity of views on the course of the war. On the other hand, the television space has become more monotonous and less interesting. This may be one of the reasons why some viewers have switched to consuming information on the Internet. However, there is also a general tendency to both decrease the importance of television and increase the importance of internet consumption due to certain advantages in news search, which are especially important during the war. Firstly, the internet allows access to news instantly, while television requires waiting for a certain time for the news to be released. Second, you can watch news on the internet anytime and from any-

---

74    N. Dankova, 'Nedoloiniinyi kanal: Shcho vidbyvaietsia za lashtunkamy "Yedynykh Novyn".' *Detector Media*, January 23, 2023, https://detector.media/prod uction/article/207480/2023-01-29-nedoliniynyy-kanal-shcho-vidbuvaietsya-za-lashtunkamy-iedynykh-novyn/.

75    K. Tyshchenko, '"Priamyi" and "Pyatyi" zaiavyly, shcho yikh vidkliuchyly vid tsyfrovoho movlennia.' *Ukrainska Pravda*, April 4, 2022, https://www.pravda.com.ua/news/2022/04/4/7337136/.

where. Third, the internet allows you to customize your news channels to get exactly the information you are interested in. Fourthly, there are many different news sources on the internet, which makes it possible to get more diverse information.

What sources of information were most important before the war? The results of the KIIS and Razumkov Center surveys76 2018-2021 are presented in Table 10.1.

**Table 10.1. "From which sources do you most often receive information about the state of affairs in Ukraine and the world? Choose up to 3 answers." (2018-2021), %**

| | 2018 KIIS) | 2019 (KIIS) | 2020 Razumkov Center) | 2021 Razumkov Center) |
|---|---|---|---|---|
| Ukrainian television (national channels) | 86 | 74 | 75 | 67 |
| Russian television | 5 | 4 | 6 | 5 |
| Ukrainian online media | 27 | 28 | 27 | 29 |
| Social networks | 24 | 24 | 44 | 44 |
| Ukrainian newspapers (national publications) | 8 | 7 | 8 | 6 |
| Ukrainian radio (national stations) | 2 | 2 | 9 | 7 |
| Local television | 6 | 4 | 9 | 9 |
| Local radio | 2 | 2 | 2 | 2 |
| Local online media | 3 | 4 | 6 | 7 |
| Local print media | 5 | 2 | 4 | 3 |
| Relatives, friends, neighbors, colleagues, acquaintances | 18 | 11 | 23 | 28 |
| Russian print media | 0 | 0 | 0 | 0 |
| Russian sites | 1 | 1 | 0 | 1 |
| LPR-DPR media (including websites) | 0 | 0 | 0 | 0 |
| Messengers (Viber, Telegram, WhatsApp, TikTok, Instagram, etc.) | --- | --- | 11 | 16 |
| Other | 1 | 1 | 2 | 1 |
| Hard to answer | --- | --- | --- | 2 |
| Total | 100 | 100 | 100 | 100 |

76 Detector Media Report, 'Mediaspozhyvannia v Ukraini: Zmina potreb media ta porazka rosiiskoi propahandy.' *Detector Media*, February 15, 2022, https://det ector.media/infospace/article/196477/2022-02-15-media-consumption-in-ukr aine-change-in-media-needs-and-defeat-of-russian-propaganda/.

As we can see, in 2018, Ukrainian television undoubtedly dominated, being the main source of information about the state of affairs in Ukraine and the world for 86% of Ukrainians. But from 2018 to 2021, this percentage decreased to 67%. At the same time, the percentage of social media users increased from 24% to 44%, and the percentage of Ukrainian online media users remained almost unchanged (from 27% to 29%). Nevertheless, television continued to dominate other sources of information in 2021, with the ratio of television to social media being 67% to 44% (a difference of 23 percentage points).

It is worth noting that due to the Covid pandemic and the need to work remotely in Ukraine, according to our data, the number of internet users has increased significantly[77]. Thus, in 2019, there were 68% internet users, in 2020, there were 74%; in 2021, there were 81%; and in 2022, there were 82%. In the first half of 2023, 88% were internet users. Therefore, the process of increasing interest in online media and social networks has been ongoing.

At the time of writing, one of the authors in Fukuyama's recent book *Liberalism and Its Contradictions* came across an interesting line about Ukraine, that all TV channels there were allegedly controlled by one oligarch (obviously, the hint was about the richest man, Rinat Akhmetov). In reality, the situation was more complicated, and in Ukraine, several large but different groups controlled different TV channels, with different emphases in the presentation of political information. In other words, there was even some quasi-pluralism and competition in the presentation of information, and consumers could generally choose what they liked best.

In July 2022, KIIS conducted a study on media consumption commissioned by the NGO "OPORA". The study included a survey representative of the population of Ukraine living in Ukraine and a diary survey. The results of the survey are shown in Graph 10.1. We asked the respondents to indicate the sources they used in the past 7 days to get news. As we can see, social networks are in the first

---

77   Data on the percentage of Internet users depends on the question and the age of the respondents (the younger the age, the more users). KIIS asks "Do you use e-mail or the Internet anywhere—at home, at work or school, or elsewhere?" and asks members of the population aged 18 and older.

place (69%), followed by Ukrainian television, "United News" (Yedyni Novyny")—57%.

**Graph 10.1. Sources used by respondents during the week to receive news, % (July 2022)**

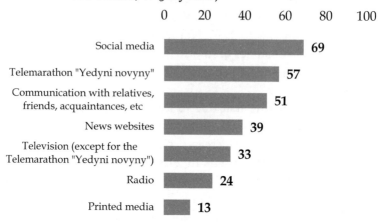

According to the results of the diary survey, there is also a tendency for online sources to dominate, especially social media, which account for 48% of total news consumption time (news sites account for 11%, television accounts for 34%). The questions asked in this study are somewhat different from the pre-war ones. Back then, we asked about the sources of information that Ukrainians most often use to get information about the state of affairs in Ukraine and the world, and now we asked about news, and not just in general, but for the last seven days. However, the difference in the wording of the question is not very large, as "information about the state of affairs in Ukraine and the world" is, in fact, synonymous with news. The biggest difference is that a significant part of the population in July 2022 did not live in the territory controlled by the government of Ukraine (refugees and those in the occupied territory), but both surveys are representative of the population living in the territory controlled by Ukraine. Therefore, we think we can compare these surveys, see Graph 10.2.

**Graph 10.2. Changes in the use of television and social media after the beginning of the war, %**

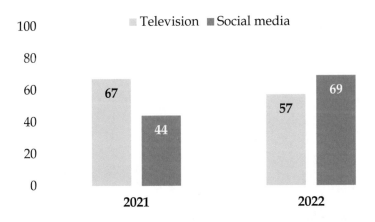

As we can see, the ratio of television and social media usage has changed dramatically, with television losing its dominance and social media becoming the main source of information. This was not so much due to a decrease in television audience (TV lost 10 percentage points of viewers) as to an increase in social media users (by 25 percentage points).

Other studies were conducted by KIIS at the request of the National Democratic Institute[78]. Respondents were asked. "Where do you get information about politics and current events? Choose all that apply". Similar studies were commissioned by us from December 2021 to November 2023. The results of the research of the Research Institute are similar to the results of the study of the Opora, see Graph 10.3.

---

78  'NDI Poll: Opportunities and Challenges Facing Ukraine's Democratic Transition.' *KIIS*, accessed 30 November 2024, https://www.kiis.com.ua/?lang=eng&cat=reports&id=1135&page=1.

**Graph 10.3. Changes in TV and social media use from December 2021 to November 2023, %**

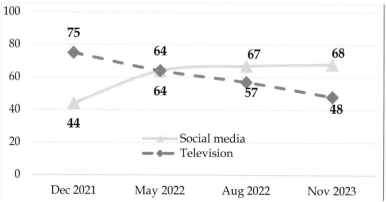

Two weeks before the war in December 2021, television dominated social media by a wide margin, and 2-3 months after the war, social media and messengers (like Telegram, YouTube, Facebook, etc.) overtook television, and in August this difference became even greater (67% social media and messengers compared to 57% television). By the end of 2023, 68% were talking about social media and messengers, while 48% mentioned television. In September 2023, KIIS conducted a survey for the European Union Advisory Mission using face-to-face interviews. When asked about the sources of information, 77% of respondents named one of the internet sources (most often telegram channels), and 43% named television. In different studies, depending on the wording of the question, the quantitative ratios differ by a few percent, but in all cases, social media is becoming more popular than television.

The fact that the number of Ukrainians who use television to get news has declined since the outbreak of the war between Ukraine and Russia, while users of social media and messengers have become more active, may be due to several factors. Social media and messengers, especially telegram channels, allow you to receive information instantly. In times of crisis and conflict, people want to receive news as quickly as possible, and social media provides this opportunity. In times of war and political crises, traditional media can be subject to government censorship or influence.

People may feel that social media offers more unbiased and independent sources of information. Telegram channels and other social platforms often offer information from specific individuals with whom users may feel a personal connection or trust, which may make the information more attractive and credible to some users. Social networks and messengers allow users not only to consume news, but also to discuss it, ask questions and share their own experiences and feedback.

Let's return to the KIIS study commissioned by the NGO OPORA (July 2022). When asked why a particular source was ranked first, the majority of respondents (46%) said that it had "true or reliable information." See Table 10.2.

**Table 10.2. Answers of respondents to the open question about the reasons why the source is important to them, % (July 2022)**

|  | Total | Social networks | Telethon „United News" | News websites |
|---|---|---|---|---|
| Truthful, reliable information | 46 | 26 | 68 | 46 |
| Easy to use | 24 | 36 | 13 | 21 |
| Lots of information, different points of view | 16 | 24 | 6 | 25 |
| Quickly/efficiently inform | 13 | 20 | 11 | 10 |
| Clear format | 2 | 3 | 1 | 2 |

The next criteria are ease of use (24%); quantity of information, the relaying of different points of view (16%); and speed of information (13%). For social networks, the most important is the ease of use (36%), and the other top-three reasons are almost the same (20-26%). The majority of those who put the United News telethon in the first place explain this primarily by the truthfulness and reliability of the information (68%), while other criteria are not as important. Respondents apparently have the idea that information broadcast on television is better controlled, unlike the Internet, where anything can be written. We also asked respondents which social networks they use to get news in general and asked them to indicate the 2 most important among them, Graph 10.4.

**Graph 10.4. Social networks used by Ukrainians in the last 7 days to receive news, % out of all adults (July 2022)**

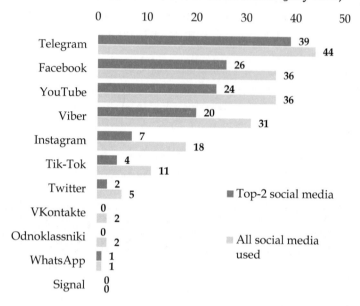

Among social media in July 2022, Telegram was the most used by respondents: 39% ranked it among their top 2 most frequently used networks, and 44% of all respondents used it in the last 7 days (data is calculated for all adults, regardless of whether they use social media at all). Facebook and YouTube are next, with 24-26% of respondents ranking them among their top 2 networks, and 36% each receiving information from them in the past week. In addition, 20% of respondents consider Viber to be one of the top 2 networks (the total use of this messenger for receiving news is 31%). Other social networks were mentioned less frequently (in particular, only 3% of respondents used one of the Russian social networks in the last week). The majority of those who receive information from the internet (news sites or social networks) prefer such types of content as short videos (62%) and short news reports (61%). Other types of content are preferred by no more than a quarter of users, see Graph 10.5.

**Graph 10.5. The most popular types of content, % of respondents who use news website and social media (July 2022)**

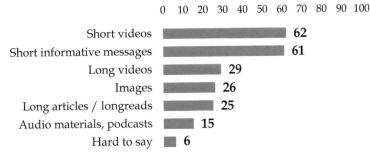

The preference for short messages and videos correlates with the results of the diary survey regarding the shift of users to Telegram for news. In the diary survey, when describing how news search and use of various platforms/information sources has changed since the outbreak of war, respondents very often mentioned the transition to Telegram. The participants explained this by the need to quickly get up-to-date operational news, a convenient way to consume information (e.g., via phone), being away from home (e.g., in shelters), and the concise format of news presentation in a rapidly changing situation. Some respondents mentioned emotional exhaustion due to very traumatic events, so a dry and short format of news presentation is more acceptable. Some examples are listed:

> "I have completely switched to Telegram. I'm interested in news from the frontline, I'm not interested in anything else." Woman, 54, Kamianske (Dnipropetrovska oblast).

> "From the first days of the war, when rockets were often falling in Kyiv and shots were heard, we had to go down to the basement, we stopped watching TV and started looking for news on our phones. We subscribed to several groups on Viber and Telegram and constantly monitored them, and the news appeared there quickly. Now we're tired of all this news, and we try to read and listen to less of it, but on automatic, and to keep up with the latest events, we still skim the text in the above groups. I like the format of the presentation, because the news is covered in a few sentences, and there is also a video or photo to go with it." Female, 30, Kyiv.

"Now I watch the news entirely on Telegram channels. Before that, I did not use Telegram as a source of news. Telegram has replaced Facebook for me." Male, 33, Vyshhorod (Kyiv region).

"Currently, I use 90% of the information only about military events and their consequences in Ukraine. I refused to watch entertainment programs that are not relevant at the moment. I use the largest Telegram channels more often, as they provide up-to-date information on military operations very quickly." Male, 36, Mykolaiv.

"When the war started, I started using Telegram—I subscribed to many channels, but later I unsubscribed from most of them—I left a few so as not to overload my information space. Telegram is very convenient for searching for different groups, and it's easy and fast to load, unlike Viber. In addition, the news format is quite short. But there is also a link to a news site if you want to read more about the news, and it's easy to share what you find interesting with your friends. Nowadays, I use Facebook less —it's hard and scary to see the loss of friends who died at the front. I am also annoyed by the photos of those who went abroad—I am happy for them on the one hand, but it is difficult for me to perceive their positive attitude, we are in different realities now ..." Woman, 52, Odesa.

"I use Telegram more. I also registered on Instagram. I rarely go to Facebook because I don't trust the information there, and when they post kebabs or jokes, it annoys me." Woman, 54, Zaporizhzhia.

The analysis of information consumption by region, gender, age, type of settlement, education, and language and ethnicity (linguistic and ethnic category) showed that the most differentiating factor in information consumption is age (which, in particular, mediates education, as younger respondents are also more educated). Thus, while 87% of 18-29 year olds rank social media as their top two sources of information, and 28% of those who are over 60 say that social media is their top source, and 61% say that Yedynyi Novyny is their top source. A similar trend applies to news sites and other television. At the same time, online is still "losing" only among the 60+ age group. In addition, the significant involvement in online is determined by the fact that while 54% of young people subscribe to official pages/channels, this indicator decreases with age to only 6% among people aged 60+. It is worth paying attention to the role of Telegram channels for younger respondents: among 18-29 year olds, 76% consider them to be among the top two social networks for themselves (the same indicator among 30-44 year olds is 52%). For the youngest, Tik Tok is especially relevant.

At the same time, Ukraine often criticizes Telegram for allegedly being controlled by Russia, which poses threats to information security. Similar accusations are made about TikTok and the influence of the Chinese government. In general, social media is perceived by many people as hostile due to the threat of spreading disinformation or propaganda. In 2018-2019, the KIIS asked respondents at the request of the NGO Detector Media the question "Do you think you are able to distinguish quality information from disinformation and fakes?". In December 2022, KIIS repeated this question in its own survey. While in February 2019, 52% said they could distinguish between quality information, in December 2022, the indicator was 78%, including an increase from 21% to 38% in the number of those who answered "yes." The decline was due to both those who consider themselves unable to distinguish quality information and those who previously could not determine their opinion (the number of representatives of both categories has decreased). Most likely, Ukrainians (as well as people in other countries) do not have the skill to avoid low-quality information for various reasons. However, the presence of subjective confidence in ability to perceive quality information gives rise to a number of information risks.

In Chapter 9 ("Attitudes toward the state, social institutions, and political forces"), we examined changes in trust in Ukrainian and Russian media (Graph 9.8 and 9.9) from December 2021 to December 2023, almost two years into the war. During this time, trust in the Ukrainian media initially increased from 32% to 57% (the balance increased from -7% to +43%), but by the end of 2023, it had dropped to 29% (the balance decreased to -11%). Trust in the Russian media was absent before, and now this absence has become even more pronounced: from 3% to 1%, there was a decline in those that reported trust in Russian media by 2%, and the balance has decreased from -76% to -92%.

The study for Opora had a more detailed list of information sources. Trust in different sources of information was measured with the following question: "Regardless of whether you use certain sources of information or not, how do you feel about the overall level of trust in the information in these sources?" Respondents were asked to give a score from 0 to 10, where 0 means „not at all" and 10 means „completely trust". Table 10.3 shows the results only for the high level of trust.[79]

**Table 10.3. Trust in information sources (July 2022), % of respondents who rated the level of trust as high**

| Regardless of whether or not you use certain sources of information, how do you feel about the overall credibility of the information in these sources? | Highest trust (scores 7-10) |
|---|---|
| Telemarathon „Yedyni Novyny" | 58 |
| Telegram channels | 35 |
| Television (except for the Telemarathon „Yedyni Novyny") | 33 |
| News websites | 28 |
| YouTube channels | 25 |
| Facebook | 21 |
| Viber | 20 |

As you can see, the Yedyni Novyny telethon was the undisputed leader in terms of trust as of summer 2022, with almost 60% of respondents having a high level of trust in it. Despite being the most popular, Telegram channels ranked second in terms of trust, just like other television (35% and 33%, respectively), followed by news websites. YouTube channels, Facebook and Viber do not differ much in terms of trust (20-25%).

The same study paid special attention to the use of Russian sources. The respondents were asked "Have you used any Russian resources to get information about current events in the last 7 days?", see Graph 10.6.

79  'Democracy, Rights and Freedoms of Citizens and Media Consumption in the Conditions of War: Results of the KIIS Survey for OPORA.' *KIIS Press Releases*, August 17, 2022, https://www.kiis.com.ua/?lang=eng&cat=reports&id=1132.

**Graph 10.6. "Did you use Russian resources?", % (July 2022)**

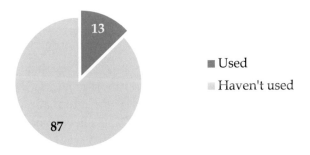

As we can see, only 13% of respondents used Russian resources. However, it should be noted that our methodological experiments showed that perhaps 6% of pro-Russian respondents refused to participate in the survey, so perhaps the percentage of those who used these resources is closer to 20%. On the other hand, the use of Russian resources does not necessarily indicate pro-Russian orientation. It turns out that users of Russian resources do not differ much from those who do not use them, see Table 10.4.

**Table 10.4. Attitudes towards pro-Russian resources of those who use them and those who do not, % (July 2022)**

| | Used Russian resources | Haven't used Russian resources |
|---|---|---|
| **Pair of statements No. 1** | | |
| The fight against the so-called pro-Russian media in Ukraine is actually an attempt to crack down on political opponents and critics of the government | 16 | 13 |
| There are too many pro-Russian media outlets in Ukraine—the state and society should take action against any suspicion of ties to Russia | 77 | 72 |
| It's hard to say | 7 | 15 |
| Total | 100 | 100 |
| **Pair of statements #2** | | |
| The Russian media provide an alternative view of the situation, so it is also important to know it for a balance of opinions | 36 | 13 |

| | | |
|---|---|---|
| To get a comprehensive and complete picture of the events, the information provided by the Ukrainian media is enough for me | 57 | 80 |
| It's hard to say | 6 | 7 |
| Total | **100** | **100** |

In particular, users of Russian resources, although to a slightly lesser extent, are also very critical of Russian and pro-Russian media. Thus, among those who have received information from Russian resources in the last seven days, 77% believe that the state and society should take measures against pro-Russian media, and only 16% see this as political reprisals. In addition, 57% say that Ukrainian media is generally sufficient for them to have a comprehensive view of the situation, although 36% believe that Russian media are important as an "alternative point of view for balance".

Another topic of interest to the researchers was the attitude towards Yedyni Novyny and the government's information policy. The fact is that the creation of the Yedyni Novyny channel caused some debate in society. In particular, it caused criticism of the owners of those channels that were not included in the Yedyni Novyny channel. For example, the management of such well-known TV channels as Channel 5 and Pryamyi, owned by former President of Ukraine Petro Poroshenko, expressed their strong dissatisfaction with this initiative[80]. Representatives of these channels argued that the creation of "Yedyni Novyny" could be aimed at usurping the airwaves and limiting plurality of opinions. In their opinion, such consolidation of news resources under one "umbrella" could lead to a loss of objectivity in reporting and a skewing of the country's information space in favor of certain political groups. This criticism by Channel 5 and Pryamyi is compounded by accusations that the government may be using Yedyni Novyny as a tool to control what information reaches the public. This, in their view, jeopardizes the principles of democracy and freedom of speech in Ukraine.

---

[80] 'Uzurpatsiia teleefiru i tinove finansuvannia kanalu "My – Ukraina": Yanina Sokolova vlashtuvala ministry Tkachenku khard-tok.' *5 Channel*, February 22, 2023, https://www.5.ua/suspilstvo/uzurpatsiia-teleefiru-i-tinove-finansuvannia-kanalu-my-ukraina-yanina-sokolova-vlashtuvala-ministru-tkachenku-khard-tok-299767.html.

Three pairs of alternative statements were formulated, and respondents had to choose the statement in each pair that was closer to their opinion. The results are presented in Table 10.5.

**Table 10.5. Attitudes towards "Yedyni Novyny" and the government's information policy, % (July 2022)**

| | % |
|---|---|
| **Pair of statements No. 1** | |
| Media should support the government's line | 32 |
| The media should be able to reasonably criticize the actions of the authorities | 60 |
| It's hard to say | 8 |
| Total | **100** |
| **Pair of statements #2** | |
| The Yedyni Novyny telethon is currently a successful initiative that unites Ukrainians and helps to form a common view of events. | 65 |
| The "Yedyni Novyny" telethon restricts access to alternative points of view, thus "encouraging" many Ukrainians to seek alternative information from dubious sources | 17 |
| It's hard to say | 18 |
| Total | **100** |
| **Pair of statements #2** | |
| To strengthen protection against the enemy, the state should more actively control information in Internet sources — news sites, social networks, Telegram channels, etc. | 60 |
| The state's attempt to more actively control information in online sources, such as news sites, social networks, Telegram channels, etc., will only lead to restrictions on the rights and freedoms of citizens | 30 |
| It's hard to say | 10 |
| Total | **100** |

In general, these results show that the majority of the population in the first year of the war approved of the government's information policy. Although only 32% believed that the media should support the government, and the majority of respondents (60%) believed that the media should be able to reasonably criticize the actions of the government, respondents did not see the government's attempts to use this to their advantage in the case of Yedyni Novyny or on the issue of information control. Regarding the Yedyni No-vyny initiative, 65% of respondents considered it successful, noting that it unites Ukrainians and contributes to the formation of a common view of events (only 17% believe that United News limits access to alternative points of view). As for the government's control over the information space, 60% of respondents expressed support for more active control of information in online sources by the state, and half as many (30%) believed that such an initiative would lead to restrictions on the rights and freedoms of citizens.

However, the previous sections have provided a lot of evidence that the first and second years of the full-scale invasion had different dynamics of attitudes, including an increase in criticism of the authorities during 2023. To understand the dynamics of the perception of "Yedyni Novyny", it is worth looking at trust from May 2022 to December 2023 under the question "How much do you trust or distrust the 'Yedyni Novyny' telethon" (Graph 10.7). As you can see, from the approval of the initiative at the beginning of the invasion when 69% demonstrated trust in the telemarathon in May 2023, criticism continued to grow, and by December 2023, only 43% trusted the telethon. Indeed, subsequent KIIS surveys also show a deepening sense of distrust. Obviously, there is a significant demand from the population for reformatting the United News initiative and finding new solutions that will meet modern challenges.

**Graph 10.7. Dynamics of the level of trust in the "Yedyni Novyny" telemarathon, %**

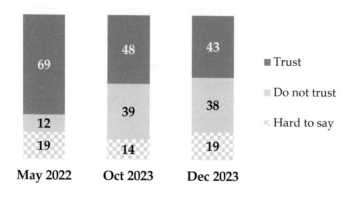

## 10.2. Changes in Internet consumption

As we have already noted, KIIS regularly includes questions about Internet use in its surveys, which allows it to accumulate data on users, assess the dynamics of the number of users and study their characteristics. When comparing data from different estimates of the number of Internet users, two aspects of the research methodology are important: 1) the questions we ask and 2) the age limits of the sample of respondents (the lower the age, the higher the percentage of users). KIIS uses the question "Do you use the internet?" with answers "yes", "no", "I don't know what it is", and those who answered "yes" are asked "How often do you use the internet?" with answers "every day or almost every day", "once or several times a week", "once or several times a month", "less than once a month". The results are shown in Graph 10.8.

**Graph 10.8. Share of internet users among the adult population, %**

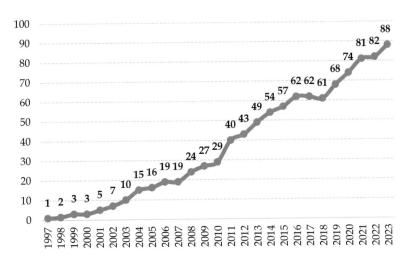

As you can see, the share of Internet users has increased significantly in recent years. The graph also demonstrates that usage increased during the war, with 81% of internet users in 2021, 82% in September 2022, and 88% in February 2023. The vast majority of users use the internet every day or almost every day (Table 10.6).

**Table 10.6. Internet usage in February 2023, %**

| | |
|---|---|
| Do not use the Internet | 12 |
| Use the Internet | 88 |
| Among them: | |
| *daily or almost daily* | *82* |
| *once or several times a week* | *4* |
| *once or several times a month or less* | *2* |

In Ukraine, there was a significant differentiation in internet use by age, education, income level, and type of settlement. For example, in 2017, the percentage of internet users among those under 40 was more than 90%, while the percentage of those aged 50-59 was 55%, those aged 60-69 only 29%, and those aged 70+ only 10%. In the same year, there were 77% of internet users in big cities, and 51% in rural areas. In February 2023, the difference in most socio-demographic characteristics decreased significantly. There is no difference by region (the one that exists is statistically insignificant), and by gender (men have a 3 percentage point higher rate, but this is because women live longer and older women use the internet less, and if you look at the difference for those under 70, this difference disappears). Internet use in villages has increased to 81%, and this is only 10 percentage points less than in the city. There are still some differences by education, income (among those with very low incomes, only 55% use the internet, although there is a significant overlap with age, as there are many older people among the least well-off), and age (56% of those over 70 use the internet, while in other groups 80% or more are internet users). It is hard, however, to say how much this is related to the war. Indeed, because of the war, the need for up-to-date information, news searches, danger warnings, air alerts has increased. But the percentage of users has also increased due to covid, and the decrease in differentiation has occurred before with the increase in the number of internet users. In addition, the relevant infrastructure in Ukraine has improved significantly in recent years.

It is important to note that the internet in Ukraine continued to work quite stably even during the war. This was due to several factors. Firstly, the decentralization of the network meant that the internet in Ukraine does not depend on a single access point, but consists of several independent networks. This makes it more resistant to attacks and damage. Another factor is the lack of strict centralized control over the networks. The government of Ukraine does not have full control over communication networks. This makes it difficult for Russia to centrally intercept or disconnect the internet. The help of Elon Musk, who provided Ukraine with Starlink satellite Internet, was also useful (although there have been and continue to be episodes of his negative interference in the course of hostilities). Of course, the internet in Ukraine was not completely resistant to interruptions. In some parts of the country, there were cases of internet outages due to infrastructure damage or attacks. However, the overall level of internet access in Ukraine remained high even during the war[81].

In October 2023, the Kyiv International Institute of Sociology conducted another all-Ukrainian survey commissioned by the United Nations Development Program in Ukraine with the support of Sweden and in partnership with the Ministry of Digital Transformation of Ukraine[82]. This is the fourth survey on the use of electronic services and the internet in Ukraine conducted by KIIS at the request of UNDP. Previously, similar surveys were conducted in September 2020, September 2021 and September 2022. The results of this study show that the level of use of electronic public services in Ukraine continues to grow despite the war. In 2023, 64% of Ukrainians used state electronic services, compared to 63% in 2022, 60% in 2021, and 53% in 2020. Thus, in fact, 3 out of 5 adult Ukrainians used electronic government services during the year. Among those who have used the services, 79% rated their experience positively.

---

81  A few weeks before the war started, we held a meeting at KIIS about possible events and considered as a very likely scenario the absence of the internet, which would completely block our work. Indeed, after the war started, all clients stopped their projects and KIIS stopped working. However, the level of stability of the internet was sufficient to allow us to resume our work three months after the war started.

82  '63% of Ukrainians Use State E-Services, User Numbers Grow for Third Year in Row.' *KIIS Press Releases*, February 1, 2023, https://www.kiis.com.ua/?lang=eng&cat=reports&id=1184&page=24.

Younger respondents, respondents with higher education, and respondents with higher income were more likely to use government e-services (all three parameters are interrelated as younger Ukrainians have better education and higher income). The most noticeable "gap" in use is observed depending on age: while 89% of 18-29 year olds have used at least one service, 30% of 70+ year olds have used at least one service. However, there has been a trend of significant use of services among all age groups since 2020. The majority of respondents (51%) used the application or portal for electronic services *Diia*[83], see Graph 10.9. This share of users has increased four times in three years: from 13% in 2020, to 30% in 2021, and to 51% in 2023. The war has neither slowed down nor accelerated the pace of Diia usage.

**Graph 10.9. Share of users of the *Diia* app, %**

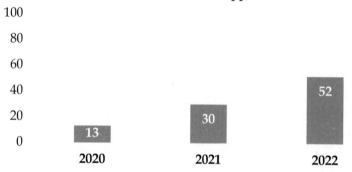

But there have been changes. Because of the war, the share of people belonging to vulnerable groups in Ukraine has increased, primarily due to the growing number of internally displaced persons. The war emphasized the importance of online interaction with the

---

83   *Diia* (action) is a mobile application, web portal and brand of the digital state in Ukraine developed by the Ministry of Digital Transformation of Ukraine. *Diia* was officially launched in 2020. The app allows you to store your driver's license, domestic and international passports, and other documents in your smartphone and use them instead of paper documents, as well as transfer copies of them when receiving banking or postal services, checking into a hotel, and in other life situations. *Diia* (the app and/or portal) can also be used to obtain public services such as child birth registration, business registration, tax payments and declarations, signing any documents, changing the place of registration, etc. The plan is to transfer 100% of public services to Diia by 2024.

state. When millions of people needed help from the state but were physically unable to use these services, perhaps because they were forced to travel, move to a new place of residence, or the administrative service center in their locality ceased to function, the ability to receive the necessary public services from their own smartphone or laptop proved to be critical.

# 11. Possible Social Problems of Post-war Ukraine

The war is causing enormous damage to Ukrainian society, the economy and its people. The challenges that Ukraine is currently facing and will face after the war are numerous. The war has caused significant damage to Ukraine's infrastructure and housing, which will require significant reconstruction and rehabilitation efforts. Unemployment and economic decline are on the rise, which will affect the overall standard of living of the Ukrainian population. The war has displaced thousands of people, resulting in a growing need for social assistance and support, particularly for refugees and internally displaced persons. The war has had negative consequences for the environment and public health, including air and water pollution, the spread of hazardous substances, and long-term health effects. The war leaves many traumas for Ukrainians, increasing the need for psychological support and trauma treatment. The psychological trauma of war can lead to increased stress and tension in families, potentially leading to more divorces and family problems. The war has affected many children in Ukraine, including those who have lost parents or been displaced. These children may face difficulties in accessing education and social support and may be more vulnerable to exploitation and violence. The list of the implications of the war goes on and on.

In his speech at the Kharkiv Readings 2022, Academician V. Bakirov, President of the SAU, noted the following:

> The fabric of social life is damaged throughout Ukraine and continues to be damaged. We are facing the problem of internally displaced persons, refugees, large masses of people who were forced to seek refuge for themselves and their families in safer places, the need to reintegrate millions of people who will return. There is a problem of reintegration of hundreds of thousands of combatants, combatants who will need to return to civilian life, find their place in it, restore or acquire the necessary knowledge, skills, professional competencies, etc. The post-war society must be prepared for anomie, for the intensification of deviant behavior, the growth of crime, drug addiction, alcoholism, the 'culture of violence,' the flourishing of 'black markets,' and the strengthening of mafia structures [...]. I believe that a big problem

will be the possible weakening and reformatting of the family institution, family relations, associated with the death of family members, territorial separation of spouses, children and parents [...]. It is possible that a system of stratification will be formed on the basis of one or another, more or less active participation in the defense of the country. Sociologists need to learn how to study these processes, assess the scale, dynamics, and impact on general social processes, and be not only consultants but also accomplices in real projects to restore normal peaceful life.

In this section, we do not consider all possible problems that may arise in Ukraine. One of the main factors affecting the ability of our society to overcome all these problems is the integration of our society, and problems with integration can be a significant obstacle to the transformation of society. This section is devoted to this problem.

Cohesion or integration[84] is one of the most important characteristics of a society. For Ukraine, which is forced to fight a powerful enemy that has been trying to divide our society for the entire period of its existence, this is a problem of the country's survival as an independent state. As the editor of *The Economist*, Arkady Ostrovsky, said, "It seems to me that Ukraine cannot be defeated from the outside. It is probably possible to undermine it internally. That's why unity is so important—both today and after the victory"[85]. Unfortunately, political forces continued to fight among themselves even after Russia's seizure of Crimea and the outbreak of war in Donbas. While in previous years the main struggle was between pro-Russian and pro-European politicians, in the last eight years, it has been mainly pro-European political forces that have been fighting among themselves. Only the full-scale war that began on February 24, 2022, changed the situation. Studies conducted by KIIS and other sociological companies, as we have seen in the previous sections, show a significant decrease in the regional and linguistic and ethnic differentiation of society and an increase in trust in the Ukrainian state, acceleration of the formation of Ukrainian identity,

---

84   Here we will not distinguish between social integration, cohesion, unity, and conciliarity and will use them as synonyms

85   Sevgil Musayeva and Mikhail Kriegel, 'Zelenskiy ne ponimaet, kak ustroyen mir. Ili ponimaet, no eto ustroystvo ego sovershenno ne ustraivayet: Arkady Ostrovsky, "The Economist".' *Ukrainska Pravda*, January 2, 2023, https://www. pravda.com.ua/.

growth of mutual support, and social unity. It is very important to maintain this after the war is over. The task of sociologists is to anticipate the emergence of certain problems and to contribute to the development of solutions to solve them or at least minimize the negative consequences. We will look at some of the processes that may affect the integration of society and that are already manifesting themselves, even before the end of the war.

## 11.1. Methodological remarks. Bogardus scale.

Since 1994, KIIS has been conducting research on the attitudes of the Ukrainian population towards certain ethnic and social groups, including a 2023 report on interethnic prejudice in Ukraine.[86] This study is based on the scale of the American sociologist Emory Bogardus (adapted by N. Panina). For each group on the list, respondents have to answer how close they are willing to be with representatives of each group. This is called social distance. The minimum social distance is 1 (I agree to allow them as a family member), the maximum is 7 (I would not allow them to enter Ukraine). The level of social distance is often interpreted as the level of prejudice against a particular group.

Now I am going to read out the names of some social and national groups. For each group, tell me if you agree to allow its representatives ... . Choose all that apply.

| As members of their family | 1 |
|---|---|
| As close friends | 2 |
| As neighbors | 3 |
| As colleagues at work | 4 |
| As residents of Ukraine | 5 |
| As guests of Ukraine | 6 |
| Would you not let them into Ukraine? | 7 |

There is a list of ethnic groups (since 1994 we have been studying attitudes toward 13 ethnic groups).

---

86   See, for example,'Inter-Ethnic Prejudices in Ukraine, October 2023.' *KIIS*, accessed [date], https://www.kiis.com.ua/?lang=eng&cat=reports&id=1364&t= 10&page=1.

| | As members of their family | As close friends | As neighbors | As colleagues at work | As residents of Ukraine | As guests of Ukraine | Would you not let them into Ukraine? |
|---|---|---|---|---|---|---|---|
| Americans | 1 | 2 | 3 | 4 | 5 | 6 | 7 |
| Belarusians | 1 | 2 | 3 | 4 | 5 | 6 | 7 |
| Jews | 1 | 2 | 3 | 4 | 5 | 6 | 7 |
| Canadians | 1 | 2 | 3 | 4 | 5 | 6 | 7 |

Etc.

In February 2023, we asked questions about attitudes toward certain social groups:

| | As members of their family | As close friends | As neighbors | As colleagues at work | As residents of Ukraine | As guests of Ukraine | Would you not let them into Ukraine? |
|---|---|---|---|---|---|---|---|
| Refugees who are currently abroad | 1 | 2 | 3 | 4 | 5 | 6 | 7 |
| Internally displaced persons who have left their homes and are living elsewhere in Ukraine | 1 | 2 | 3 | 4 | 5 | 6 | 7 |
| Ukrainians who ended up in the occupied territory after February 24, 2022 and still live there | 1 | 2 | 3 | 4 | 5 | 6 | 7 |
| Russian-speaking citizens of Ukraine | 1 | 2 | 3 | 4 | 5 | 6 | 7 |
| Citizens of Ukraine who are Russian by nationality | 1 | 2 | 3 | 4 | 5 | 6 | 7 |

Table 11.1 below shows the distribution of answers, which combines the percentage of people who are ready to accept refugees, IDPs and representatives of other groups as family members,

friends, neighbors or work colleagues (score 1-4). If we use the terminology of E. Golovakha and N. Panina, this attitude can be called tolerant. The attitude towards a particular category of the population, which means that a person would not like to see representatives of this category in his or her environment, but does not object to these people being citizens of Ukraine (score 5), can be called social exclusion by analogy with the terminology of Ye. Golovakha and N. Panina. Disagreement with the fact that people of this social category should be able to live in Ukraine can be called xenophobia. If they do not object to these people coming as guests (score 6), this is a lower level of xenophobia, and if they do not even perceive them as guests (score 7—would not let them into Ukraine at all), this is the highest level of xenophobia.

The results of the survey on social groups conducted in February 2023 are shown in Table 11.1. Table 11.1 below shows the distribution of answers, which combines the percentage of people who are ready to accept refugees, IDPs and representatives of other groups as family members, friends, neighbors or work colleagues (score 1-4), i.e., tolerant attitude.

**Table 11.1. How much social distance are Ukrainians willing to allow for representatives of several social categories, % (March 2023)**

| We agree to allow representatives of these groups as... | Refugees who are now abroad | Internally displaced persons (IDPs) | Ukrainians who found themselves in the occupied territory after February 24, 2022 | Russian-speaking citizens of Ukraine | Citizens of Ukraine who are Russian by na-... |
|---|---|---|---|---|---|
| ...family members, friends, neighbors, colleagues | 46 | 53 | 44 | 43 | 29 |
| ...the people of Ukraine | 42 | 42 | 46 | 43 | 35 |
| ...guests of Ukraine | 8 | 5 | 4 | 8 | 14 |
| I would not let them into Ukraine | 5 | 1 | 7 | 7 | 23 |
| Total | 100 | 100 | 100 | 100 | 100 |
| Average social distance | 3.67 | 3.37 | 3.73 | 3.83 | 4.71 |

The use of the Bogardus scale provides somewhat more specific, detailed and diverse information about attitudes toward certain groups than direct assessments. However, the results generally correlate with direct assessments of attitudes toward certain groups. Table 11.2. contains data from a survey conducted by the School of Political Analysis of the National University of Kyiv-Mohyla Academy and the sociological group "Rating", where 2000 respondents were interviewed using the CATI method.[87]

---

87  'Reintehratsiia zvilnenykh hromad ta sotsialna zhurtovanist.' Accessed March 2, 2024, https://www.ukma.edu.ua/RG_ShPA_Reintegration_2000_102023-1.pdf.

**Table 11.2. "Please rate your attitude towards the following social or national groups.", % (October 2023)**

|  | Negative | Neutral | Positive |
|---|---|---|---|
| Internally displaced persons who have left their homes and are living elsewhere in Ukraine | 4 | 28 | 67 |
| Ukrainians who left Ukraine after the outbreak of war and are now abroad | 14 | 50 | 34 |
| Ukrainians who ended up in the occupied territory after February 24, 2022 and still live there | 14 | 47 | 37 |
| Ukrainians who have been in the occupied territory since 2014 and still live there | 26 | 49 | 23 |
| Russian-speaking citizens of Ukraine | 23 | 42 | 33 |
| Russian citizens who oppose the war through their actions | 14 | 32 | 52 |
| Russian citizens in general | 72 | 22 | 5 |

As we can see, there is a clear negative attitude towards Russian citizens and Ukrainians in the territory occupied in 2014 (because a significant number of them left those territories, and some of our former citizens who remained there (but not all of them) became collaborators), and the situation with IDPs is relatively unproblematic (with 4% having a negative attitude), there is a not very significant negative attitude towards refugees, those who have recently stayed in the occupied territory and Russians who oppose the war (14% for each of these categories), and almost a quarter of respondents (23%) have a negative attitude towards Russian-speaking citizens of Ukraine.

## 11.2. Russian language in Ukraine

The use of the Russian language in Ukraine and the coexistence of Ukrainian and Russian has been a controversial issue in Ukraine since the first years of independence. Since the 1990s, politicians have been more actively using this factor in their political struggle, exaggerating real problems to mobilize their electorate (although in polls, when we asked which problems are most urgent, both

Ukrainian and Russian-speaking citizens always put the language issue at the bottom of the list in terms of importance). Now this problem seems less serious, as the vast majority of Ukrainians (84%) believed that there were no problems in May 2023 (Table 11.3). Even among Russian speakers, 81% believed that there were no problems.[88] But a year earlier, in May 2022, 95% of respondents believed that there were no problems (and 90% among Russian-speaking respondents), a statistically significant negative trend.

**Table 11.3. "There are many versions and explanations of the events in the information space today. I will read you pairs of statements, and you will tell me which statement you agree with to a greater extent.", % (May 2023)**

|  | In Ukraine, there are no problems with the use of the Russian language and Russian-speaking citizens are not harassed or persecuted | In Ukraine, Russian-speaking citizens are systematically harassed and persecuted because of their language | It's hard to say | Total |
|---|---|---|---|---|
| All respondents | 84 | 8 | 8 | 100 |
| Russian speakers | 81 | 13 | 6 | 100 |

Measurements using the Bogardus scale in March 2023 also did not raise any particular concerns (see Table 11.1). The social distance index was 3.83, which is below average; 43% are ready to allow Russian-speaking Ukrainians into their environment, and the same number agree that Russian-speaking Ukrainians should live in Ukraine, although they do not want them in their close social circle (86% in total). Only 14% have a xenophobic attitude toward them. Yet this does not mean that this problem cannot escalate. Posts on

---

88   KIIS CATI survey of 984 respondents, May 2023. 'Are Russian-Speaking Citizens of Ukraine Oppressed and Persecuted Because of the Russian Language?' *KIIS*, June 13, 2023, https://kiis.com.ua/?lang=eng&cat=reports&id=1245&page=1..

Facebook and in the media show that there may be no compromise or agreement on this issue. Supporters of ousting the Russian language from use in Ukraine believe that the war has proven that there is nothing to argue about: it is the language of the enemy and has no place in Ukraine. Russian-speaking Ukrainians who are defending Ukraine with arms in their hands draw the opposite conclusion: the war has proven that the language issue is imposed by political struggle, Russian-speaking citizens are no less patriotic than Ukrainian-speaking citizens, and they fight side by side. The line of thinking goes: "We give our lives for Ukraine, and we are accused of using the Russian language."

In this section, we do not consider ways to solve these problems as this requires special consideration. I will only mention an interesting proposal by the famous historian Timothy Snyder:

> I am in favor of Ukrainization. I believe that there should be a language that is spoken in politics and public life, and this language should be Ukrainian [...]. If it were up to me, there would be more Ukrainian in public life... However, if there is an important second language in your country-and this is the case elsewhere in the world-you should have some kind of ownership over this language. The Ukrainian situation is extremely unusual. It is not normal when you have another important language, but you do not determine its standards and rules. The global norm is when you write your own dictionaries, textbooks, and choose your own spelling and grammar. I speak American English. I can tell at a glance whether a text is written in British English or American English. I propose to do it the way it happens in the world. In other words, Ukraine is giving Russia an absolutely unnatural advantage by not creating a standard of the Russian language in Ukraine on its own, by not creating its own dictionaries of the Russian language for Ukraine. This means that Ukrainians cannot tell whether a Russian-speaking person is from Russia or Ukraine. But there is another aspect: it is an offensive weapon. It is not just a defense. If you define the standards of the Russian language in Ukraine yourself, you are protecting yourself from Russia and creating the possibility of offensive political actions against Russia[89].

So far, the results of our surveys indicate an accelerated formation of Ukrainian civic identity, where both Ukrainian and Russian-speaking communities share basic views on the future of Ukraine.

---

89   Timothy Snyder, 'Potribno zaprovadyty ukrainsku rosiisku movu iz vlasnymy standartamy.' *Ukrainski Novyny*, July 10, 2019, https://ukranews.com/ua/ne ws/641398-timoti-snajder-potribno-zaprovadyty-ukrayinsku-rosijsku-movu-i z-vlasnymy-standartamy.

The language issue leaves some room for debate, although, as shown in Chapter 8 on the teaching of Russian in schools, there is a public consensus on the Ukrainian language as an important symbol of statehood and support for the ideal that it should be the only official state language with further expansion of its use (e.g., expansion of available Ukrainian-language content on the internet, etc.). At the same time, everyday use of the Russian language cannot be grounds for social exclusion, discrimination, or restriction. In fact, the vast majority of Ukrainians, according to our surveys, fully share this prudent and wise position. However, unfortunately, there are enough Ukrainian actors and enemies alike who resort to emotionally colored speculation, which is especially amplified by social media. The problem of attitudes towards the Russian-speaking population and the problem of relations between Russian and Ukrainian-speaking citizens of Ukraine are not objectively present at the moment, but in the event of an undesirable development, they could significantly reduce the integration of society, so the state of these relations should be constantly monitored.

## 11.3. Russian opposition to the government ("good Russians")

In Chapter 6, we analyzed the dynamics of the attitudes of Ukrainians toward Russia and its inhabitants. In particular, before 2014, 80-90% of Ukrainians had a positive attitude toward Russia; in the first half of February 2022, before the outbreak of war, a third of the Ukrainian population (34%) had a positive attitude toward Russia; after the outbreak of war, this figure dropped to 2%.

Attitudes toward Russians have changed in a similar way. Studies that we have conducted since 1994 using the Bogardus Social Distance Scale have shown that Russians were the closest group to Ukrainians, with a social distance that was less than that to Belarusians and other ethnic groups. After the outbreak of war, Russians moved to the last place among all the groups we studied.[90]

---

90   'Inter-Ethnic Prejudice in Ukraine, September 2022.' *KIIS*, https://www.kiis.com.ua/?lang=eng&cat=reports&id=1150&page=1.

Of course, these trends in changing attitudes toward Russia and Russians are natural and positive; Ukrainians have finally seen the light and realized what kind of monster their neighboring country has become. But at the same time, differentiation of attitudes toward Russians disappears, and negative attitudes are transferred to the enemies of the Putin regime. Common theses are: "Russian liberalism ends where the Ukrainian issue begins"; "Navalny said that Crimea is not a sandwich to be taken and given away"; "Nevzorov supported special forces in Lithuania in 1991"; "they are all like that" etc.

The absence of differential treatment of Russians, which can be called the problem of "good Russians," is morally perfectly understandable and in fact justified (it is difficult to sympathize and have a good attitude towards those who continue to represent the aggressor who kills your fellow citizens every day), but it is a dangerous trend. Why is this so?

The survival of Ukraine as an independent state now depends on the actions of the Armed Forces, citizens of Ukraine and international support. But in the future, from a strategic perspective, the most important thing for us is to neutralize Russia as an aggressive state. If the government in Russia does not change, its defeat will not lead to a lasting peace, but to a temporary truce until it gathers strength for new attacks. Ukraine will be forced to invest a disproportionate share of its budget in military spending and live under the threat of a new war (this will have a negative impact on living standards and migration processes). Another way to encourage the survival of the state of Ukraine is to change the government in Russia and turn it into a more or less democratic country that does not pose a threat to its neighbors. Now this seems unrealistic, but Germany, which contributed to a terrible catastrophe, the deaths of tens of millions of people, and burned people on an industrial scale, not only does not pose a threat to other countries, but is now hosting almost a million Ukrainian refugees. Discussing the possibilities of change in Russia is not the purpose of this chapter, but in my opinion, the Russian population is very sensitive to propaganda and public opinion is easily controlled and can change quickly (for example, a positive attitude towards Stalin changed from 28% to 60%

in 10 years). Therefore, it is critically important for us to know who will come to power in Russia and what strategic path the new government will choose.

From this point of view, we must support the opponents of the Putin regime in every way possible, even if some of their views are not to our liking, and their opinions and advice on affairs in Ukraine look arrogant and indicate a lack of understanding of the situation. Their influence on the situation in Russia is important to us. The economist Volodymyr Dubrovsky, posted on Facebook: "We are more interested than anyone else in ensuring that the small minority of Russians who now want Ukraine to win somehow unite and seize the moment when it comes. No one has to like them, but at this stage they are our allies and very valuable."[91] Which Russians can we hope to support Ukraine if we treat them all the same? Ukrainians will not come to power in Russia, it must be Russians. We must approach this issue pragmatically, not emotionally, and do everything that is useful to Ukraine, not alienate our allies (besides, there are many Russians who sincerely want Ukraine to win and do everything they can to do so). Therefore, we consider a negative attitude toward the very few, but existing "good Russians" or decent Russians to be a certain threat to sustainable peace in Ukraine's future. At the same time, it should be understood that a thorough transformation of Russia is possible if the West has a strategic plan, in which Ukraine is one of the important participants and within which pragmatic relations with the Russian opposition can be developed. Without a strategic desire and a long-term plan to transform Russia into a normal state, the reference to the scenario of a defeated Nazi Germany will not be convincing, let alone realistic.

---

91   Economist Volodymyr Dubrovskyi, post on Facebook, Access date 12 May 2023.

## 11.4. Ukrainian Russians or ethnic Ukrainians.

Another problem is the attitude towards Ukrainians (citizens of Ukraine) who are ethnic Russians and ethnic Belarusians. According to the 2001 census, there were 17% of Russians in Ukraine; the census has not been conducted in Ukraine for more than 20 years, so we only have data from selective sociological studies. After 2014, some Russians remained in the occupied territories (in Crimea and the occupied part of Donbas), and some began to identify themselves as Ukrainians as children of mixed marriages and others. According to KIIS research, in December 2021, there were 7% of ethnic Russians in Ukraine, and in September 2022, only 4% of them remained, and in February 2023 only 2% remained.

When measuring social distance using the Bogardus scale, it should be taken into account that some groups live only outside of Ukraine (e.g., Americans, French), some live mainly in Ukraine (e.g., Ukrainians, Crimean Tatars), and some live both in Ukraine and abroad (e.g., Russians, Belarusians). Therefore, we have divided some ethnic groups, such as Russians and Belarusians, into residents of Ukraine and residents of countries where they are the largest ethnic group (see Table 11.4).

Table 11.4. **Dynamics of social distance from the adult population of Ukraine to Belarusians, Russians, and Jews from October 2018 to October 2022, %**

| Social distance to... | 2018 October | 2022 October | The difference |
|---|---|---|---|
| Russians — residents of Ukraine | 3.24 | 5.03 | 1.79 |
| Russians — residents of Russia | 3.89 | 6.39 | 2.50 |
| Belarusians — residents of Ukraine | 2.95 | 4.37 | 1.42 |
| Belarusians — residents of Belarus | 3.58 | 5.34 | 1.76 |
| Jews living in Ukraine | 3.83 | 3.80 | -0.03 |

As we can see, since the beginning of the war, social distance to Russians (i.e. those who are residents of Russia) has increased significantly: it is 6.39 with a maximum of 7 (remember, 7 means "would not let them into Ukraine"). This score is higher than to any ethnic group in the 29 years of measuring social distance. Since

2018, it has increased more than for other groups. The distance to Belarusians—residents of Belarus—is somewhat lower, but still very high, at 5.34. It means, that attitudes toward Russians—residents of Russia and toward Belarusians—residents of Belarus have, as expected, deteriorated significantly. Unexpectedly, attitudes toward Russians and Belarusians living in Ukraine have also deteriorated. The index of social distance for Ukrainians who are ethnic Russians increased from 3.24 to 5.03, and 43% of the population would not allow them to enter Ukraine. The situation with Ukrainians who are ethnic Belarusians is slightly better, with social distance increasing from 2.95 to 4.37, and 26% of respondents would not allow them to enter Ukraine. This attitude is obviously irrational and unfair, because sociological research shows that in general, the views of Ukrainian citizens who are ethnic Russians differ somewhat from those of ethnic Ukrainians, but not very significantly, and these citizens also defend Ukraine from its enemies. Of course, the attitude towards Russian citizens of Ukraine is much better than towards Russian citizens of Russia, who would not be allowed into Ukraine even as guests by 80% of respondents, but this situation is still worrying and may have a negative impact on the unity of our society. Perhaps there are methodological aspects that influenced the results; the situation during the war is so tense that the level of understanding of questions involving Russians is decreasing. For many people, "Russian" evokes political associations, which is why this deterioration in attitudes is possible, and more detailed research, perhaps even methodological experiments, are needed to understand whether respondents adequately understand this question. And now, many people of Russian nationality call themselves Ukrainians in the survey because they have this civic identification. In addition, according to our research, 78% of those ethnic Russian-speaking Russians who continue to call themselves Russians consider themselves citizens of Ukraine in the first place[92].The negative attitude towards ethnic Russian Ukrainians may also be due to the fact that before the war, a significant number

---

92  'Indicators of National-Civic Ukrainian Identity.' *KIIS*, August 16, 2022, https://www.kiis.com.ua/?lang=eng&cat=reports&id=1131&page=1.

of them supported pro-Russian political forces in Ukraine, the Party of Regions, Yanukovych, and Medvedchuk. Now the situation has changed, but not everyone realizes it.

Ukrainians who are ethnic Russians, according to research, do not fundamentally differ from ethnic Ukrainians on key issues (including attitudes toward Russia, Ukraine's independence, the EU, and NATO) and are just as likely to defend Ukraine in the ranks of the Armed Forces as they are to engage in volunteer and other activities. Citizens of Ukraine are Ukrainians regardless of their ethnic origin, and only this approach allows us to preserve the unity of Ukraine. We must clearly distinguish between real enemies and compatriots, brothers-in-arms who are fighting alongside us. We hope that the government, NGOs, media, and opinion leaders will fight this negative trend and promote the integration of our society.

## 11.5. Status by behavior during the war as a new basis for social differentiation.

There is also a risk of contradictions (as after World War II) and a new social differentiation of Ukrainian citizens based on their behavior during the war and efforts to defend Ukraine. In fact, it is possible to distinguish at least five groups on this basis: 1) those who fought in the ranks of the Ukrainian Defense Forces; 2) those who remained in Ukraine during the war and did not leave their homes; 3) internally displaced persons 4) those who left the country (refugees) (a separate distinction should be made between refugees who legally left the territory of Ukraine and men who illegally left the country); 5) those who were in the occupied territory (here, too, different problems may arise in the case of the „old" territories occupied in 2014 and the „new" territories occupied in the last two years).

1) The Defense Forces of Ukraine. As we have already noted, trust in the Armed Forces of Ukraine reached 94% in September 2022, and after the war is over, the Armed Forces soldiers can be a driving force in the fight for justice, fighting corruption, and rebuilding the

country. At the same time, reintegrating more than a million combatants may prove to be a difficult process. Professor Fedir Shandor, who is currently a company commander in the Armed Forces of Ukraine, noted in his speech at the Kharkiv Readings 2022 that his in-depth interviews suggest that a significant number of the Armed Forces soldiers will not return to their jobs but will look for a new field of activity, including some who will join private military companies and even criminal organizations. Therefore, the problem of reintegration of the Armed Forces requires special attention.

**2) Those who stayed in Ukraine during the war.** This is, in fact, the largest and main group of the population of Ukraine, now it embodies the population of Ukraine, and it is this group that sociologists mainly study (studies of refugees are not yet representative). There are some discussions about how people should behave during the war. Those who are safe are accused of having fun and enjoying a "normal" life during the war. According to the Rating company[93], 59% of respondents consider it necessary to significantly limit themselves in entertainment and shopping, 62% consider it unacceptable to go to restaurants, and the same number consider it unacceptable to buy expensive food and clothing. The logic of others, including soldiers of the Armed Forces of Ukraine, is that we are fighting for the country and our families to live a normal life, as much as possible during the war. In any case, these discussions are not a problem that can significantly affect the unity of the country.

**3) Internally displaced persons (IDPs).** This is a separate category among those who remained in Ukraine, see Table 11.1. IDPs are the best treated of the groups we studied this time. With a social distance index of 3.37, which is significantly lower than the average for ethnic groups, 53% are ready to let them into their environment, and another 42% agree that they should live in Ukraine (95% in total). Only 5% have a xenophobic attitude towards them (the same

---

93   'Chotyrnadtsiate zahalnonatsionalne opytuvannia: Psykholohichni markery viiny (June 18–19, 2022).' *Rating Group*, https://ratinggroup.ua/research/ukr aine/chetyrnadcatyy_obschenacionalnyy_opros_psihologicheskie_markery_ voyny_18-19_iyunya_2022.html.

number as towards Ukrainian-speaking Ukrainians). The situation with IDPs looks quite satisfactory (both in terms of IDPs' attitudes toward the new community and the community's attitudes toward IDPs).

**4) Those who went abroad as refugees.** According to estimates by the United Nations High Commissioner for Refugees (UNHCR) as of December 2, 2022[94], since the beginning of the hostilities, approximately one third of Ukrainians have been forced to flee their homes, with more than 7.9 million refugees in Europe alone. According to later estimates, as of December 19, 2023, the number of refugees abroad in Ukraine was already less, 6.3 million, but it is still one of the largest crises of human displacement in the modern world[95]. The return of refugees after the end of the war is critically important for Ukraine, and one of the factors that affect this is the attitude towards them in Ukraine.

In September 2022, KIIS conducted a study of the attitudes of Ukrainians living in Ukraine towards Ukrainian refugees in Europe. To study the attitudes towards certain categories of refugees, we conducted a split-sample experiment, identifying five equivalent subgroups, in each subgroup we asked questions about only one of the categories. In addition to the general attitude towards Ukrainian refugees in Europe, we also formulated five more detailed categories of refugees (see Table 11.5).

---

94  'Ukraine Situation Flash Update #36.' December 2, 2022, https://reliefweb.int/report/ukraine/ukraine-situation-flash-update-36-2-december-2022.

95  'Ukraine Situation Flash Update #62.' December 27, 2023, https://reliefweb.int/report/ukraine/ukraine-situation-flash-update-62-27-december-2023.

**Table 11.5. „And what is your overall attitude to... ?", % (September 2022)**

| | They understand and do not judge | Upset and condemn | It's hard to say |
|---|---|---|---|
| General attitude, without specification | 90 | 5 | 4 |
| A 38-year-old woman with a young child. They moved to Europe, and the husband stayed in Ukraine | 90 | 6 | 4 |
| A 25-year-old girl who has no children and has moved to Europe | 87 | 9 | 5 |
| A 72-year-old professor who was in Europe during the invasion for personal reasons and continued to stay there | 83 | 10 | 7 |
| A 31-year-old man who lives in Ukraine but occasionally works in Poland. During the invasion, he was in Poland and decided not to return but to continue working in Poland. | 75 | 19 | 6 |

The question for the baseline scenario which represents attitudes in general was "As you know, many Ukrainians have left the country and become refugees because of the Russian invasion. Some residents of Ukraine who stayed behind are sympathetic to the refugees and do not condemn them for leaving and not returning. Other people, on the contrary, are upset by this choice and condemn them for leaving and not returning. What is your general attitude towards Ukrainian refugees in Europe?" Other questions were similar.

The results show that, in general, the vast majority of Ukrainians (83-90%) understood and did not condemn refugees, with a slightly worse attitude towards men, especially those of conscription age (75%). It should be noted that in addition to the security and socio-economic conditions of return, the problem of overcoming the negative attitudes of those who stayed and now live in

Ukraine toward those who went abroad may become relevant. Moreover, these narratives ("they left and are enjoying Europe while we are suffering here under shelling and blackouts") are readily broadcast by Russian propaganda, which is trying to split Ukraine. The survey results now show that overall, attitudes are fairly normal, which creates the right background for returnees when conditions are right. The relevant narrative (that Ukrainians in Ukraine are sincerely waiting for the return of their fellow citizens) should be broadcast at different levels and for different audiences. This should be understood by those Ukrainians who are currently living in Ukraine. Ukrainians abroad should also understand and feel this[96].

Another approach is to use the Bogardus scale. As can be seen from Table 11.1, 46% of respondents have a completely tolerant attitude, and almost 42% agree that they should return to Ukraine (87% in total). Only 13% would not like to see them in Ukraine. In principle, these data are consistent with the findings of a study we conducted in September 2022[97].

The average social distance from the Ukrainian population to refugees is 3.67, which is lower than the average for the 13 ethnic groups we are constantly studying. The average for the 13 groups is 4.00. For a better understanding of the results of this study, we also present the results of a Bogardus scale survey that we conducted in September 2022 for two groups: those with minimal social distance (Ukrainian-speaking Ukrainians, average distance 2.22) and those with maximum social distance (Russians — residents of Russia, average distance 6.39). See Table 11.6.

---

96   'Attitude of Ukrainians Who Are Currently in Ukraine Towards Ukrainian Refugees in Europe.' *KIIS*, November 1, 2022, https://www.kiis.com.ua/?lang=eng&cat=reports&id=1160&page=1.

97   'Attitude of Ukrainians Who Are Currently in Ukraine Towards Ukrainian Refugees in Europe.' *KIIS*, November 1, 2022, https://www.kiis.com.ua/?lang=eng&cat=reports&id=1160&page=1.

Table 11.6. How much social distance are residents of Ukraine willing to tolerate between Ukrainian-speaking Ukrainians and Russian-speaking Russians, % (September 2022)

| We agree to allow representatives of these groups as... | Ukrainian-speaking Ukrainians | Russians — residents of Russia |
|---|---|---|
| ...family members, friends, neighbors, colleagues | 76 | 10 |
| ...the people of Ukraine | 20 | 2 |
| ...guests of Ukraine | 4 | 8 |
| I would not let them into Ukraine | 1 | 80 |
| Total | 100 | 100 |
| Average social distance | 2.22 | 6.39 |

As we can see, even for Ukrainian-speaking Ukrainians, the social distance is not equal to 1. Approximately 25% of the population would not like to see them among their immediate environment and 5% have a xenophobic attitude towards them. Therefore, the 13% negative attitude toward refugees is not particularly worrisome.

## Persons who were in the occupied territory

The attitude towards those in the occupied territories is very important for the return of the territories and for the reintegration of the population living there. Adequate communication about who is considered a collaborator is particularly important. Obviously, there is a difference between voluntary collaboration and forced collaboration. There is also a difference depending on the consequences of cooperation with the occupation administration. Some activities can be considered not very significant, but at the same time they can lead to the torture and death of innocent people. The example of teachers at school is illustrative of the complexities of deficits and relevant punishments. On the one hand, one can understand some teachers who, knowing the consequences in Bucha, Hostomel, Irpin, Izyum, etc., work under the fear of death (although it should also be understood that the mass exodus of people from the occupation means that many of them have ways to leave).

On the other hand, if a teacher is sincerely engaged in propaganda and "turns in" the parents of children who are simultaneously studying online at a Ukrainian school to the occupiers, there can be no excuses. As far as we understand, the authorities are working to formalize this differentiation, and it will be important to communicate it properly to the public. In September 2022, KIIS conducted a survey on attitudes toward those who remained in the occupied territories[98]. The results are presented in Table 11.7.

**Table 11.7. "A couple of statements about the attitude towards those who now live in the territories occupied after February 24. Which of these statements is closer to your point of view?", % (September 2022)**

| Statement | % |
| --- | --- |
| Most residents who still live in the territories occupied after February 24 continue to live there because they really support the Russians or simply do not care about Ukraine | 12 |
| The majority of residents still living in the territories occupied after February 24 are victims of circumstances, and they would like to see Ukraine regain control of these territories. | 72 |
| It is difficult to say whether refusal to answer | 16 |
| Total | 100 |

12% of respondents agree that the majority of residents still living in the territories occupied after February 24, 2022, continue to live there because they really support the Russians or simply do not care about Ukraine. However, 72% disagree, believing that most residents still living in the territories occupied after February 24 are victims of circumstances and would like to see Ukraine regain control of these territories. In the situation of de-occupation, it is important to understand that most citizens in the territories occupied after February 24 are victims of circumstances who are actually waiting for the Ukrainian armed forces and want to be liberated. Episodes of cooperation with the occupiers should be investigated and punished, but we must remember that most residents are our fellow citizens and patriots. The narrative about the "predominance

---

98   'Do Ukrainians Share the Narratives of the "Split"?' *KIIS*, September 19, 2022, https://www.kiis.com.ua/?lang=eng&cat=reports&id=1134&page=1.

of collaborators and traitors" will complicate the return of the territories to Ukrainian rule and threaten the strengthening of unity."

Another study was conducted by KIIS at the request of the NGO OPORA (CATI, July 2022, n=1000), results in Table 11.8)[99].

**Table 11.8. "Should there be criminal liability in the following cases …", % who answered "yes" (July 2022)**

| Cases | % |
|---|---|
| The person agreed to take a leadership position in the occupation administration to ensure the livelihood of the | 69 |
| A local businessman keeps jobs, provides goods or services, but pays taxes to the occupation administration | 52 |
| A person in the temporarily occupied territories received a Russian passport | 51 |
| The teacher continues to teach children, but has agreed to teach subjects according to the Russian curriculum | 49 |
| Pensioner applies for Russian social benefits | 37 |
| An employee of a utility company supports the operation of critical infrastructure, but receives his salary from the occupation administration | 33 |
| The doctor provides medical services, but according to Russian standards | 25 |

In our opinion, there are serious problems in the attitude of the Ukrainian population towards those who remained in the occupied territory. The 72% of those who believe that the occupied population wants Ukraine to regain control of the territory is not enough to sympathize with and support the occupied, who are in terrible conditions (the liberation of Bucha, Irpin, Kherson and other settlements provides more and more evidence of the horrors of the occupation). Half of the population believes that teachers who were forced to teach should be tried for collaboration, 37% believe that pensioners who have lost their Ukrainian pensions, have no means of subsistence and have applied for Russian payments should be tried, one third would like to see utility workers convicted, and a quarter would like to see doctors convicted (but to be fair, if we had specified the descriptions, the level of criticism would have been

---

99   'Do Ukrainians Share the Narratives of the "Split"?'

lower). These are the consequences of the government's incompletely conceived communication with the population, which can cause serious problems with the liberation and reintegration of the liberated territories and reduce the integration of our society.

The main message to the population should be that the population of the occupied territories are our fellow citizens who are in trouble and need sympathy and support. As for the collaborators, these are isolated cases that should be identified by the SBU and punished in accordance with the law; we should not treat everyone with suspicion because of individual collaborators. This, by the way, is where the destructive position of social media and the media (not only Ukrainian, but also Western) comes into play. As sociologists, we rely on representative samples and statistics that can show that a certain practice is marginal and not so widespread. At the same time, some emotional stories in social media and the media create a false impression of widespread activity (for example, collaboration, when at the same time there may be much more insurgent activity).

In a February 2023 survey using the Bogardus scale (see Table 11.1), the social distance index is 3.73, which is below average, 44% of respondents are ready to let them into their environment, and another 46% agree that they should live in Ukraine (90% in total). Only 10% have a xenophobic attitude towards them.

## 11.6. Migrants from less developed countries

It is very difficult to estimate the possible demographic situation in the country now, because it depends heavily on when the war ends. The longer the war lasts, the more refugees will take root in Europe and other countries, learn the language, find adequate work, children will succeed in school, and gain friends and prospects. After the war, we will see another wave of migration: men will go to their wives and children who decided not to return.

The authors of a study funded by the EU Council conclude that Ukraine's population could decline by 24-33% depending on

288   WAR AND THE TRANSFORMATION OF UKRAINIAN SOCIETY

the duration of the war[100]. The effect would be especially noticeable for children and the population of productive age. Under unfavorable conditions, Ukraine's population could drop to 25 million. Ella Libanova gives more optimistic estimates[101]. In any case, it is clear that the demographic situation in Ukraine will be difficult and there will be a shortage of labor. It can be assumed that the labor shortage in Ukraine will be largely compensated by migration from less developed countries (presumably Muslim), as is the case in many other countries (for example, Turks helped rebuild Germany in their time). Ukraine is not yet ready for this, we do not have the appropriate infrastructure and the population has no experience of communicating with representatives of other cultures. This could also become one of the likely sources of conflict and a decrease in Ukraine's integration.

* * *

Now, at a heavy price, Ukraine has achieved perhaps the greatest level of unity and cohesion in its history. It is very important not to lose it. Sociologists should anticipate possible conflicts and suggest ways to avoid or mitigate them. We have examined possible sources of conflict that could affect the level of social unity or that could undermine Ukraine's security. We believe that among this list of problems and threats to the unity of Ukraine, the most serious are the undifferentiated attitude towards Russians, the lack of a pragmatic attitude towards the enemies of Putin's system, the attitude towards refugees, and the attitude towards our fellow citizens in the occupied territory. Very often, an emotional approach to the formation of social relations dominates the pragmatic approach, according to which the only criterion for our behavior is to consider what is useful and what is harmful for Ukraine.

---

100   Jose Miguel Guzman, 'Demohrafichna trahediia Ukrainy: druhyi holodomor?' *Ukrainska Pravda*, June 28, 2022, https://www.epravda.com.ua/publications/2022/06/28/688487/.

101   'Do Ukrainy mozhe ne povernutysia 5 mln liudei: Libanova pro novu ekonomiku ta prirvu z rosiianamy.' *ICTV Fakty*, December 5, 2022, https://fakty.com.ua/.

# 12. Conclusions
## The Main Trends of Changes in Ukrainian Society

In this last chapter of our book, we would like to draw attention to some important aspects and limitations of our work. The first limitation is the time limit. When we started writing the book, various experts said that the war could end within a year. We had some hope that the war would end before we finished writing the book. And then we would record what changes have taken place in Ukrainian society during this time. Unfortunately, this did not happen. The Ukrainian counter-offensive of 2023 did not meet the expectations of the Ukrainian population and the leadership of the Allies. We are not military experts and cannot analyze the reasons for this although it has been attributed to delays and insufficient supply of necessary weapons. Indeed, at the time of the book's completion, Ukraine had not yet received the promised aircraft and many other types of weapons, and this gave Russia sufficient time to prepare powerful defensive lines. But not the least among reasons for the disappointments associated with the counter-offensive are the inflated expectations that were formed by representatives of the West and the Ukrainian authorities ("all the necessary weapons for a counteroffensive have been transferred", "we will be in Crimea in the summer", etc.). As Ukrainian Armed Forces Commander-in-Chief V. Zaluzhnyi said in an interview with the Washington Post: "This is not a show that the whole world is watching and placing bets or something. Every day, every meter is given to us in blood."[102] Now none of the experts can predict when the war will end, and so, in fact, in our book, we record the changes in Ukrainian society that took place during the first two years of the war, or rather from February 24, 2022, to December 31, 2023.

---

102  Isabelle Khurshudyan, 'Ukraine's Top General, Valery Zaluzhny, Wants Shells, Planes and Patience.' *The Washington Post*, June 30, 2023, https://www.washingtonpost.com/world/2023/06/30/valery-zaluzhny-ukraine-general-interview/.

The second limitation of our findings is that it is an overview of trends, not a scientific theory. During the two years of the war, we prepared press releases that now form the basis of this book. Each press release was based on sociological research that allowed us to track the main trends in public opinion and values. Our approach was to identify these trends, not to build a scientific theory. A scientific theory requires more sophisticated methodologies: testing various hypotheses, analyzing interrelationships, building computer models of social processes, discussions at conferences, and much more time for research. Although our work is not aimed at creating such theories, it nevertheless reflects important changes in people's beliefs and values during the war.

We realize that our book cannot be considered an exhaustive scientific study. However, we hope that it will serve as an important source for understanding public opinion in times of great change and extraordinary circumstances. We provide data and observations that may be useful for further analyses and research in this area. Most of our research data has been transferred to the National Data Bank "Kyiv Archive"[103] and researchers have the opportunity to conduct a more detailed analysis.

## 12.1. Socio-economic changes

The war in Ukraine has caused significant social and economic damage. The destruction of infrastructure and industrial facilities has led to a decline in production and an increase in unemployment. Economic losses have worsened the lives of millions of Ukrainians, reducing incomes and increasing poverty. The war has caused a humanitarian crisis, forcing one-third of the population to flee their homes, making it difficult to provide basic social services. The war has caused great environmental damage: the explosion of the Kakhovka hydroelectric power plant alone caused significant economic and environmental losses.

---

103   National Data Bank, 'Kyiv Archive.' Accessed October 19, 2024, https://ukra ine.survey-archive.com/.

Economists estimate the socio-economic consequences of war based on statistical information. But statistical information is not always more accurate than survey data. Surveys provide a more accurate picture of the economic situation and social well-being, as they reveal the real level of unemployment, falling incomes, and stressful conditions that may not be fully reflected in official statistics. Surveys also help to collect subjective and objective information about people's lives, including their psychological state, readiness for resistance and compromise, and they complement official statistics, providing a more complete understanding of the impact of the war on the socio-economic situation.

Surveys reveal the devastating consequences of the war. At the beginning of 2023, 68% of respondents reported a decrease in their income. Mental and physical health has also been significantly affected by the war. According to the survey, 64% of respondents experienced a deterioration in their mental health and 50% experienced negative changes in their physical well-being, both of which have increased compared to May 2022. The war also led to the separation of families, with 46% of respondents reporting experiencing separation from their families, and this figure is gradually increasing (in May and August 2022, it was 38% and 42%, respectively). However, the most severe and traumatic consequence of the war is the loss of loved ones, which cannot be restored, and it also destroys the health and lives of loved ones. Every day of the war, they are increasing. While in May 2020, 20% of respondents had lost a friend or family member, in August 2020, the number was already 28%, and in January, 37%. The population also faced the loss of property (11%) and the loss of housing (9%), which amounts to about 4 million people. According to the study, only 13% did not experience any stressful situations, 87% experienced some kind of stressful situation during 2022, and this is the highest rate in the last 10 years of measurements.

The war has also created profound material discomforts. According to our data, 50% of Ukraine's population has lived without electricity many times. It is not surprising that under such conditions, Ukrainians had to do without access to the Internet (26%), other means of communication (21%), and heating (13%) many times or permanently, while 33% lived without heating from time to time, 12% have been often or permanently without water supply, with another 38% without a water supply from time to time.

## 12.2. Migration, refugees

According to the Ptukha Institute of Demography and Social Studies, out of 12 million working-age people in Ukraine, only 8-9 million are in permanent residence, which is 45-50% of the pre-war number. This raises the question of the source of labor for postwar recovery. The situation is further complicated by the fact that many Ukrainians have moved abroad. For example, 6.5 million left for Europe, and 1.5-2 million for Russia (and to a large extent, this is a case of forced displacement to Russia, especially of children). The number of internally displaced persons (IDPs) exceeds 5 million.

Over time, these people adapt to new living conditions. They learn the language of the host country, which facilitates their integration into society. Finding a job is a key element of this process, as it not only provides financial stability, but also helps with socialization and adaptation to a new way of life. However, the longer the war lasts, the less likely refugees are to return to Ukraine. Many of them manage to take root in the host countries, especially women with children, for whom stability and future prospects for their children are a priority. Children have the opportunity to attend local schools and receive quality education, which opens up new opportunities for them. While in April 2022, 75% of refugees surveyed in Europe said they definitely planned to return, a year later (in April 2023), only half of them (52%) said so.[104]

After the war is over, a new wave of emigration is likely to occur, as men who are currently unable to leave Ukraine due to martial law will join their families. This could lead to entire families remaining in the countries they emigrated to instead of returning to Ukraine. This, in turn, could have long-term consequences for the demographic situation in Ukraine and for the countries hosting

---

104  'Yak zminylosia zhyttia ta plany ukraintsiv, yaki vyikhaly za kordon: Rezultaty doslidzhennia u dynamitsi.' *NV*, July 17, 2023, https://nv.ua/ukr/article/example-url.

Ukrainian refugees. To mitigate the consequences, there should be a government policy that includes the restoration of housing, infrastructure, the labor market, wages, social assistance programs, and compensation. It is also important to create a favorable social and psychological climate and maintain ties with those who have left. There are many negative statements on social media about those who have left Ukraine, and negative attitudes toward refugees can be an obstacle to their return, even if other conditions are met. Our research shows that so far, attitudes towards refugees are generally neutral to positive, with 90% of Ukrainians treating them "with understanding and not condemning" them. By contrast, only 5% condemn them, but they are more active on social media. Certain categories of refugees may be treated worse, for example, men of military age who were in the army before the war started and did not return (and even more so those who left Ukraine illegally after the invasion). The attitude of Ukrainians toward internally displaced persons (IDPs) is even more positive. But the situation can change, and constant monitoring of attitudes toward refugees and IDPs and the implementation of measures to maintain a positive attitude toward them are needed.

## 12.3. Geopolitical orientations of the population of Ukraine

Ukraine is located between Russia and Europe and has been making its geopolitical choice throughout the period of independence. In most parliamentary and presidential elections, attitudes toward Russia and the EU were among the most important issues. The country's presidents changed, each with a different vision of foreign policy, from pro-Russian to pro-European. Until 2014, Ukrainian society had fluctuating attitudes toward a possible alliance with Russia or accession to the EU and NATO. At the same time, fluctuations in the geopolitical vector did not mean fluctuations in Ukraine's independence — Ukrainians in all regions saw Ukraine as an independent state. Moreover, the pro-European vector did not mean anti-Russian sentiment. Among those who supported EU accession, the vast majority had a good attitude toward Russia and wanted good neighborly relations.

With regard to NATO, the situation was even more complicated: in 2009, only 16% of the population supported Ukraine's accession to NATO, and most politicians did not even include this item in their election programs because it was unpopular. We, as sociologists, did not ask this question very often, given the consensus at that time on Ukraine's military neutrality. At the same time, Putin was very popular in Ukraine, with about 60% of the population having a positive attitude toward him, while Ukrainian politicians could not boast of such support (the most popular Ukrainian politicians on the eve of the 2010 presidential election had no more than 30% support). Positive attitudes toward Russia were even higher, at around 90%, making NATO membership almost impossible in terms of public support. It is important to recall that the NATO issue was not even a demand of the protesters during the Revolution of Dignity in 2013-2014, and even EU membership was demanded by a much smaller number of protesters than dignity and justice.

The situation changed dramatically after Russia annexed Crimea in 2014. This act of aggression caused a significant increase in support for Ukraine's accession to NATO among the population, reaching 48%. This demonstrates that the claim that Russia is attacking Ukraine because it wants to join NATO is false. In fact, Ukraine's desire to join NATO emerged as a reaction to Russia's aggression. Although after 2014, the population as a whole was more likely to want to join NATO, there was a significant regional differentiation, with the East and South being more likely to be against joining NATO. Thus, although Ukraine's geopolitical choice in favor of the EU and NATO was made (and, in particular, included in the Constitution of Ukraine), it cannot be said for certain that this choice was irreversible in the eyes of Ukrainian citizens. It was only after Russia's full-scale invasion of Ukraine on February 24, 2022, that the majority of Ukrainians in all regions regardless of the language spoken began to support both EU and NATO membership. Thus, as early as July 2022, according to KIIS, if a referendum were held, 81% of all respondents would vote in favor of joining the EU and 71% would vote for joining NATO. When recalculated based on the respondents who would participate in the voting, 96% would vote in favor of the referendum on EU membership, and 91% would vote in favor of the referendum on NATO membership.

It can be said that Ukraine has made its final and irreversible geopolitical choice in favor of Europe and Western civilization in general.

## 12.4. Attitudes of Ukrainians towards Russia and Belarus

The attitude of Ukrainians toward Russia from 2008 (and possibly earlier) until May 2014 can be described as unrequited love. During this period, in different years, between 80% and 90% of Ukrainians had a positive attitude toward Russia, while the share of Russians living in Russia who sympathized with Ukraine ranged from 30% to 70%. For example, after the Russian-Georgian war in August 2008, Russians' attitudes toward Ukraine deteriorated significantly: by January 2009, only 29% of Russians had a positive attitude toward Ukraine, while 90% of Ukrainians continued to have a positive attitude toward Russia.

The collapse of Ukrainians' positive attitudes toward Russia began after the occupation of Crimea and continued after the outbreak of the war in Donbas, and by March 2015, only 30% of Ukrainians had a positive attitude toward Russia. However, after the end of active hostilities, the positive attitude of Ukrainians toward Russia gradually recovered, and by September 2018, 48% of Ukrainians had a positive attitude toward Russia. Of course, this is due to the positive attitude towards ordinary Russians: in our November 2021 poll, 75% of Ukrainians had a positive attitude towards Russians, while only 13% of the population had a positive attitude towards the Russian leadership. But Ukrainians apparently did not want to see that the problem was not only with the leadership and that the vast majority of Russians were sincerely happy to see the "return of Crimea" and shared imperial foreign policy views. Over the past three years, before the full-scale invasion, there was a gradual decline in positive attitudes toward Russia, but even despite several months of escalation near Ukraine's borders, 34% of the Ukrainian population had a good attitude toward Russia in early February 2022, mainly due to positive attitudes toward Russians themselves.

However, after the outbreak of the war in May 2022, attitudes toward Russia deteriorated dramatically, with only 2% of citizens having a good attitude toward Russia, while 92% had a bad attitude. At the same time, regional differentiation in attitudes towards Russia has virtually disappeared. In all regions of Ukraine, the vast majority of residents have a bad attitude towards Russia, in particular, 90% in the South have a bad attitude, and 85% in the East. By comparison, before the war began in early February 2022, 45% and 53%, respectively, had a good attitude towards Russia. A few percent have a positive attitude toward Russia, 4% in the East.

A radical change in the situation after the outbreak of the war in February 2022 was that attitudes toward not only Russia but also Russians deteriorated catastrophically. In November 2021, 75% of the population of Ukraine had a positive attitude towards ordinary Russians, and in May 2022, 82% already had a negative attitude towards them. Ukrainians have completely lost the illusion that only the Russian leadership is responsible for the attack on Ukraine. Some observers, both in the West and among Russia's opposition, have tried to appeal to Russians' "protests" immediately after the invasion as an indicator that ordinary Russians are actually against it. Interestingly, the independent Russian research center Levada itself refutes this and, citing methodological experiments, proves that despite the insincerity of some respondents, the overall results of polls showing Russian support for the war are quite representative of the Russian population. At the same time, according to the KIIS, in November 2021, more than 40% of Ukrainians (especially in the South and East) had close relatives in Russia with whom they had communicated. Obviously, after the invasion, there were many attempts to "talk" between Ukrainians and their relatives and friends in Russia. It is clear how these conversations mostly ended: relatives and friends in Russia shared the narratives of the Russian authorities, ignoring the real facts of the horrific killings, shelling, and destruction. A special watershed was Bucha and the merciless destruction of the besieged Mariupol. All these events broke the old family and friendship ties and proved to Ukrainians that the problem was not only with the Russian authorities, but also with the people themselves (not all of them, of course, but the vast majority).

With the beginning of a new stage of the war in February 2022, the situation in the attitude of Ukrainians toward Belarus has also changed. Not only did Belarus not condemn Russia's attack on Ukraine, but it actually became an accomplice in Putin's invasion of Ukraine, serving as a springboard for Russian military units attacking Ukraine from the north. Thanks to this support, Russian troops quickly approached Kyiv, took Chornobyl and other cities in northern Ukraine. Belarus provided its infrastructure to the Russian army. Rockets were fired from Belarusian territory towards Ukraine, and Belarusian railways and medical infrastructure were used in the attack. It is clear that this has led to a significant deterioration in the attitude of Ukrainians toward Belarus. In May 2023, when asked the question "Do you think Belarus is an accomplice to the military conflict in Ukraine?" 84% of Ukrainians answered this question in the affirmative, while only 10% answered "no". Another question was "How has your attitude toward Belarusians changed since Russia attacked Ukraine on February 24, 2022?". The results were as follows: 68% answered that "It has worsened"; 24% answerred that "it has not changed"; 3% answered that "it has improved". When asked about their attitude toward Belarusians, 43% had a positive attitude, while 48% had a negative attitude.

It is clear that this has also led to a significant deterioration in the attitude of Ukrainians towards Belarus (as we know, this assessment integrates the attitude of the population and other leaders of the country). In February-March 2023, only 12% of Ukrainians had a positive attitude toward Belarus. This was a sharp drop compared to the 85% positive attitude we recorded in 2014.

## 12.5. Moral and psychological state and readiness to resist the enemy

The moral and psychological state of the population is a critical factor in the context of any military conflict, especially during a full-scale war. It affects the readiness for self-defense, the will to win, and patience under stress and unusual circumstances. According to two waves of SHARP research (November 2022 and August 2023), the level of social cohesion in Ukraine is very high. It is characterized by a sense of belonging to one's country; Ukrainian identity; a high level of trust in state institutions (although this indicator declined slightly in 2023, although it remained high); a focus on the common good and actions for the common good notably community cooperation and civic engagement. The level of mutual assistance, the level of trust in volunteers, and the prevalence of volunteer activity have increased significantly. The homogeneity of views has increased, and regional and linguistic and ethnic differentiation has significantly decreased.

One of the most important indicators of the moral and psychological level of the population is subjective life satisfaction and the level of happiness in society. Self-assessment of happiness is sensitive to the slightest changes in these areas, and therefore can serve as a reliable indicator of the general state of society. For over 20 years, KIIS has been asking Ukrainians the question "Do you consider yourself a happy person?". In December 2021, on the eve of the invasion, 71% of Ukrainians considered themselves happy, while 15% did not. In May 2023, despite more than a year of full-scale war, the figures remained almost the same: 70% of Ukrainians considered themselves happy, while only 15% did not consider themselves happy. In December 2023, the level of happiness slightly decreased: 63% of people were happy, and the number of unhappy people increased to 17%. The decline in happiness was most likely due to the unrealized expectations of the Armed Forces' counteroffensive, which was overestimated. However, the level of happiness at 63% is equal to the level that it was in Ukraine in May 2018 when figures stood at 63% of happy people and 17% of unhappy people.

In October 2022, the majority of Ukrainians (60%) felt part of the national resistance, and another 32% felt at least partially involved in the resistance to the enemy. At the same time, only 4% of respondents did not feel part of the resistance to the enemy. 84% of respondents began to speak Ukrainian more often, and 55% began to wear national symbols and colors. Support for the Armed Forces has increased, with 81% indicating that they have donated money to the Armed Forces and 21% joining the Ukrainian Defense Forces or Territorial Defense units.

An important indicator of the resilience of Ukraine's population is the readiness (or rather, unreadiness) of the population to make territorial concessions to achieve peace and preserve independence as soon as possible. In the first six surveys that we regularly conducted from May 2022 to May 2023, there were virtually no changes in the indicators. About 8-10% of respondents were generally ready for some territorial concessions, and the vast majority—82-87%—consistently opposed any concessions. From May to December 2023, there was a gradual increase in the share of those who were ready for territorial concessions: from 10% in May to 14% in October and to 19% in December. At the same time, there is a downward trend in the share of those who oppose territorial concessions: from 84% in May to 80% in October and to 74% in December. However, as of now, a clear majority of Ukrainians still believe that Ukraine should not give up any of its territories. In the wake of the full-scale invasion, Ukraine saw a mobilization of society and a surge of optimism, supported by bright victories in the north of Ukraine, Kharkiv and Kherson regions, but amid a difficult 2023 and problems with the counteroffensive, optimism has declined slightly. The situation is particularly aggravated by the wavering of some of Ukraine's Western allies, especially the blocking of vital US aid at the end of 2023. Going forward, the situation will depend mainly on adequate Western assistance and the situation at the front.

If more detailed options for compromise are formulated (e.g., "continuing to counter Russian aggression until the liberation of the entire territory of Ukraine, except Crimea, and Crimea will be under UN protectorate", etc.), the number of those who agree may be somewhat higher. KIIS, as well as other reputable sociological companies, has conducted dozens of nationwide polls in which various customers—Western scholars, analysts, journalists, etc.—tried to "feel" the limits of acceptable compromises for Ukrainians using different wording and methods. The results of the surveys show that Ukrainians are not interested in mere "peace," they realize that without additional serious conditions, a mere ceasefire will only postpone further Russian aggression, so the fight must continue and there can be no concessions.

One of the components of resilience, and perhaps a factor that influences resilience, is the level of optimism among the population about Ukraine's development prospects. In October 2022 and December 2023, we asked people what they thought Ukraine would be like in 10 years: a prosperous country within the European Union or a country with a ruined economy and a large outflow of people. We are indeed seeing an increase in pessimism (the number of those who believe that in 10 years Ukraine will be a country with a ruined economy and a large outflow of people has increased from 5% to 19%). However, the overwhelming majority of Ukrainians (73%) still believe that in 10 years Ukraine will be a prosperous country within the EU (the figure stood at 88% in October 2022).

## 12.6. Value orientations and nation building

The process of national identification of Ukrainians is dynamic and deeply rooted, as evidenced by the growing share of the population that identifies itself primarily as a citizen of Ukraine. This trend has intensified in response to Russian aggression, demonstrating the strengthening of national consciousness and self-identification despite historical challenges and external threats. If from 1992 to 2004, about 40% of Ukrainians believed that they were primarily citizens of Ukraine, and then a resident of their city, a representative of a nationality, etc.; in 2025-2013 the number was about 50%; in 2014-2021 the number was 60%; and after the outbreak of war in 2022-2023 this figure jumped to 80%. It is also important that among the Russian-speaking population, including ethnic Russians, this figure was also almost 80%. That is, since the declaration of independence in 1991, and especially against the backdrop of the war with Russia, Ukraine has been forming a civic nation, regardless of ethnicity or other aspects.

There have also been significant changes in attitudes toward the Russian language in Ukraine. In 2019, despite the occupation of Crimea and Russia's war in Donbas, 81% of Ukrainians still believed that Russian should be taught in schools, and only 8% were against it. And in 2023, the majority of respondents (52%) opposed the teaching of Russian in schools, believing that it has no place in the educational program. This indicates a desire to distance themselves from Russian cultural influence (and this sentiment is typical for all regions of Ukraine).

Ukrainians are showing a growing affinity for public holidays that reflect national identity and patriotism, especially in the context of Russian aggression. Easter, Christmas, and New Year's remain the most popular holidays among the population, but there has also been a marked increase in the popularity of holidays that are directly related to Ukrainian statehood. In 2021, only 37% honored Independence Day the most (in 2013, before the occupation of Crimea and Russia's war in Donbas, only 12% honored it), and in 2023, 63% did. The Day of Defenders of Ukraine has increased from 29% to 54%, and Constitution Day has increased from 14% to 29%. In addition, there are three other holidays that have a strong association with the Soviet past and for which the continuation of "decommunization of consciousness" is evident. From 34% to 25%, there are fewer people who like International Women's Day, from 30% to 13%; there are also fewer people who like Victory Day; and fewer people who like Labor Day, from 12% to 5%. The sharp increase in respectful attitudes toward national holidays is a reflection of the nation-building processes that Ukraine is currently undergoing.

Significant changes have also occurred in attitudes toward controversial aspects of history: the figure of Stalin and the activities of the Organization of Ukrainian Nationalists and the Ukrainian Insurgent Army (OUN-UPA) during World War II. The number of Stalin supporters decreased from 23% in 2012 to 4% in 2023. This is in stark contrast to the trends of changing values in Russia, where over the same period the number of Stalin supporters increased from 28% to 60%, and Stalin has actually become a national hero in Russia. Attitudes toward the OUN-UPA show positive dynamics among Ukrainians, with the share of those who positively assess their activities during World War II increasing from 20% to 43% after the Russian invasion. And in October 2023, KIIS conducted a survey for the Center for the Study of the Liberation Movement, and 90% of respondents who knew the UPA were positive about recognizing them as fighters for Ukraine's independence. This reflects a nationwide rethinking of the role of the OUN-UPA as fighters for Ukraine's independence in the context of current challenges and efforts to defend national identity and sovereignty.

The majority of Ukrainians continue to identify themselves as Orthodox, with the vast majority belonging to the OCU. This reflects an increase in support for the OCU, from 42% in 2021 to 54% in 2022, while the UOC (MP) lost ground among believers, dropping from 18% to 4%. This shift reflects the broader context of national and religious identification, especially in light of the Russian invasion and Ukraine's efforts to strengthen its independence and national identity.

The process of formation of European values is complex and gradual, and studying it has certain methodological difficulties. For example, when respondents were asked to choose between "traditional Ukrainian values" and "modern European/Western values," the vast majority chose traditional Ukrainian values. However, when traditional values were associated with the common values of Eastern Slavs (Ukrainians, Russians, Belarusians), most respondents preferred modern European/Western values.

Ukrainians want Ukraine to become a fully functioning democracy. On the eve of the invasion, 76% of Ukrainians wanted this, and in 2023, 95% wanted it. As for the main criteria of democracy, most respondents mentioned fair justice for all (64%), freedom of speech (59%), and free and fair elections (44%).

Gender equality is not a high priority for most Ukrainians compared to other socio-economic and political issues. However, there is high support for equality between men and women in various spheres of life, including politics and work under martial law.

Regarding the LGBT+ community, although homophobia is still present in Ukrainian society, polls show growing support for the rights of LGBT+ people, including civil partnerships and the right to participate in demonstrations. At the same time, society is divided on the issue of adoption of children by LGBT+ couples, with a significant portion not supporting the idea.

## 12.7. Attitudes towards the state and social institutions

The situation with attitudes toward the state and social institutions looks rather paradoxical. Since the outbreak of the war, living standards in Ukraine have declined significantly, poverty rates have increased, unemployment rates have risen significantly, and the assessment of the situation has improved. Two months before the war, in November 2021, only 5% believed that the central government was coping with almost all of its responsibilities, and 44% believed that it was almost not coping. And after eight months of war, in December 2022, the estimates were almost reversed: 41% believed that it was coping and only 9% believed that it was not coping. However, in 2023, the indicators slightly deteriorated. The same applies to assessments of Ukraine's future. Before the war, Ukrainians were quite pessimistic in their assessments: 35% believed that the situation was likely to deteriorate and only 13% thought it would improve. And in December 2022, the number of pessimists decreased from 35% to 8%, while the number of optimists increased dramatically to 76%. Again, at the end of 2023, the level of pessimism increased, although optimism still prevails.

The Armed Forces are the most trusted in Ukraine, and in the first year of the war, between December 2021 and December 2022, the level of trust increased from 72% to 96%. This is followed by trust in the President of Ukraine and trust in volunteers. In December 2021, 27% trusted the President (and the balance was negative - 23%, i.e. there were more people who did not trust than trusted), but in a year and by December 2022, the figure rose to 84%, and the balance was +80%. The perception of the Government and the Parliament (Verkhovna Rada) also improved significantly over the year. Trust in the Government increased from 14% to 52% (the balance increased from -46% to +33%). In the case of the parliament, although the overall trust indicators are not high, there has also been a significant increase in trust: from 11% to 35%, and the balance has increased from -56% to +2%. This data confirms the concept of "rally around the flag". This is the theory of rallying the population around a leader in very difficult situations, especially in times of war.

After another year of war (from December 2022 to December 2023), the effect of rallying around the flag has somewhat diminished, but all indicators are higher than before the war. Trust in the President has dropped from 84% to 62%, but this is still much higher than the pre-war figure of 27%. Trust in the parliament and the government has also declined: the share of those who trust the Verkhovna Rada has dropped from 35% to 15% (before the war in December 2021 it was 11%), and trust in the government has dropped from 52% to 26% (before the war it was 14%).

In general, it can be said that the possibility of losing statehood made Ukrainians reassess their pre-war views. Ukrainians began to value their state much more. Comparing democratic Ukraine to totalitarian Russia has made us appreciate our own sovereignty, freedom and citizens' rights more. War helps unite a nation against a common enemy. This sense of unity and common purpose leads to an increase in patriotism and pride in one's country and state. What may have seemed like disadvantages, uninteresting or unsatisfactory before, may now look attractive in comparison to the war, and be perceived as valuable and important. A successful confrontation with Russia, despite all the difficulties, can strengthen national pride and faith in the state's own strengths and capabilities.

## 12.8. Changes in media and consumption

Since the outbreak of war on February 24, 2022, Ukraine's media space has undergone significant changes. One of the most important was the creation of United News, a joint project of public and private TV channels aimed at informing citizens about the situation at the front and in. In fact, the channels stopped working independently, and each channel has several hours to broadcast its content as part of a single project called "United News" («Yedyni Novyny»).

What were the most important sources of information before the war? In 2018, Ukrainian television undoubtedly dominated, being the main source of information about the state of affairs in Ukraine and the world for 86% of Ukrainians. It is worth noting that due to the Covid pandemic and the need to work remotely in Ukraine, according to our data, the number of internet users has increased significantly. Thus, in 2019, 68% were internet users; in 2020, 74% were internet users; in 2021, 81% were internet users; in 2022, 82% were internet users; and in the first half of 2023, 88% were internet users. Therefore, the process of increasing interest in online media and social networks was ongoing. But after the outbreak of war, there were dramatic changes.

Two weeks before the war, in December 2021, television dominated social media as a news source by a wide margin (TV was a news source for 75%, social media for 44%), and 2-3 months after the war, social media and messengers (Viber, Telegram, WhatsApp, TikTok, Instagram, etc.) overtook television, and in August this difference became even greater (67% social media and messengers compared to 57% television). Among social networks in July 2022, Telegram was the most used by respondents: 39% ranked it among their top two most frequently used networks. This was followed by Facebook and YouTube, which were listed by 24-26% of respondents as their top two networks. In addition, 20% of respondents ranked Viber among their top two networks. In September 2023, among the various sources of information, most people talked about Telegram.

Amid the war, the level of use of electronic public services in Ukraine continued to grow: 53% in 2020; 60% in 2021; and 63% in 2022. The Diia app became the main tool for providing electronic services to Ukrainians, with usage increasing four times from 2020 to 2022, reaching 52%. The war did not affect the growth rate of the Diia app, but it did emphasize the importance of online interaction with the state, especially for vulnerable groups, including internally displaced persons. For millions of citizens, the ability to receive public services online has become critical in wartime.

In 2023, some disappointment with the counteroffensive and the realization that the war is a long term affair somewhat reduced the effect of rallying around the flag. In addition to the decline in trust in the government, trust in the Ukrainian media also declined from 57% to 29% between December 2022 and December 2023. Trust in the United News telethon has also declined. While between May 2022 and October 2023, the share of those who trusted it dropped from 69% to 48%, by December 2023, the figure had fallen to 43%.

## 12.9. Possible social problems of post-war Ukraine

As already mentioned, the level of cohesion in our society has increased significantly since the outbreak of the war. But at the same time, there are also problems of a new social differentiation of our society based on behavior during the war and efforts to protect Ukraine, the phenemonon of "where one was and what one did during the war". In fact, it is possible to distinguish at least five groups on this basis: 1) those who fought in the ranks of the Defense Forces; 2) those who stayed in Ukraine during the war and did not leave their homes; 3) internally displaced persons; 4) those who went abroad (refugees); 5) persons who were in the occupied territory (and here, too, different problems may arise in the case of the "old" territories occupied in 2014 and the "new" territories occupied in the last two years).

There may be some friction between these groups, which could turn into serious tensions if society does not take care to prevent possible problems. For example, those in the ranks of the Armed Forces may accuse those who are safe of having fun and a "normal" life during the war. Those who stayed in Ukraine may accuse refugees living in Europe of lacking patriotism and enjoying life in the EU, while other Ukrainians suffer from constant missile and drone attacks by the enemy. This is actively discussed on social media and may be one of the reasons why refugees are less motivated to return home. And those who stayed in the occupied territories are treated by some Ukrainians as collaborators (although the vast majority maintain a normal and positive attitude).

Of all the problem groups, IDPs are treated the best, and there is hope that there will be fewer problems of social tension than with other groups. The relatively worst attitude is towards those who live in the occupied territories. In general, only 12% of respondents believe that most residents who still live in the territories occupied after February 24 continue to live there because they really support the Russians or simply do not care about Ukraine. But the situation is worse for specific categories of people. Half of the population believes that teachers who were forced to teach should be tried for collaboration, 37% believe that pensioners who have lost their Ukrainian pensions, have no means of subsistence and have applied for Russian payments should be tried, one third would like to see utility workers convicted, and a quarter would like to see doctors convicted. These are the consequences of improper communication between the government and the population, which can cause serious problems with the liberation and reintegration of the liberated territories and reduce the integration of our society. Adequate communication about who is considered a collaborator is especially important; the population of the occupied territories and other citizens of Ukraine should clearly know who the state does and does not consider a collaborator.

Another problem is the attitude toward Ukrainians (citizens of Ukraine) who are ethnic Russians and ethnic Belarusians. Attitudes toward them have deteriorated significantly, with 44% of the population not wanting to see Ukrainians who are ethnic Russians as citizens of Ukraine and 22% not wanting to see Ukrainians who are ethnic Belarusians as citizens of Ukraine. It is possible that the deterioration in attitudes toward Russians living in Ukraine and Russian-speaking Ukrainians is due to the fact that before the outbreak of full-scale war, they had a higher percentage of those who supported pro-Russian parties than Ukrainian-speaking Ukrainians. But now the situation has changed radically. All the polls conducted by KIIS and other sociological companies after February 24,

2022, show that although Ukrainian citizens who are ethnic Russians and Russian-speaking Ukrainians differ somewhat in their views, in fact, most of them are quite pro-Ukrainian. Perhaps not everyone is aware of the radical changes that have taken place in our society.

Over almost two years of war, attitudes toward Russian-speaking Ukrainians have also deteriorated, although unlike the situation with Russians, more than 80% are ready to coexist with them as citizens of Ukraine. In fact, most Ukrainians are aware of the new reality that our citizens—ethnic Russians, Russian-speaking Ukrainians, and representatives of other ethnic groups—are fighting the enemy side by side. However, this issue can be artificially exacerbated and turned into a problem. The enemy is not among us, but is waging an active information war to sow enmity between us, including between linguistic and ethnic groups. We must closely monitor the interethnic relations of Ukrainian citizens to counteract negative trends that could reduce the integration of our society.

Of course, these trends in changing attitudes toward Russia and Russians are natural and positive; Ukrainians have finally seen the light and realized the threat posed by their neighbor. But at the same time, the differentiation of attitudes toward Russians is disappearing, and negative attitudes are being transferred to the enemies of the Putin regime. A common thesis is "Russian liberalism ends where the Ukrainian issue begins." The lack of differential treatment of Russians, which can be called the problem of "good Russians," can be a dangerous trend. The fact is that Ukraine's survival as an independent state now depends on the actions of the Armed Forces, Ukrainian citizens, and international support. But in the future, in a strategic perspective, the most important thing for us is to neutralize Russia as an aggressive state. If the government in Russia does not change, its defeat will not lead to sustainable peace, but to a temporary truce until it gathers strength for new attacks. Therefore, it is critically important for us who will come to power in Russia and what strategic path it will choose. From this point of view, we must support the opponents of the Putin regime in every way possible, even if we do not like some of their views.

Finally, after the war, there may be a problem of interaction with migrants. It can be assumed that the labor shortage in Ukraine will be largely compensated by migration from less developed countries (probably Muslim countries), as is the case in many other countries. Ukraine is not yet ready for this, we do not have the appropriate infrastructure and the population has no experience of communicating with representatives of other cultures. This could also become one of the likely sources of conflict and a decrease in Ukraine's integration.

## 12.10. Summary

A summary can be formulated in the following conclusions.

1.  The war in Ukraine has caused significant human losses and socio-economic damage, including the destruction of infrastructure and rising unemployment. The mental and physical health of Ukrainians has been significantly affected by the war. The war has torn families apart and caused the loss of loved ones, increasing the psychological and social burden.

2.  Mass migration in Ukraine is on an unprecedented scale: millions of Ukrainians (approximately one-third of the population) have moved abroad or become internally displaced.

3.  Ukraine has made a final and irreversible geopolitical choice—the overwhelming majority of Ukrainians support joining the EU and NATO, both nationally and in all regions of Ukraine.

4.  The attitude of Ukrainians towards Russia, which deteriorated significantly in 2014 after the occupation of Crimea, has deteriorated even further, with the percentage of supporters of Russia dropping to 2%. Attitudes towards Russians living in Russia have also deteriorated sharply, from 75% in 2021 to 3% of positive attitudes. Similar changes have occurred in attitudes toward Belarus, which most Ukrainians consider a party to the war.

5. The war has contributed to the unification of the nation, increased social cohesion, Ukrainian identity, the use of the Ukrainian language, and increased patriotism and pride in the country. The level of mutual assistance, the level of trust in volunteers, and the prevalence of volunteer activities have all increased. Regional and linguistic and ethnic differentiation has significantly decreased.

6. The process of forming Ukrainian national identity has accelerated, demonstrating dynamic growth and deep penetration into various aspects of public life, from strengthening citizens' self-identification as Ukrainians to rethinking historical heritage and cultural influences. For example, the percentage of citizens who consider themselves primarily Ukrainian citizens has increased from 40% in 1992-2004 to 80% after the outbreak of war in 2022-2023. The popularity of national holidays has increased. The majority of respondents in 2023 spoke out against the teaching of Russian in schools, indicating a desire to distance themselves from Russian cultural influence. Support for the Orthodox Church of Ukraine (OCU) has increased, and attitudes toward the OUN-UPA have improved.

7. There is some difficulty in choosing between traditional Ukrainian and modern European/Western values. However, there has been significant progress in this area, with 95% of Ukrainians actively supporting the idea of the country's transition to a full-fledged democracy. Together with the positive dynamics in relation to gender equality and the rights of the LGBT+ community, these processes indicate the active formation of the Ukrainian nation based on the values of freedom, equality and openness to change.

8. Attitudes toward the state as a whole and toward the authorities — the President, the government, and the parliament — have improved significantly, with trust increasing but declining slightly at the end of 2023 (although the level of trust remains higher than before the war). Attitudes toward other social institutions have also improved.

9. The resilience of the population remains high. Since the beginning of the war, the majority of Ukrainians (84%-87%) did not support territorial concessions to achieve peace and advocated the liberation of all territories inclusive of Crimea and Donbas, but in December 2023, this figure dropped to 74%. Despite all the hardships, Ukrainians' happiness remained at a fairly high level at 63%, which is only slightly lower than before the war. Optimism about Ukraine's future as a prosperous country within the EU has grown significantly, and although it declined slightly at the end of 2023, from 88% to 73%, it remains well above pre-war levels.

10. There have been significant changes in media consumption. Television channels stopped operating independently and united under a single project called United News. Trust in the Ukrainian media increased dramatically after the start of the war, but by the end of 2023, it had declined. Consumption of television as a news source has declined, and television has lost ground to social media, primarily telegram channels.

11. New potential sources of social tension have emerged, including a new basis for social differentiation: the status and behavior of a person during the war. Potential social conflicts are possible between different groups of Ukrainians, including refugees abroad, internally displaced persons, the mainstream population that has not changed their place of residence, and those who lived in the occupied territory. Attitudes toward Russian-speaking Ukrainians and Ukrainians who are ethnically Russian have also deteriorated.

# Appendices
## Some Tables

## To Chapter 3.

**Table D.3.1. Stressful situations experienced by Ukrainians, % of all respondents**

|  | 2013 | 2014 | 2015 | 2016 | 2017 | 2018 | 2019 | 2020 | 2021 | 2022 |
|---|---|---|---|---|---|---|---|---|---|---|
| Survive a serious illness or surgery | 9 | 7 | 11 | 11 | 9 | 12 | 15 | 15 | 18 | 13 |
| Surviving a serious illness of loved ones | 12 | 10 | 14 | 13 | 12 | 9 | 13 | 16 | 16 | 17 |
| Surviving the death of loved ones | 7 | 6 | 9 | 9 | 7 | 9 | 9 | 16 | 19 | 16 |
| Living in a state of near-suicide | 0 | 1 | 0 | 0 | 1 | 1 | 1 | 1 | 1 | - |
| Lose your job and be forced to be unemployed | 6 | 8 | 9 | 6 | 7 | 5 | 6 | 13 | 11 | 19 |
| Suffer from an attack or robbery | 1 | 1 | 1 | 1 | 1 | 1 | 1 | 1 | 1 | 3 |
| Suffer from theft or fraud | 2 | 2 | 3 | 4 | 2 | 2 | 2 | 4 | 4 | 7 |
| To find yourself without a livelihood | 5 | 6 | 6 | 9 | 8 | 6 | 3 | 6 | 6 | 9 |
| Feeling helpless | 12 | 12 | 13 | 13 | 13 | 10 | 5 | 5 | 7 | 18 |
| Apply to the court for help | 2 | 2 | 2 | 1 | 2 | 3 | 1 | 2 | 3 | 2 |
| Losing faith in people, facing meanness | 9 | 8 | 9 | 14 | 8 | 8 | 6 | 10 | 10 | 11 |
| Losing faith in your own abilities | 6 | 5 | 7 | 8 | 7 | 6 | 4 | 3 | 3 | - |

| | | | | | | | | | | |
|---|---|---|---|---|---|---|---|---|---|---|
| Seriously conflict with others | 2 | 4 | 3 | 3 | 3 | 2 | 1 | 2 | 2 | - |
| To be subjected to threats, intimidation | - | 2 | 1 | 1 | 2 | 2 | 0 | 2 | 2 | - |
| Survive bombing, shelling | - | 7 | 6 | 1 | 1 | 1 | 0 | 2 | 2 | 32 |
| To experience other stressful situations | 15 | 28 | 22 | 12 | 16 | 13 | 9 | 11 | 14 | 12 |
| I have not experienced any stressful situations | 48 | 35 | 34 | 37 | 42 | 38 | 49 | 32 | 29 | 13 |
| Hard to say / refusal to answer | 2 | 4 | 2 | 5 | 5 | 10 | 1 | 2 | 2 | 3 |

## To Chapter 5.

Table D.5.1. Please imagine that a referendum on whether Ukraine should join the European Union is being held now. What is your choice?

| Year | For accession | Against accession | Will not vote | Hard to say | Total |
|------|---------------|-------------------|---------------|-------------|-------|
| 2005 | 34 | 39 | 8 | 19 | 100 |
| 2007 | 47 | 28 | 6 | 18 | 100 |
| 2009 | 42 | 28 | 10 | 20 | 100 |
| 2010 | 44 | 26 | 7 | 24 | 100 |
| 2012 | 42 | 32 | 7 | 19 | 100 |
| 2013 | 41 | 33 | 10 | 16 | 100 |
| 2014 | 48 | 31 | 8 | 13 | 100 |
| 2015 | 50 | 27 | 11 | 13 | 100 |
| 2016 | 49 | 27 | 10 | 14 | 100 |
| 2017 | 53 | 24 | 10 | 13 | 100 |
| 2018 | 49 | 25 | 12 | 14 | 100 |
| 2019 | 51 | 23 | 9 | 17 | 100 |
| 2020 | 52 | 26 | 9 | 13 | 100 |
| 2021 | 52 | 19 | 25 | 4 | 100 |
| 2022 | 81 | 4 | 11 | 4 | 100 |

**Table D.5.2. Please imagine that a referendum on whether Ukraine should join NATO is being held now. What is your choice?**

| Year | For accession | Against accession | Will not vote | Hard to say | Total |
|------|---------------|-------------------|---------------|-------------|-------|
| 2005 | 16 | 57 | 9 | 19 | 100 |
| 2007 | 19 | 60 | 6 | 15 | 100 |
| 2008 | 19 | 62 | 6 | 12 | 100 |
| 2009 | 17 | 63 | 8 | 12 | 100 |
| 2014 | 44 | 38 | 7 | 11 | 100 |
| 2015 | 37 | 36 | 11 | 16 | 100 |
| 2016 | 39 | 31 | 18 | 12 | 100 |
| 2017 | 42 | 30 | 10 | 18 | 100 |
| 2019 | 40 | 31 | 8 | 20 | 100 |
| 2020 | 44 | 31 | 10 | 16 | 100 |
| 2021 | 48 | 24 | 23 | 5 | 100 |
| 2022 | 71 | 7 | 15 | 7 | 100 |

# To Chapter 6.

Table D.6.1. How do you feel about Ukraine/Russia in general now?

| Date | Attitudes towards Russia in Ukraine, % | | | | Date | Russia's attitude to Ukraine, % | | | |
|---|---|---|---|---|---|---|---|---|---|
| | Good | Bad | Hard to say | Total | | Good | Bad | Hard to say | Total |
| Apr.08 | 88 | 7 | 5 | 100 | Mar.08 | 55 | 33 | 12 | 100 |
| Sep. 08 | 88 | 9 | 3 | 100 | Sept.08 | 38 | 53 | 10 | 100 |
| Feb. 09 | 91 | 5 | 4 | 100 | Jan. 09 | 29 | 62 | 10 | 100 |
| May. 09 | 93 | 4 | 3 | 100 | May.09 | 33 | 56 | 11 | 100 |
| Oct. 09 | 92 | 6 | 3 | 100 | Sept.09 | 46 | 44 | 10 | 100 |
| Sep.10 | 90 | 6 | 4 | 100 | Mar.10 | 59 | 29 | 12 | 100 |
| Jun.10 | 92 | 6 | 3 | 100 | July 10 | 70 | 22 | 9 | 100 |
| Oct.10 | 93 | 4 | 3 | 100 | Oct. 10 | 67 | 21 | 12 | 100 |
| Nov.11 | 80 | 13 | 7 | 100 | Sept.11 | 68 | 23 | 9 | 100 |
| Feb. 12 | 85 | 9 | 6 | 100 | Jan. 12 | 64 | 25 | 12 | 100 |
| Sep. 12 | 83 | 11 | 6 | 100 | Sept.12 | 74 | 17 | 10 | 100 |
| Feb. 13 | 85 | 8 | 7 | 100 | Feb. 13 | 69 | 21 | 9 | 100 |
| May. 13 | 81 | 10 | 9 | 100 | May.13 | 72 | 18 | 9 | 100 |
| Nov.13 | 82 | 10 | 8 | 100 | Sept.13 | 69 | 22 | 8 | 100 |
| Feb. 14 | 78 | 13 | 9 | 100 | Jan. 14 | 66 | 26 | 9 | 100 |
| May. 14 | 52 | 38 | 10 | 100 | May 14 | 35 | 49 | 17 | 100 |
| Sep. 14 | 48 | 41 | 11 | 100 | Sept.14 | 32 | 55 | 13 | 100 |
| Dec.14 | 37 | 48 | 16 | 100 | Jan. 15 | 24 | 63 | 13 | 100 |

| Date | | | | | Date | | | | |
|---|---|---|---|---|---|---|---|---|---|
| Feb. 15 | 34 | 51 | 15 | 100 | Mar.15 | 31 | 56 | 13 | 100 |
| May. 15 | 30 | 56 | 14 | 100 | May 15 | 26 | 59 | 14 | 100 |
| Sep. 15 | 34 | 53 | 13 | 100 | Sept.15 | 33 | 56 | 11 | 100 |
| Feb. 16 | 36 | 47 | 13 | 100 | Feb. 16 | 27 | 59 | 14 | 100 |
| May. 16 | 42 | 43 | 15 | 100 | May 16 | 39 | 47 | 13 | 100 |
| Sep. 16 | 40 | 46 | 14 | 100 | Sept.16 | 26 | 56 | 17 | 100 |
| Dec.16 | 40 | 47 | 13 | 100 | Dec.16 | 34 | 54 | 13 | 100 |
| Feb. 17 | 39 | 46 | 15 | 100 | Jan. 17 | 34 | 54 | 13 | 100 |
| May. 17 | 44 | 37 | 19 | 100 | May 17 | 26 | 59 | 15 | 100 |
| Sep. 17 | 37 | 46 | 17 | 100 | Sept.17 | 32 | 53 | 15 | 100 |
| Dec.17 | 42 | 39 | 19 | 100 | Dec.17 | 28 | 56 | 17 | 100 |
| Feb. 18 | 45 | 38 | 18 | 100 | Mar.18 | 33 | 55 | 12 | 100 |
| Sep. 18 | 48 | 32 | 19 | 100 | Sept.18 | 33 | 56 | 12 | 100 |
| Feb. 19 | 57 | 27 | 17 | 100 | Feb. 19 | 34 | 55 | 10 | 100 |
| Sep. 19 | 54 | 35 | 11 | 100 | Sept.19 | 56 | 31 | 13 | 100 |
| Feb. 20 | 54 | 33 | 13 | 100 | Jan. 20 | 41 | 47 | 12 | 100 |
| Sep. 20 | 42 | 42 | 16 | 100 | Aug. 20 | 48 | 43 | 9 | 100 |
| Feb. 21 | 41 | 42 | 17 | 100 | Feb.21 | 54 | 31 | 13 | 100 |
| Nov.21 | 39 | 47 | 14 | 100 | Nov.21 | 45 | 43 | 12 | 100 |
| Feb. 21 | 34 | 50 | 15 | 100 | --- | --- | --- | --- | --- |
| May.22 | 2 | 92 | 6 | 100 | --- | --- | --- | --- | --- |

Table D.6.2. What would you like to see in Ukraine's relations with Russia?

| Date | Ukraine's relations with Russia should be the same as with other countries—with closed borders, visas, customs | Ukraine and Russia should be independent, but friendly states—with open borders, without visas and customs | Ukraine and Russia should unite into one state | Hard to say | Total |
|---|---|---|---|---|---|
| Apr. 08 | 10 | 67 | 20 | 3 | 100 |
| Sep. 08 | 17 | 66 | 16 | 2 | 100 |
| Feb. 09 | 8 | 68 | 23 | 1 | 100 |
| May. 09 | 10 | 65 | 23 | 2 | 100 |
| Oct. 09 | 11 | 67 | 19 | 3 | 100 |
| Sep. 10 | 11 | 67 | 19 | 3 | 100 |
| Jun. 10 | 12 | 70 | 16 | 2 | 100 |
| Oct. 10 | 10 | 67 | 20 | 2 | 100 |
| Nov. 11 | 13 | 67 | 16 | 1 | 100 |
| Feb. 12 | 13 | 69 | 16 | 2 | 100 |
| Sep. 12 | 11 | 72 | 14 | 3 | 100 |
| Feb. 13 | 13 | 68 | 16 | 3 | 100 |
| May. 13 | 11 | 69 | 14 | 5 | 100 |
| Nov. 13 | 12 | 73 | 9 | 6 | 100 |
| Feb. 14 | 15 | 68 | 12 | 5 | 100 |
| May. 14 | 32 | 54 | 8 | 5 | 100 |
| Sep. 14 | 45 | 44 | 5 | 6 | 100 |
| Dec. 14 | 50 | 42 | 3 | 5 | 100 |
| Feb. 15 | 48 | 43 | 4 | 6 | 100 |
| May. 15 | 45 | 46 | 2 | 7 | 100 |
| Sep. 15 | 46 | 45 | 2 | 7 | 100 |
| Feb. 16 | 42 | 43 | 4 | 11 | 100 |
| May. 16 | 44 | 44 | 3 | 9 | 100 |
| Sep. 16 | 49 | 43 | 3 | 6 | 100 |
| Dec. 16 | 45 | 46 | 3 | 7 | 100 |
| Feb. 17 | 47 | 43 | 2 | 7 | 100 |
| May 17 | 43 | 47 | 4 | 6 | 100 |

| Sep. 17 | 49 | 40 | 4 | 8 | 100 |
|---|---|---|---|---|---|
| Dec. 17 | 45 | 40 | 4 | 11 | 100 |
| Feb. 18 | 44 | 44 | 3 | 9 | 100 |
| Sep. 18 | 38 | 50 | 4 | 8 | 100 |
| Feb. 19 | 39 | 48 | 4 | 9 | 100 |
| Sep. 19 | 41 | 49 | 3 | 7 | 100 |
| Feb. 20 | 39 | 51 | 3 | 7 | 100 |
| Sep. 20 | 39 | 51 | 5 | 5 | 100 |
| Feb. 21 | 39 | 49 | 6 | 6 | 100 |
| Jul. 22 | 79 | 11 | 1 | 8 | 100 |
| May. 23 | 79 | 10 | 1 | 10 | 100 |

# To Chapter 7.

Table D.7.1. Self-assessment of happiness by the population of Ukraine (2001-2023), % of all Respondents

| Date | Yes | More likely yes than no | Yes and no | More likely no than yes | No | Hard to say | Total |
|---|---|---|---|---|---|---|---|
| Jan. 01 | 20 | 18 | 28 | 14 | 19 | 2 | 100 |
| Nov.02 | 23 | 26 | 22 | 17 | 10 | 2 | 100 |
| Nov.03 | 24 | 28 | 24 | 14 | 8 | 2 | 100 |
| Dec.05 | 22 | 25 | 27 | 14 | 11 | 1 | 100 |
| Oct.06 | 23 | 29 | 25 | 11 | 9 | 3 | 100 |
| Dec.07 | 28 | 26 | 21 | 12 | 11 | 2 | 100 |
| Mar.08 | 28 | 29 | 21 | 12 | 8 | 3 | 100 |
| Jun.09 | 30 | 28 | 21 | 10 | 7 | 3 | 100 |
| Jun.10 | 33 | 32 | 19 | 9 | 5 | 2 | 100 |
| Feb.11 | 34 | 29 | 17 | 9 | 8 | 3 | 100 |
| Feb.-Nov.12 | 22 | 35 | 26 | 9 | 4 | 4 | 100 |
| Feb.-Nov.13 | 24 | 34 | 24 | 10 | 5 | 3 | 100 |
| Feb.14 | 22 | 38 | 23 | 8 | 4 | 5 | 100 |
| May.15 | 24 | 34 | 21 | 10 | 7 | 4 | 100 |
| May.15 | 26 | 28 | 21 | 13 | 9 | 4 | 100 |
| May.16 | 23 | 31 | 25 | 11 | 8 | 2 | 100 |

| May.17 | 24 | 29 | 24 | 12 | 7 | 3 | 100 |
|--------|----|----|----|----|----|----|-----|
| May.18 | 37 | 26 | 16 | 8 | 9 | 4 | 100 |
| Apr.20 | 45 | 23 | 14 | 6 | 10 | 2 | 100 |
| Apr.21 | 44 | 24 | 12 | 6 | 11 | 3 | 100 |
| Dec.21 | 44 | 26 | 13 | 7 | 8 | 2 | 100 |
| Sep.22 | 43 | 25 | 17 | 6 | 7 | 2 | 100 |
| Dec.23 | 41 | 28 | 13 | 8 | 9 | 1 | 100 |

Table D.8.2. Which of these holidays are the most important or favorite for you? Please indicate no more than 5 holidays.

| | 2013 | 2016 | 2017 | 2018 | 2020 | 2021 | 2023 |
|--------|------|------|------|------|------|------|------|
| New Year | 81 | 74 | 76 | 79 | 74 | 55 | 52 |
| Christmas | 79 | 79 | 80 | 81 | 79 | 63 | 69 |
| International Women's Day | 49 | 37 | 49 | 45 | 40 | 34 | 25 |
| Labor Day | 10 | 7 | 12 | 9 | 11 | 12 | 5 |
| Easter | 83 | 81 | 80 | 82 | 77 | 72 | 70 |
| Victory Day | 40 | 35 | 37 | 31 | 33 | 30 | 13 |
| Trinity | 36 | 34 | 29 | 35 | 31 | 17 | 22 |
| Constitution Day of Ukraine | 4 | 5 | 5 | 5 | 7 | 14 | 29 |
| Independence Day of Ukraine | 12 | 20 | 17 | 16 | 19 | 37 | 63 |
| Day of Defenders of Ukraine | --- | --- | 10 | 11 | 13 | 29 | 54 |
| None | 2 | 2 | 2 | 3 | 2 | 1 | 2 |
| Hard to say | 1 | 0 | 1 | 0 | 1 | 1 | 1 |

## To Chapter 10

Table D.10.1.Share of Internet users among the adult population, %. According to the KIIS poll "Do you personally use the Internet?"

| Year | % of Internet users |
|---|---|
| 1997 | 1 |
| 1998 | 2 |
| 1999 | 3 |
| 2000 | 3 |
| 2001 | 5 |
| 2002 | 7 |
| 2003 | 10 |
| 2004 | 15 |
| 2005 | 16 |
| 2006 | 19 |
| 2007 | 19 |
| 2008 | 24 |
| 2009 | 27 |
| 2010 | 29 |
| 2011 | 40 |
| 2012 | 43 |
| 2013 | 49 |
| 2014 | 54 |
| 2015 | 57 |
| 2016 | 62 |
| 2017 | 62 |
| 2018 | 61 |
| 2019 | 68 |
| 2020 | 74 |
| 2021 | 81 |
| 2022 | 82 |
| 2023 | 88 |

# SOVIET AND POST-SOVIET POLITICS AND SOCIETY
Edited by Dr. Andreas Umland | ISSN 1614-3515

1  *Андреас Умланд (ред.)* | Воплощение Европейской конвенции по правам человека в России. Философские, юридические и эмпирические исследования | ISBN 3-89821-387-0

2  *Christian Wipperfürth* | Russland – ein vertrauenswürdiger Partner? Grundlagen, Hintergründe und Praxis gegenwärtiger russischer Außenpolitik | Mit einem Vorwort von Heinz Timmermann | ISBN 3-89821-401-X

3  *Manja Hussner* | Die Übernahme internationalen Rechts in die russische und deutsche Rechtsordnung. Eine vergleichende Analyse zur Völkerrechtsfreundlichkeit der Verfassungen der Russländischen Föderation und der Bundesrepublik Deutschland | Mit einem Vorwort von Rainer Arnold | ISBN 3-89821-438-9

4  *Matthew Tejada* | Bulgaria's Democratic Consolidation and the Kozloduy Nuclear Power Plant (KNPP). The Unattainability of Closure | With a foreword by Richard J. Crampton | ISBN 3-89821-439-7

5  *Марк Григорьевич Меерович* | Квадратные метры, определяющие сознание. Государственная жилищная политика в СССР. 1921 – 1941 гг | ISBN 3-89821-474-5

6  *Andrei P. Tsygankov, Pavel A. Tsygankov (Eds.)* | New Directions in Russian International Studies | ISBN 3-89821-422-2

7  *Марк Григорьевич Меерович* | Как власть народ к труду приучала. Жилище в СССР – средство управления людьми. 1917 – 1941 гг. | С предисловием Елены Осокиной | ISBN 3-89821-495-8

8  *David J. Galbreath* | Nation-Building and Minority Politics in Post-Socialist States. Interests, Influence and Identities in Estonia and Latvia | With a foreword by David J. Smith | ISBN 3-89821-467-2

9  *Алексей Юрьевич Безугольный* | Народы Кавказа в Вооруженных силах СССР в годы Великой Отечественной войны 1941-1945 гг. | С предисловием Николая Бугая | ISBN 3-89821-475-3

10  *Вячеслав Лихачев и Владимир Прибыловский (ред.)* | Русское Национальное Единство, 1990-2000. В 2-х томах | ISBN 3-89821-523-7

11  *Николай Бугай (ред.)* | Народы стран Балтии в условиях сталинизма (1940-е – 1950-е годы). Документированная история | ISBN 3-89821-525-3

12  *Ingmar Bredies (Hrsg.)* | Zur Anatomie der Orange Revolution in der Ukraine. Wechsel des Elitenregimes oder Triumph des Parlamentarismus? | ISBN 3-89821-524-5

13  *Anastasia V. Mitrofanova* | The Politicization of Russian Orthodoxy. Actors and Ideas | With a foreword by William C. Gay | ISBN 3-89821-481-8

14  *Nathan D. Larson* | Alexander Solzhenitsyn and the Russo-Jewish Question | ISBN 3-89821-483-4

15  *Guido Houben* | Kulturpolitik und Ethnizität. Staatliche Kunstförderung im Russland der neunziger Jahre | Mit einem Vorwort von Gert Weisskirchen | ISBN 3-89821-542-3

16  *Leonid Luks* | Der russische „Sonderweg"? Aufsätze zur neuesten Geschichte Russlands im europäischen Kontext | ISBN 3-89821-496-6

17  *Евгений Мороз* | История «Мёртвой воды» – от страшной сказки к большой политике. Политическое неоязычество в постсоветской России | ISBN 3-89821-551-2

18  *Александр Верховский и Галина Кожевникова (ред.)* | Этническая и религиозная интолерантность в российских СМИ. Результаты мониторинга 2001-2004 гг. | ISBN 3-89821-569-5

19  *Christian Ganzer* | Sowjetisches Erbe und ukrainische Nation. Das Museum der Geschichte des Zaporoger Kosakentums auf der Insel Chortycja | Mit einem Vorwort von Frank Golczewski | ISBN 3-89821-504-0

20  *Эльза-Баир Гучинова* | Помнить нельзя забыть. Антропология депортационной травмы калмыков | С предисловием Кэролайн Хамфри | ISBN 3-89821-506-7

21  *Юлия Лидерман* | Мотивы «проверки» и «испытания» в постсоветской культуре. Советское прошлое в российском кинематографе 1990-х годов | С предисловием Евгения Марголита | ISBN 3-89821-511-3

22  *Tanya Lokshina, Ray Thomas, Mary Mayer (Eds.)* | The Imposition of a Fake Political Settlement in the Northern Caucasus. The 2003 Chechen Presidential Election | ISBN 3-89821-436-2

23  *Timothy McCajor Hall, Rosie Read (Eds.)* | Changes in the Heart of Europe. Recent Ethnographies of Czechs, Slovaks, Roma, and Sorbs | With an afterword by Zdeněk Salzmann | ISBN 3-89821-606-3

24  *Christian Autengruber* | Die politischen Parteien in Bulgarien und Rumänien. Eine vergleichende Analyse seit Beginn der 90er Jahre | Mit einem Vorwort von Dorothée de Nève | ISBN 3-89821-476-1

25  *Annette Freyberg-Inan with Radu Cristescu* | The Ghosts in Our Classrooms, or: John Dewey Meets Ceauşescu. The Promise and the Failures of Civic Education in Romania | ISBN 3-89821-416-8

26  *John B. Dunlop* | The 2002 Dubrovka and 2004 Beslan Hostage Crises. A Critique of Russian Counter-Terrorism | With a foreword by Donald N. Jensen | ISBN 3-89821-608-X

27  *Peter Koller* | Das touristische Potenzial von Kam''janec'–Podil's'kyj. Eine fremdenverkehrsgeographische Untersuchung der Zukunftsperspektiven und Maßnahmenplanung zur Destinationsentwicklung des „ukrainischen Rothenburg" | Mit einem Vorwort von Kristiane Klemm | ISBN 3-89821-640-3

28  *Françoise Daucé, Elisabeth Sieca-Kozlowski (Eds.)* | Dedovshchina in the Post-Soviet Military. Hazing of Russian Army Conscripts in a Comparative Perspective | With a foreword by Dale Herspring | ISBN 3-89821-616-0

29  *Florian Strasser* | Zivilgesellschaftliche Einflüsse auf die Orange Revolution. Die gewaltlose Massenbewegung und die ukrainische Wahlkrise 2004 | Mit einem Vorwort von Egbert Jahn | ISBN 3-89821-648-9

30  *Rebecca S. Katz* | The Georgian Regime Crisis of 2003-2004. A Case Study in Post-Soviet Media Representation of Politics, Crime and Corruption | ISBN 3-89821-413-3

31  *Vladimir Kantor* | Willkür oder Freiheit. Beiträge zur russischen Geschichtsphilosophie | Ediert von Dagmar Herrmann sowie mit einem Vorwort versehen von Leonid Luks | ISBN 3-89821-589-X

32  *Laura A. Victoir* | The Russian Land Estate Today. A Case Study of Cultural Politics in Post-Soviet Russia | With a foreword by Priscilla Roosevelt | ISBN 3-89821-426-5

33  *Ivan Katchanovski* | Cleft Countries. Regional Political Divisions and Cultures in Post-Soviet Ukraine and Moldova| With a foreword by Francis Fukuyama | ISBN 3-89821-558-X

34  *Florian Mühlfried* | Postsowjetische Feiern. Das Georgische Bankett im Wandel | Mit einem Vorwort von Kevin Tuite | ISBN 3-89821-601-2

35  *Roger Griffin, Werner Loh, Andreas Umland (Eds.)* | Fascism Past and Present, West and East. An International Debate on Concepts and Cases in the Comparative Study of the Extreme Right | With an afterword by Walter Laqueur | ISBN 3-89821-674-8

36  *Sebastian Schlegel* | Der „Weiße Archipel". Sowjetische Atomstädte 1945-1991 | Mit einem Geleitwort von Thomas Bohn | ISBN 3-89821-679-9

37  *Vyacheslav Likhachev* | Political Anti-Semitism in Post-Soviet Russia. Actors and Ideas in 1991-2003 | Edited and translated from Russian by Eugene Veklerov | ISBN 3-89821-529-6

38  *Josette Baer (Ed.)* | Preparing Liberty in Central Europe. Political Texts from the Spring of Nations 1848 to the Spring of Prague 1968 | With a foreword by Zdeněk V. David | ISBN 3-89821-546-6

39  *Михаил Лукьянов* | Российский консерватизм и реформа, 1907-1914 | С предисловием Марка Д. Стейнберга | ISBN 3-89821-503-2

40  *Nicola Melloni* | Market Without Economy. The 1998 Russian Financial Crisis | With a foreword by Eiji Furukawa | ISBN 3-89821-407-9

41  *Dmitrij Chmelnizki* | Die Architektur Stalins | Bd. 1: Studien zu Ideologie und Stil | Bd. 2: Bilddokumentation | Mit einem Vorwort von Bruno Flierl | ISBN 3-89821-515-6

42  *Katja Yafimava* | Post-Soviet Russian-Belarussian Relationships. The Role of Gas Transit Pipelines | With a foreword by Jonathan P. Stern | ISBN 3-89821-655-1

43  *Boris Chavkin* | Verflechtungen der deutschen und russischen Zeitgeschichte. Aufsätze und Archivfunde zu den Beziehungen Deutschlands und der Sowjetunion von 1917 bis 1991 | Ediert von Markus Edlinger sowie mit einem Vorwort versehen von Leonid Luks | ISBN 3-89821-756-6

44  *Anastasija Grynenko in Zusammenarbeit mit Claudia Dathe* | Die Terminologie des Gerichtswesens der Ukraine und Deutschlands im Vergleich. Eine übersetzungswissenschaftliche Analyse juristischer Fachbegriffe im Deutschen, Ukrainischen und Russischen | Mit einem Vorwort von Ulrich Hartmann | ISBN 3-89821-691-8

45  *Anton Burkov* | The Impact of the European Convention on Human Rights on Russian Law. Legislation and Application in 1996-2006 | With a foreword by Françoise Hampson | ISBN 978-3-89821-639-5

46  *Stina Torjesen, Indra Overland (Eds.)* | International Election Observers in Post-Soviet Azerbaijan. Geopolitical Pawns or Agents of Change? | ISBN 978-3-89821-743-9

47  *Taras Kuzio* | Ukraine – Crimea – Russia. Triangle of Conflict | ISBN 978-3-89821-761-3

48  *Claudia Šabić* | „Ich erinnere mich nicht, aber L'viv!" Zur Funktion kultureller Faktoren für die Institutionalisierung und Entwicklung einer ukrainischen Region | Mit einem Vorwort von Melanie Tatur | ISBN 978-3-89821-752-1

49  *Marlies Bilz* | Tatarstan in der Transformation. Nationaler Diskurs und Politische Praxis 1988-1994 | Mit einem Vorwort von Frank Golczewski | ISBN 978-3-89821-722-4

50  *Марлен Ларюэль (ред.)* | Современные интерпретации русского национализма | ISBN 978-3-89821-795-8

51  *Sonja Schüler* | Die ethnische Dimension der Armut. Roma im postsozialistischen Rumänien | Mit einem Vorwort von Anton Sterbling | ISBN 978-3-89821-776-7

52  *Галина Кожевникова* | Радикальный национализм в России и противодействие ему. Сборник докладов Центра «Сова» за 2004-2007 гг. | С предисловием Александра Верховского | ISBN 978-3-89821-721-7

53  *Галина Кожевникова и Владимир Прибыловский* | Российская власть в биографиях I. Высшие должностные лица РФ в 2004 г. | ISBN 978-3-89821-796-5

54  *Галина Кожевникова и Владимир Прибыловский* | Российская власть в биографиях II. Члены Правительства РФ в 2004 г. | ISBN 978-3-89821-797-2

55  *Галина Кожевникова и Владимир Прибыловский* | Российская власть в биографиях III. Руководители федеральных служб и агентств РФ в 2004 г.| ISBN 978-3-89821-798-9

56  *Ileana Petroniu* | Privatisierung in Transformationsökonomien. Determinanten der Restrukturierungs-Bereitschaft am Beispiel Polens, Rumäniens und der Ukraine | Mit einem Vorwort von Rainer W. Schäfer | ISBN 978-3-89821-790-3

57  *Christian Wipperfürth* | Russland und seine GUS-Nachbarn. Hintergründe, aktuelle Entwicklungen und Konflikte in einer ressourcenreichen Region| ISBN 978-3-89821-801-6

58  *Togzhan Kassenova* | From Antagonism to Partnership. The Uneasy Path of the U.S.-Russian Cooperative Threat Reduction | With a foreword by Christoph Bluth | ISBN 978-3-89821-707-1

59  *Alexander Höllwerth* | Das sakrale eurasische Imperium des Aleksandr Dugin. Eine Diskursanalyse zum postsowjetischen russischen Rechtsextremismus | Mit einem Vorwort von Dirk Uffelmann | ISBN 978-3-89821-813-9

60  *Олег Рябов* | «Россия-Матушка». Национализм, гендер и война в России XX века | С предисловием Елены Гощило | ISBN 978-3-89821-487-2

61  *Ivan Maistrenko* | Borot'bism. A Chapter in the History of the Ukrainian Revolution | With a new Introduction by Chris Ford | Translated by George S. N. Luckyj with the assistance of Ivan L. Rudnytsky | Second, Revised and Expanded Edition ISBN 978-3-8382-1107-7

62  *Maryna Romanets* | Anamorphosic Texts and Reconfigured Visions. Improvised Traditions in Contemporary Ukrainian and Irish Literature | ISBN 978-3-89821-576-3

63  *Paul D'Anieri and Taras Kuzio (Eds.)* | Aspects of the Orange Revolution I. Democratization and Elections in Post-Communist Ukraine | ISBN 978-3-89821-698-2

64  *Bohdan Harasymiw in collaboration with Oleh S. Ilnytzkyj (Eds.)* | Aspects of the Orange Revolution II. Information and Manipulation Strategies in the 2004 Ukrainian Presidential Elections | ISBN 978-3-89821-699-9

65  *Ingmar Bredies, Andreas Umland and Valentin Yakushik (Eds.)* | Aspects of the Orange Revolution III. The Context and Dynamics of the 2004 Ukrainian Presidential Elections | ISBN 978-3-89821-803-0

66  *Ingmar Bredies, Andreas Umland and Valentin Yakushik (Eds.)* | Aspects of the Orange Revolution IV. Foreign Assistance and Civic Action in the 2004 Ukrainian Presidential Elections | ISBN 978-3-89821-808-5

67  *Ingmar Bredies, Andreas Umland and Valentin Yakushik (Eds.)* | Aspects of the Orange Revolution V. Institutional Observation Reports on the 2004 Ukrainian Presidential Elections | ISBN 978-3-89821-809-2

68  *Taras Kuzio (Ed.)* | Aspects of the Orange Revolution VI. Post-Communist Democratic Revolutions in Comparative Perspective | ISBN 978-3-89821-820-7

69  *Tim Bohse* | Autoritarismus statt Selbstverwaltung. Die Transformation der kommunalen Politik in der Stadt Kaliningrad 1990-2005 | Mit einem Geleitwort von Stefan Troebst | ISBN 978-3-89821-782-8

70  *David Rupp* | Die Rußländische Föderation und die russischsprachige Minderheit in Lettland. Eine Fallstudie zur Anwaltspolitik Moskaus gegenüber den russophonen Minderheiten im „Nahen Ausland" von 1991 bis 2002 | Mit einem Vorwort von Helmut Wagner | ISBN 978-3-89821-778-1

71  *Taras Kuzio* | Theoretical and Comparative Perspectives on Nationalism. New Directions in Cross-Cultural and Post-Communist Studies | With a foreword by Paul Robert Magocsi | ISBN 978-3-89821-815-3

72  *Christine Teichmann* | Die Hochschultransformation im heutigen Osteuropa. Kontinuität und Wandel bei der Entwicklung des postkommunistischen Universitätswesens | Mit einem Vorwort von Oskar Anweiler | ISBN 978-3-89821-842-9

73  *Julia Kusznir* | Der politische Einfluss von Wirtschaftseliten in russischen Regionen. Eine Analyse am Beispiel der Erdöl- und Erdgasindustrie, 1992-2005 | Mit einem Vorwort von Wolfgang Eichwede | ISBN 978-3-89821-821-4

74   *Alena Vysotskaya* | Russland, Belarus und die EU-Osterweiterung. Zur Minderheitenfrage und zum Problem der Freizügigkeit des Personenverkehrs | Mit einem Vorwort von Katlijn Malfliet | ISBN 978-3-89821-822-1

75   *Heiko Pleines (Hrsg.)* | Corporate Governance in post-sozialistischen Volkswirtschaften | ISBN 978-3-89821-766-8

76   *Stefan Ihrig* | Wer sind die Moldawier? Rumänismus versus Moldowanismus in Historiographie und Schulbüchern der Republik Moldova, 1991-2006 | Mit einem Vorwort von Holm Sundhaussen | ISBN 978-3-89821-466-7

77   *Galina Kozhevnikova in collaboration with Alexander Verkhovsky and Eugene Veklerov* | Ultra-Nationalism and Hate Crimes in Contemporary Russia. The 2004-2006 Annual Reports of Moscow's SOVA Center | With a foreword by Stephen D. Shenfield | ISBN 978-3-89821-868-9

78   *Florian Küchler* | The Role of the European Union in Moldova's Transnistria Conflict | With a foreword by Christopher Hill | ISBN 978-3-89821-850-4

79   *Bernd Rechel* | The Long Way Back to Europe. Minority Protection in Bulgaria | With a foreword by Richard Crampton | ISBN 978-3-89821-863-4

80   *Peter W. Rodgers* | Nation, Region and History in Post-Communist Transitions. Identity Politics in Ukraine, 1991-2006 | With a foreword by Vera Tolz | ISBN 978-3-89821-903-7

81   *Stephanie Solywoda* | The Life and Work of Semen L. Frank. A Study of Russian Religious Philosophy | With a foreword by Philip Walters | ISBN 978-3-89821-457-5

82   *Vera Sokolova* | Cultural Politics of Ethnicity. Discourses on Roma in Communist Czechoslovakia | ISBN 978-3-89821-864-1

83   *Natalya Shevchik Ketenci* | Kazakhstani Enterprises in Transition. The Role of Historical Regional Development in Kazakhstan's Post-Soviet Economic Transformation | ISBN 978-3-89821-831-3

84   *Martin Malek, Anna Schor-Tschudnowskaja (Hgg.)* | Europa im Tschetschenienkrieg. Zwischen politischer Ohnmacht und Gleichgültigkeit | Mit einem Vorwort von Lipchan Basajewa | ISBN 978-3-89821-676-0

85   *Stefan Meister* | Das postsowjetische Universitätswesen zwischen nationalem und internationalem Wandel. Die Entwicklung der regionalen Hochschule in Russland als Gradmesser der Systemtransformation | Mit einem Vorwort von Joan DeBardeleben | ISBN 978-3-89821-891-7

86   *Konstantin Sheiko in collaboration with Stephen Brown* | Nationalist Imaginings of the Russian Past. Anatolii Fomenko and the Rise of Alternative History in Post-Communist Russia | With a foreword by Donald Ostrowski | ISBN 978-3-89821-915-0

87   *Sabine Jenni* | Wie stark ist das „Einige Russland"? Zur Parteibindung der Eliten und zum Wahlerfolg der Machtpartei im Dezember 2007 | Mit einem Vorwort von Klaus Armingeon | ISBN 978-3-89821-961-7

88   *Thomas Borén* | Meeting-Places of Transformation. Urban Identity, Spatial Representations and Local Politics in Post-Soviet St Petersburg | ISBN 978-3-89821-739-2

89   *Aygul Ashirova* | Stalinismus und Stalin-Kult in Zentralasien. Turkmenistan 1924-1953 | Mit einem Vorwort von Leonid Luks | ISBN 978-3-89821-987-7

90   *Leonid Luks* | Freiheit oder imperiale Größe? Essays zu einem russischen Dilemma | ISBN 978-3-8382-0011-8

91   *Christopher Gilley* | The 'Change of Signposts' in the Ukrainian Emigration. A Contribution to the History of Sovietophilism in the 1920s | With a foreword by Frank Golczewski | ISBN 978-3-89821-965-5

92   *Philipp Casula, Jeronim Perovic (Eds.)* | Identities and Politics During the Putin Presidency. The Discursive Foundations of Russia's Stability | With a foreword by Heiko Haumann | ISBN 978-3-8382-0015-6

93   *Marcel Viëtor* | Europa und die Frage nach seinen Grenzen im Osten. Zur Konstruktion ,europäischer Identität' in Geschichte und Gegenwart | Mit einem Vorwort von Albrecht Lehmann | ISBN 978-3-8382-0045-3

94   *Ben Hellman, Andrei Rogachevskii* | Filming the Unfilmable. Casper Wrede's 'One Day in the Life of Ivan Denisovich' | Second, Revised and Expanded Edition | ISBN 978-3-8382-0044-6

95   *Eva Fuchslocher* | Vaterland, Sprache, Glaube. Orthodoxie und Nationenbildung am Beispiel Georgiens | Mit einem Vorwort von Christina von Braun | ISBN 978-3-89821-884-9

96   *Vladimir Kantor* | Das Westlertum und der Weg Russlands. Zur Entwicklung der russischen Literatur und Philosophie | Ediert von Dagmar Herrmann | Mit einem Beitrag von Nikolaus Lobkowicz | ISBN 978-3-8382-0102-3

97   *Kamran Musayev* | Die postsowjetische Transformation im Baltikum und Südkaukasus. Eine vergleichende Untersuchung der politischen Entwicklung Lettlands und Aserbaidschans 1985-2009 | Mit einem Vorwort von Leonid Luks | Ediert von Sandro Henschel | ISBN 978-3-8382-0103-0

98   *Tatiana Zhurzhenko* | Borderlands into Bordered Lands. Geopolitics of Identity in Post-Soviet Ukraine | With a foreword by Dieter Segert | ISBN 978-3-8382-0042-2

99 *Кирилл Галушко, Лидия Смола (ред.)* | Пределы падения – варианты украинского буду-
щего. Аналитико-прогностические исследования | ISBN 978-3-8382-0148-1

100 *Michael Minkenberg (Ed.)* | Historical Legacies and the Radical Right in Post-Cold War Central
and Eastern Europe | With an afterword by Sabrina P. Ramet | ISBN 978-3-8382-0124-5

101 *David-Emil Wickström* | Rocking St. Petersburg. Transcultural Flows and Identity Politics in the St. Petersburg
Popular Music Scene | With a foreword by Yngvar B. Steinholt | Second, Revised and Expanded Edition |
ISBN 978-3-8382-0100-9

102 *Eva Zabka* | Eine neue „Zeit der Wirren"? Der spät- und postsowjetische Systemwandel 1985-2000 im Spiegel
russischer gesellschaftspolitischer Diskurse | Mit einem Vorwort von Margareta Mommsen | ISBN 978-3-8382-0161-0

103 *Ulrike Ziemer* | Ethnic Belonging, Gender and Cultural Practices. Youth Identitites in Contemporary Russia |
With a foreword by Anoop Nayak | ISBN 978-3-8382-0152-8

104 *Ksenia Chepikova* | ‚Einiges Russland' - eine zweite KPdSU? Aspekte der Identitätskonstruktion einer post-
sowjetischen „Partei der Macht" | Mit einem Vorwort von Torsten Oppelland | ISBN 978-3-8382-0311-9

105 *Леонид Люкс* | Западничество или евразийство? Демократия или идеократия? Сборник статей
об исторических дилеммах России | С предисловием Владимира Кантора | ISBN 978-3-8382-0211-2

106 *Anna Dost* | Das russische Verfassungsrecht auf dem Weg zum Föderalismus und zurück. Zum
Konflikt von Rechtsnormen und -wirklichkeit in der Russländischen Föderation von 1991 bis 2009 | Mit einem Vorwort von Ale-
xander Blankenagel | ISBN 978-3-8382-0292-1

107 *Philipp Herzog* | Sozialistische Völkerfreundschaft, nationaler Widerstand oder harmloser Zeit-
vertreib? Zur politischen Funktion der Volkskunst im sowjetischen Estland | Mit einem Vorwort von Andreas Kappeler | ISBN
978-3-8382-0216-7

108 *Marlène Laruelle (Ed.)* | Russian Nationalism, Foreign Policy, and Identity Debates in Putin's
Russia. New Ideological Patterns after the Orange Revolution | ISBN 978-3-8382-0325-6

109 *Michail Logvinov* | Russlands Kampf gegen den internationalen Terrorismus. Eine kritische Bestands-
aufnahme des Bekämpfungsansatzes | Mit einem Geleitwort von Hans-Henning Schröder und einem Vorwort von Eckhard Jesse
| ISBN 978-3-8382-0329-4

110 *John B. Dunlop* | The Moscow Bombings of September 1999. Examinations of Russian Terrorist Attacks at
the Onset of Vladimir Putin's Rule | Second, Revised and Expanded Edition | ISBN 978-3-8382-0388-1

111 *Андрей А. Ковалёв* | Свидетельство из-за кулис российской политики I. Можно ли делать добро
из зла? (Воспоминания и размышления о последних советских и первых послесоветских годах) | With a foreword by Peter
Reddaway | ISBN 978-3-8382-0302-7

112 *Андрей А. Ковалёв* | Свидетельство из-за кулис российской политики II. Угроза для себя и окру-
жающих (Наблюдения и предостережения относительно происходящего после 2000 г.) | ISBN 978-3-8382-0303-4

113 *Bernd Kappenberg* | Zeichen setzen für Europa. Der Gebrauch europäischer lateinischer Sonderzeichen in der
deutschen Öffentlichkeit | Mit einem Vorwort von Peter Schlobinski | ISBN 978-3-89821-749-1

114 *Ivo Mijnssen* | The Quest for an Ideal Youth in Putin's Russia I. Back to Our Future! History, Modernity, and
Patriotism according to Nashi, 2005-2013 | With a foreword by Jeronim Perović | Second, Revised and Expanded Edition |
ISBN 978-3-8382-0368-3

115 *Jussi Lassila* | The Quest for an Ideal Youth in Putin's Russia II. The Search for Distinctive Conformism in
the Political Communication of Nashi, 2005-2009 | With a foreword by Kirill Postoutenko | Second, Revised and Expanded Edi-
tion | ISBN 978-3-8382-0415-4

116 *Valerio Trabandt* | Neue Nachbarn, gute Nachbarschaft? Die EU als internationaler Akteur am Beispiel ihrer
Demokratieförderung in Belarus und der Ukraine 2004-2009 | Mit einem Vorwort von Jutta Joachim | ISBN 978-3-8382-0437-6

117 *Fabian Pfeiffer* | Estlands Außen- und Sicherheitspolitik I. Der estnische Atlantizismus nach der wiedererlang-
ten Unabhängigkeit 1991-2004 | Mit einem Vorwort von Helmut Hubel | ISBN 978-3-8382-0127-6

118 *Jana Podßuweit* | Estlands Außen- und Sicherheitspolitik II. Handlungsoptionen eines Kleinstaates im Rah-
men seiner EU-Mitgliedschaft (2004-2008) | Mit einem Vorwort von Helmut Hubel | ISBN 978-3-8382-0440-6

119 *Karin Pointner* | Estlands Außen- und Sicherheitspolitik III. Eine gedächtnispolitische Analyse estnischer Ent-
wicklungskooperation 2006-2010 | Mit einem Vorwort von Karin Liebhart | ISBN 978-3-8382-0435-2

120 *Ruslana Vovk* | Die Offenheit der ukrainischen Verfassung für das Völkerrecht und die europäi-
sche Integration | Mit einem Vorwort von Alexander Blankenagel | ISBN 978-3-8382-0481-9

121 *Mykhaylo Banakh* | Die Relevanz der Zivilgesellschaft bei den postkommunistischen Transformationsprozessen in mittel- und osteuropäischen Ländern. Das Beispiel der spät- und postsowjetischen Ukraine 1986-2009 | Mit einem Vorwort von Gerhard Simon | ISBN 978-3-8382-0499-4

122 *Michael Moser* | Language Policy and the Discourse on Languages in Ukraine under President Viktor Yanukovych (25 February 2010–28 October 2012) | ISBN 978-3-8382-0497-0 (Paperback edition) | ISBN 978-3-8382-0507-6 (Hardcover edition)

123 *Nicole Krome* | Russischer Netzwerkkapitalismus Restrukturierungsprozesse in der Russischen Föderation am Beispiel des Luftfahrtunternehmens „Aviastar" | Mit einem Vorwort von Petra Stykow | ISBN 978-3-8382-0534-2

124 *David R. Marples* | 'Our Glorious Past'. Lukashenka's Belarus and the Great Patriotic War | ISBN 978-3-8382-0574-8 (Paperback edition) | ISBN 978-3-8382-0675-2 (Hardcover edition)

125 *Ulf Walther* | Russlands „neuer Adel". Die Macht des Geheimdienstes von Gorbatschow bis Putin | Mit einem Vorwort von Hans-Georg Wieck | ISBN 978-3-8382-0584-7

126 *Simon Geissbühler (Hrsg.)* | Kiew – Revolution 3.0. Der Euromaidan 2013/14 und die Zukunftsperspektiven der Ukraine | ISBN 978-3-8382-0581-6 (Paperback edition) | ISBN 978-3-8382-0681-3 (Hardcover edition)

127 *Andrey Makarychev* | Russia and the EU in a Multipolar World. Discourses, Identities, Norms | With a foreword by Klaus Segbers | ISBN 978-3-8382-0629-5

128 *Roland Scharff* | Kasachstan als postsowjetischer Wohlfahrtsstaat. Die Transformation des sozialen Schutzsystems | Mit einem Vorwort von Joachim Ahrens | ISBN 978-3-8382-0622-6

129 *Katja Grupp* | Bild Lücke Deutschland. Kaliningrader Studierende sprechen über Deutschland | Mit einem Vorwort von Martin Schulz | ISBN 978-3-8382-0552-6

130 *Konstantin Sheiko, Stephen Brown* | History as Therapy. Alternative History and Nationalist Imaginings in Russia, 1991-2014 | ISBN 978-3-8382-0665-3

131 *Elisa Kriza* | Alexander Solzhenitsyn: Cold War Icon, Gulag Author, Russian Nationalist? A Study of the Western Reception of his Literary Writings, Historical Interpretations, and Political Ideas | With a foreword by Andrei Rogatchevski | ISBN 978-3-8382-0589-2 (Paperback edition) | ISBN 978-3-8382-0690-5 (Hardcover edition)

132 *Serghei Golunov* | The Elephant in the Room. Corruption and Cheating in Russian Universities | ISBN 978-3-8382-0570-0

133 *Manja Hussner, Rainer Arnold (Hgg.)* | Verfassungsgerichtsbarkeit in Zentralasien I. Sammlung von Verfassungstexten | ISBN 978-3-8382-0595-3

134 *Nikolay Mitrokhin* | Die „Russische Partei". Die Bewegung der russischen Nationalisten in der UdSSR 1953-1985 | Aus dem Russischen übertragen von einem Übersetzerteam unter der Leitung von Larisa Schippel | ISBN 978-3-8382-0024-8

135 *Manja Hussner, Rainer Arnold (Hgg.)* | Verfassungsgerichtsbarkeit in Zentralasien II. Sammlung von Verfassungstexten | ISBN 978-3-8382-0597-7

136 *Manfred Zeller* | Das sowjetische Fieber. Fußballfans im poststalinistischen Vielvölkerreich | Mit einem Vorwort von Nikolaus Katzer | ISBN 978-3-8382-0757-5

137 *Kristin Schreiter* | Stellung und Entwicklungspotential zivilgesellschaftlicher Gruppen in Russland. Menschenrechtsorganisationen im Vergleich | ISBN 978-3-8382-0673-8

138 *David R. Marples, Frederick V. Mills (Eds.)* | Ukraine's Euromaidan. Analyses of a Civil Revolution | ISBN 978-3-8382-0660-8

139 *Bernd Kappenberg* | Setting Signs for Europe. Why Diacritics Matter for European Integration | With a foreword by Peter Schlobinski | ISBN 978-3-8382-0663-9

140 *René Lenz* | Internationalisierung, Kooperation und Transfer. Externe bildungspolitische Akteure in der Russischen Föderation | Mit einem Vorwort von Frank Ettrich | ISBN 978-3-8382-0751-3

141 *Juri Plusnin, Yana Zausaeva, Natalia Zhidkevich, Artemy Pozanenko* | Wandering Workers. Mores, Behavior, Way of Life, and Political Status of Domestic Russian Labor Migrants | Translated by Julia Kazantseva | ISBN 978-3-8382-0653-0

142 *David J. Smith (Eds.)* | Latvia – A Work in Progress? 100 Years of State- and Nation-Building | ISBN 978-3-8382-0648-6

143 *Инна Чувычкина (ред.)* | Экспортные нефте- и газопроводы на постсоветском пространстве. Анализ трубопроводной политики  в свете теории международных отношений | ISBN 978-3-8382-0822-0

144 *Johann Zajaczkowski* | Russland – eine pragmatische Großmacht? Eine rollentheoretische Untersuchung russischer Außenpolitik am Beispiel der Zusammenarbeit mit den USA nach 9/11 und des Georgienkrieges von 2008 | Mit einem Vorwort von Siegfried Schieder | ISBN 978-3-8382-0837-4

145 *Boris Popivanov* | Changing Images of the Left in Bulgaria. The Challenge of Post-Communism in the Early 21st Century | ISBN 978-3-8382-0667-7

146 *Lenka Krátká* | A History of the Czechoslovak Ocean Shipping Company 1948-1989. How a Small, Landlocked Country Ran Maritime Business During the Cold War | ISBN 978-3-8382-0666-0

147 *Alexander Sergunin* | Explaining Russian Foreign Policy Behavior. Theory and Practice | ISBN 978-3-8382-0752-0

148 *Darya Malyutina* | Migrant Friendships in a Super-Diverse City. Russian-Speakers and their Social Relationships in London in the 21st Century | With a foreword by Claire Dwyer | ISBN 978-3-8382-0652-3

149 *Alexander Sergunin, Valery Konyshev* | Russia in the Arctic. Hard or Soft Power? | ISBN 978-3-8382-0753-7

150 *John J. Maresca* | Helsinki Revisited. A Key U.S. Negotiator's Memoirs on the Development of the CSCE into the OSCE | With a foreword by Hafiz Pashayev | ISBN 978-3-8382-0852-7

151 *Jardar Østbø* | The New Third Rome. Readings of a Russian Nationalist Myth | With a foreword by Pål Kolstø | ISBN 978-3-8382-0870-1

152 *Simon Kordonsky* | Socio-Economic Foundations of the Russian Post-Soviet Regime. The Resource-Based Economy and Estate-Based Social Structure of Contemporary Russia | With a foreword by Svetlana Barsukova | ISBN 978-3-8382-0775-9

153 *Duncan Leitch* | Assisting Reform in Post-Communist Ukraine 2000–2012. The Illusions of Donors and the Disillusion of Beneficiaries | With a foreword by Kataryna Wolczuk | ISBN 978-3-8382-0844-2

154 *Abel Polese* | Limits of a Post-Soviet State. How Informality Replaces, Renegotiates, and Reshapes Governance in Contemporary Ukraine | With a foreword by Colin Williams | ISBN 978-3-8382-0845-9

155 *Mikhail Suslov (Ed.)* | Digital Orthodoxy in the Post-Soviet World. The Russian Orthodox Church and Web 2.0 | With a foreword by Father Cyril Hovorun | ISBN 978-3-8382-0871-8

156 *Leonid Luks* | Zwei „Sonderwege"? Russisch-deutsche Parallelen und Kontraste (1917-2014). Vergleichende Essays | ISBN 978-3-8382-0823-7

157 *Vladimir V. Karacharovskiy, Ovsey I. Shkaratan, Gordey A. Yastrebov* | Towards a New Russian Work Culture. Can Western Companies and Expatriates Change Russian Society? | With a foreword by Elena N. Danilova | Translated by Julia Kazantseva | ISBN 978-3-8382-0902-9

158 *Edmund Griffiths* | Aleksandr Prokhanov and Post-Soviet Esotericism | ISBN 978-3-8382-0963-0

159 *Timm Beichelt, Susann Worschech (Eds.)* | Transnational Ukraine? Networks and Ties that Influence(d) Contemporary Ukraine | ISBN 978-3-8382-0944-9

160 *Mieste Hotopp-Riecke* | Die Tataren der Krim zwischen Assimilation und Selbstbehauptung. Der Aufbau des krimtatarischen Bildungswesens nach Deportation und Heimkehr (1990-2005) | Mit einem Vorwort von Swetlana Czerwonnaja | ISBN 978-3-89821-940-2

161 *Olga Bertelsen (Ed.)* | Revolution and War in Contemporary Ukraine. The Challenge of Change | ISBN 978-3-8382-1016-2

162 *Natalya Ryabinska* | Ukraine's Post-Communist Mass Media. Between Capture and Commercialization | With a foreword by Marta Dyczok | ISBN 978-3-8382-1011-7

163 *Alexandra Cotofana, James M. Nyce (Eds.)* | Religion and Magic in Socialist and Post-Socialist Contexts. Historic and Ethnographic Case Studies of Orthodoxy, Heterodoxy, and Alternative Spirituality | With a foreword by Patrick L. Michelson | ISBN 978-3-8382-0989-0

164 *Nozima Akhrarkhodjaeva* | The Instrumentalisation of Mass Media in Electoral Authoritarian Regimes. Evidence from Russia's Presidential Election Campaigns of 2000 and 2008 | ISBN 978-3-8382-1013-1

165 *Yulia Krasheninnikova* | Informal Healthcare in Contemporary Russia. Sociographic Essays on the Post-Soviet Infrastructure for Alternative Healing Practices | ISBN 978-3-8382-0970-8

166 *Peter Kaiser* | Das Schachbrett der Macht. Die Handlungsspielräume eines sowjetischen Funktionärs unter Stalin am Beispiel des Generalsekretärs des Komsomol Aleksandr Kosarev (1929-1938) | Mit einem Vorwort von Dietmar Neutatz | ISBN 978-3-8382-1052-0

167 *Oksana Kim* | The Effects and Implications of Kazakhstan's Adoption of International Financial Reporting Standards. A Resource Dependence Perspective | With a foreword by Svetlana Vlady | ISBN 978-3-8382-0987-6

168 *Anna Sanina* | Patriotic Education in Contemporary Russia. Sociological Studies in the Making of the Post-Soviet Citizen | With a foreword by Anna Oldfield | ISBN 978-3-8382-0993-7

169 *Rudolf Wolters* | Spezialist in Sibirien Faksimile der 1933 erschienenen ersten Ausgabe | Mit einem Vorwort von Dmitrij Chmelnizki | ISBN 978-3-8382-0515-1

170 *Michal Vít, Magdalena M. Baran (Eds.)* | Transregional versus National Perspectives on Contemporary Central European History. Studies on the Building of Nation-States and Their Cooperation in the 20th and 21st Century | With a foreword by Petr Vágner | ISBN 978-3-8382-1015-5

171 *Philip Gamaghelyan* | Conflict Resolution Beyond the International Relations Paradigm. Evolving Designs as a Transformative Practice in Nagorno-Karabakh and Syria | With a foreword by Susan Allen | ISBN 978-3-8382-1057-5

172 *Maria Shagina* | Joining a Prestigious Club. Cooperation with Europarties and Its Impact on Party Development in Georgia, Moldova, and Ukraine 2004–2015 | With a foreword by Kataryna Wolczuk | ISBN 978-3-8382-1084-1

173 *Alexandra Cotofana, James M. Nyce (Eds.)* | Religion and Magic in Socialist and Post-Socialist Contexts II. Baltic, Eastern European, and Post-USSR Case Studies | With a foreword by Anita Stasulane | ISBN 978-3-8382-0990-6

174 *Barbara Kunz* | Kind Words, Cruise Missiles, and Everything in Between. The Use of Power Resources in U.S. Policies towards Poland, Ukraine, and Belarus 1989–2008 | With a foreword by William Hill | ISBN 978-3-8382-1065-0

175 *Eduard Klein* | Bildungskorruption in Russland und der Ukraine. Eine komparative Analyse der Performanz staatlicher Antikorruptionsmaßnahmen im Hochschulsektor am Beispiel universitärer Aufnahmeprüfungen | Mit einem Vorwort von Heiko Pleines | ISBN 978-3-8382-0995-1

176 *Markus Soldner* | Politischer Kapitalismus im postsowjetischen Russland. Die politische, wirtschaftliche und mediale Transformation in den 1990er Jahren | Mit einem Vorwort von Wolfgang Ismayr | ISBN 978-3-8382-1222-7

177 *Anton Oleinik* | Building Ukraine from Within. A Sociological, Institutional, and Economic Analysis of a Nation-State in the Making | ISBN 978-3-8382-1150-3

178 *Peter Rollberg, Marlene Laruelle (Eds.)* | Mass Media in the Post-Soviet World. Market Forces, State Actors, and Political Manipulation in the Informational Environment after Communism | ISBN 978-3-8382-1116-9

179 *Mikhail Minakov* | Development and Dystopia. Studies in Post-Soviet Ukraine and Eastern Europe | With a foreword by Alexander Etkind | ISBN 978-3-8382-1112-1

180 *Aijan Sharshenova* | The European Union's Democracy Promotion in Central Asia. A Study of Political Interests, Influence, and Development in Kazakhstan and Kyrgyzstan in 2007–2013 | With a foreword by Gordon Crawford | ISBN 978-3-8382-1151-0

181 *Andrey Makarychev, Alexandra Yatsyk (Eds.)* | Boris Nemtsov and Russian Politics. Power and Resistance | With a foreword by Zhanna Nemtsova | ISBN 978-3-8382-1122-0

182 *Sophie Falsini* | The Euromaidan's Effect on Civil Society. Why and How Ukrainian Social Capital Increased after the Revolution of Dignity | With a foreword by Susann Worschech | ISBN 978-3-8382-1131-2

183 *Valentyna Romanova, Andreas Umland (Eds.)* | Ukraine's Decentralization. Challenges and Implications of the Local Governance Reform after the Euromaidan Revolution | ISBN 978-3-8382-1162-6

184 *Leonid Luks* | A Fateful Triangle. Essays on Contemporary Russian, German and Polish History | ISBN 978-3-8382-1143-5

185 *John B. Dunlop* | The February 2015 Assassination of Boris Nemtsov and the Flawed Trial of his Alleged Killers. An Exploration of Russia's "Crime of the 21st Century" | ISBN 978-3-8382-1188-6

186 *Vasile Rotaru* | Russia, the EU, and the Eastern Partnership. Building Bridges or Digging Trenches? | ISBN 978-3-8382-1134-3

187 *Marina Lebedeva* | Russian Studies of International Relations. From the Soviet Past to the Post-Cold-War Present | With a foreword by Andrei P. Tsygankov | ISBN 978-3-8382-0851-0

188 *Tomasz Stępniewski, George Soroka (Eds.)* | Ukraine after Maidan. Revisiting Domestic and Regional Security | ISBN 978-3-8382-1075-9

189 *Petar Cholakov* | Ethnic Entrepreneurs Unmasked. Political Institutions and Ethnic Conflicts in Contemporary Bulgaria | ISBN 978-3-8382-1189-3

190 *A. Salem, G. Hazeldine, D. Morgan (Eds.)* | Higher Education in Post-Communist States. Comparative and Sociological Perspectives | ISBN 978-3-8382-1183-1

191 *Igor Torbakov* | After Empire. Nationalist Imagination and Symbolic Politics in Russia and Eurasia in the Twentieth and Twenty-First Century | With a foreword by Serhii Plokhy | ISBN 978-3-8382-1217-3

192 *Aleksandr Burakovskiy* | Jewish-Ukrainian Relations in Late and Post-Soviet Ukraine. Articles, Lectures and Essays from 1986 to 2016 | ISBN 978-3-8382-1210-4

193 *Natalia Shapovalova, Olga Burlyuk (Eds.)* | Civil Society in Post-Euromaidan Ukraine. From Revolution to Consolidation | With a foreword by Richard Youngs | ISBN 978-3-8382-1216-6

194 *Franz Preissler* | Positionsverteidigung, Imperialismus oder Irredentismus? Russland und die „Russischsprachigen", 1991–2015 | ISBN 978-3-8382-1262-3

195 *Marian Madeła* | Der Reformprozess in der Ukraine 2014-2017. Eine Fallstudie zur Reform der öffentlichen Verwaltung | Mit einem Vorwort von Martin Malek | ISBN 978-3-8382-1266-1

196 *Anke Giesen* | „Wie kann denn der Sieger ein Verbrecher sein?" Eine diskursanalytische Untersuchung der russlandweiten Debatte über Konzept und Verstaatlichungsprozess der Lagergedenkstätte „Perm'-36" im Ural | ISBN 978-3-8382-1284-5

197 *Victoria Leukavets* | The Integration Policies of Belarus and Ukraine vis-à-vis the EU and Russia. A Comparative Analysis Through the Prism of a Two-Level Game Approach | ISBN 978-3-8382-1247-0

198 *Oksana Kim* | The Development and Challenges of Russian Corporate Governance I. The Roles and Functions of Boards of Directors | With a foreword by Sheila M. Puffer | ISBN 978-3-8382-1287-6

199 *Thomas D. Grant* | International Law and the Post-Soviet Space I. Essays on Chechnya and the Baltic States | With a foreword by Stephen M. Schwebel | ISBN 978-3-8382-1279-1

200 *Thomas D. Grant* | International Law and the Post-Soviet Space II. Essays on Ukraine, Intervention, and Non-Proliferation | ISBN 978-3-8382-1280-7

201 *Slavomír Michálek, Michal Štefansky* | The Age of Fear. The Cold War and Its Influence on Czechoslovakia 1945–1968 | ISBN 978-3-8382-1285-2

202 *Iulia-Sabina Joja* | Romania's Strategic Culture 1990–2014. Continuity and Change in a Post-Communist Country's Evolution of National Interests and Security Policies | With a foreword by Heiko Biehl | ISBN 978-3-8382-1286-9

203 *Andrei Rogatchevski, Yngvar B. Steinholt, Arve Hansen, David-Emil Wickström* | War of Songs. Popular Music and Recent Russia-Ukraine Relations | With a foreword by Artemy Troitsky | ISBN 978-3-8382-1173-2

204 *Maria Lipman (Ed.)* | Russian Voices on Post-Crimea Russia. An Almanac of Counterpoint Essays from 2015–2018 | ISBN 978-3-8382-1251-7

205 *Ksenia Maksimovtsova* | Language Conflicts in Contemporary Estonia, Latvia, and Ukraine. A Comparative Exploration of Discourses in Post-Soviet Russian-Language Digital Media | With a foreword by Ammon Cheskin | ISBN 978-3-8382-1282-1

206 *Michal Vít* | The EU's Impact on Identity Formation in East-Central Europe between 2004 and 2013. Perceptions of the Nation and Europe in Political Parties of the Czech Republic, Poland, and Slovakia | With a foreword by Andrea Petö | ISBN 978-3-8382-1275-3

207 *Per A. Rudling* | Tarnished Heroes. The Organization of Ukrainian Nationalists in the Memory Politics of Post-Soviet Ukraine | ISBN 978-3-8382-0999-9

208 *Kaja Gadowska, Peter Solomon (Eds.)* | Legal Change in Post-Communist States. Progress, Reversions, Explanations | ISBN 978-3-8382-1312-5

209 *Pawel Kowal, Georges Mink, Iwona Reichardt (Eds.)* | Three Revolutions: Mobilization and Change in Contemporary Ukraine I. Theoretical Aspects and Analyses on Religion, Memory, and Identity | ISBN 978-3-8382-1321-7

210 *Pawel Kowal, Georges Mink, Adam Reichardt, Iwona Reichardt (Eds.)* | Three Revolutions: Mobilization and Change in Contemporary Ukraine II. An Oral History of the Revolution on Granite, Orange Revolution, and Revolution of Dignity | ISBN 978-3-8382-1323-1

211 *Li Bennich-Björkman, Sergiy Kurbatov (Eds.)* | When the Future Came. The Collapse of the USSR and the Emergence of National Memory in Post-Soviet History Textbooks | ISBN 978-3-8382-1335-4

212 *Olga R. Gulina* | Migration as a (Geo-)Political Challenge in the Post-Soviet Space. Border Regimes, Policy Choices, Visa Agendas | With a foreword by Nils Muižnieks | ISBN 978-3-8382-1338-5

213 *Sanna Turoma, Kaarina Aitamurto, Slobodanka Vladiv-Glover (Eds.)* | Religion, Expression, and Patriotism in Russia. Essays on Post-Soviet Society and the State. ISBN 978-3-8382-1346-0

214 *Vasif Huseynov* | Geopolitical Rivalries in the "Common Neighborhood". Russia's Conflict with the West, Soft Power, and Neoclassical Realism | With a foreword by Nicholas Ross Smith | ISBN 978-3-8382-1277-7

215 *Mikhail Suslov* | Geopolitical Imagination. Ideology and Utopia in Post-Soviet Russia | With a foreword by Mark Bassin | ISBN 978-3-8382-1361-3

216 *Alexander Etkind, Mikhail Minakov (Eds.)* | Ideology after Union. Political Doctrines, Discourses, and Debates in Post-Soviet Societies | ISBN 978-3-8382-1388-0

217 *Jakob Mischke, Oleksandr Zabirko (Hgg.)* | Protestbewegungen im langen Schatten des Kreml. Aufbruch und Resignation in Russland und der Ukraine | ISBN 978-3-8382-0926-5

218 *Oksana Huss* | How Corruption and Anti-Corruption Policies Sustain Hybrid Regimes. Strategies of Political Domination under Ukraine's Presidents in 1994-2014 | With a foreword by Tobias Debiel and Andrea Gawrich | ISBN 978-3-8382-1430-6

219 *Dmitry Travin, Vladimir Gel'man, Otar Marganiya* | The Russian Path. Ideas, Interests, Institutions, Illusions | With a foreword by Vladimir Ryzhkov | ISBN 978-3-8382-1421-4

220 *Gergana Dimova* | Political Uncertainty. A Comparative Exploration | With a foreword by Todor Yalamov and Rumena Filipova | ISBN 978-3-8382-1385-9

221 *Torben Waschke* | Russland in Transition. Geopolitik zwischen Raum, Identität und Machtinteressen | Mit einem Vorwort von Andreas Dittmann | ISBN 978-3-8382-1480-1

222 *Steven Jobbitt, Zsolt Bottlik, Marton Berki (Eds.)* | Power and Identity in the Post-Soviet Realm. Geographies of Ethnicity and Nationality after 1991 | ISBN 978-3-8382-1399-6

223 *Daria Buteiko* | Erinnerungsort. Ort des Gedenkens, der Erholung oder der Einkehr? Kommunismus-Erinnerung am Beispiel der Gedenkstätte Berliner Mauer sowie des Soloveckij-Klosters und -Museumsparks | ISBN 978-3-8382-1367-5

224 *Olga Bertelsen (Ed.)* | Russian Active Measures. Yesterday, Today, Tomorrow | With a foreword by Jan Goldman | ISBN 978-3-8382-1529-7

225 *David Mandel* | "Optimizing" Higher Education in Russia. University Teachers and their Union "Universitetskaya solidarnost'" | ISBN 978-3-8382-1519-8

226 *Mikhail Minakov, Gwendolyn Sasse, Daria Isachenko (Eds.)* | Post-Soviet Secessionism. Nation-Building and State-Failure after Communism | ISBN 978-3-8382-1538-9

227 *Jakob Hauter (Ed.)* | Civil War? Interstate War? Hybrid War? Dimensions and Interpretations of the Donbas Conflict in 2014–2020 | With a foreword by Andrew Wilson | ISBN 978-3-8382-1383-5

228 *Tima T. Moldogaziev, Gene A. Brewer, J. Edward Kellough (Eds.)* | Public Policy and Politics in Georgia. Lessons from Post-Soviet Transition | With a foreword by Dan Durning | ISBN 978-3-8382-1535-8

229 *Oxana Schmies (Ed.)* | NATO's Enlargement and Russia. A Strategic Challenge in the Past and Future | With a foreword by Vladimir Kara-Murza | ISBN 978-3-8382-1478-8

230 *Christopher Ford* | Ukapisme – Une Gauche perdue. Le marxisme anti-colonial dans la révolution ukrainienne 1917-1925 | Avec une préface de Vincent Présumey | ISBN 978-3-8382-0899-2

231 *Anna Kutkina* | Between Lenin and Bandera. Decommunization and Multivocality in Post-Euromaidan Ukraine | With a foreword by Juri Mykkänen | ISBN 978-3-8382-1506-8

232 *Lincoln E. Flake* | Defending the Faith. The Russian Orthodox Church and the Demise of Religious Pluralism | With a foreword by Peter Martland | ISBN 978-3-8382-1378-1

233 *Nikoloz Samkharadze* | Russia's Recognition of the Independence of Abkhazia and South Ossetia. Analysis of a Deviant Case in Moscow's Foreign Policy | With a foreword by Neil MacFarlane | ISBN 978-3-8382-1414-6

234 *Arve Hansen* | Urban Protest. A Spatial Perspective on Kyiv, Minsk, and Moscow | With a foreword by Julie Wilhelmsen | ISBN 978-3-8382-1495-5

235 *Eleonora Narvselius, Julie Fedor (Eds.)* | Diversity in the East-Central European Borderlands. Memories, Cityscapes, People | ISBN 978-3-8382-1523-5

236 *Regina Elsner* | The Russian Orthodox Church and Modernity. A Historical and Theological Investigation into Eastern Christianity between Unity and Plurality | With a foreword by Mikhail Suslov | ISBN 978-3-8382-1568-6

237 *Bo Petersson* | The Putin Predicament. Problems of Legitimacy and Succession in Russia | With a foreword by J. Paul Goode | ISBN 978-3-8382-1050-6

238 *Jonathan Otto Pohl* | The Years of Great Silence. The Deportation, Special Settlement, and Mobilization into the Labor Army of Ethnic Germans in the USSR, 1941–1955 | ISBN 978-3-8382-1630-0

239 *Mikhail Minakov (Ed.)* | Inventing Majorities. Ideological Creativity in Post-Soviet Societies | ISBN 978-3-8382-1641-6

240 *Robert M. Cutler* | Soviet and Post-Soviet Foreign Policies I. East-South Relations and the Political Economy of the Communist Bloc, 1971–1991 | With a foreword by Roger E. Kanet | ISBN 978-3-8382-1654-6

241 *Izabella Agardi* | On the Verge of History. Life Stories of Rural Women from Serbia, Romania, and Hungary, 1920–2020 | With a foreword by Andrea Pető | ISBN 978-3-8382-1602-7

242 *Sebastian Schäffer (Ed.)* | Ukraine in Central and Eastern Europe. Kyiv's Foreign Affairs and the International Relations of the Post-Communist Region | With a foreword by Pavlo Klimkin and Andreas Umland| ISBN 978-3-8382-1615-7

243 *Volodymyr Dubrovskyi, Kalman Mizsei, Mychailo Wynnyckyj (Eds.)* | Eight Years after the Revolution of Dignity. What Has Changed in Ukraine during 2013–2021? | With a foreword by Yaroslav Hrytsak | ISBN 978-3-8382-1560-0

244 *Rumena Filipova* | Constructing the Limits of Europe Identity and Foreign Policy in Poland, Bulgaria, and Russia since 1989 | With forewords by Harald Wydra and Gergana Yankova-Dimova | ISBN 978-3-8382-1649-2

245 *Oleksandra Keudel* | How Patronal Networks Shape Opportunities for Local Citizen Participation in a Hybrid Regime A Comparative Analysis of Five Cities in Ukraine | With a foreword by Sabine Kropp | ISBN 978-3-8382-1671-3

246 *Jan Claas Behrends, Thomas Lindenberger, Pavel Kolar (Eds.)* | Violence after Stalin Institutions, Practices, and Everyday Life in the Soviet Bloc 1953–1989 | ISBN 978-3-8382-1637-9

247 *Leonid Luks* | Macht und Ohnmacht der Utopien Essays zur Geschichte Russlands im 20. und 21. Jahrhundert | ISBN 978-3-8382-1677-5

248 *Iuliia Barshadska* | Brüssel zwischen Kyjiw und Moskau Das auswärtige Handeln der Europäischen Union im ukrainisch-russischen Konflikt 2014-2019 | Mit einem Vorwort von Olaf Leiße | ISBN 978-3-8382-1667-6

249 *Valentyna Romanova* | Decentralisation and Multilevel Elections in Ukraine Reform Dynamics and Party Politics in 2010–2021 | With a foreword by Kimitaka Matsuzato | ISBN 978-3-8382-1700-0

250 *Alexander Motyl* | National Questions. Theoretical Reflections on Nations and Nationalism in Eastern Europe | ISBN 978-3-8382-1675-1

251 *Marc Dietrich* | A Cosmopolitan Model for Peacebuilding. The Ukrainian Cases of Crimea and the Donbas | With a foreword by Rémi Baudouï | ISBN 978-3-8382-1687-4

252 *Eduard Baidaus* | An Unsettled Nation. Moldova in the Geopolitics of Russia, Romania, and Ukraine | With forewords by John-Paul Himka and David R. Marples | ISBN 978-3-8382-1582-2

253 *Igor Okunev, Petr Oskolkov (Eds.)* | Transforming the Administrative Matryoshka. The Reform of Autonomous Okrugs in the Russian Federation, 2003–2008 | With a foreword by Vladimir Zorin | ISBN 978-3-8382-1721-5

254 *Winfried Schneider-Deters* | Ukraine's Fateful Years 2013–2019. Vol. I: The Popular Uprising in Winter 2013/2014 | ISBN 978-3-8382-1725-3

255 *Winfried Schneider-Deters* | Ukraine's Fateful Years 2013–2019. Vol. II: The Annexation of Crimea and the War in Donbas | ISBN 978-3-8382-1726-0

256 *Robert M. Cutler* | Soviet and Post-Soviet Russian Foreign Policies II. East-West Relations in Europe and the Political Economy of the Communist Bloc, 1971–1991 | With a foreword by Roger E. Kanet | ISBN 978-3-8382-1727-7

257 *Robert M. Cutler* | Soviet and Post-Soviet Russian Foreign Policies III. East-West Relations in Europe and Eurasia in the Post-Cold War Transition, 1991–2001 | With a foreword by Roger E. Kanet | ISBN 978-3-8382-1728-4

258 *Paweł Kowal, Iwona Reichardt, Kateryna Pryshchepa (Eds.)* | Three Revolutions: Mobilization and Change in Contemporary Ukraine III. Archival Records and Historical Sources on the 1990 Revolution on Granite | ISBN 978-3-8382-1376-2

259 *Mikhail Minakov (Ed.)* | Philosophy Unchained. Developments in Post-Soviet Philosophical Thought. | With a foreword by Christopher Donohue | ISBN 978-3-8382-1768-0

260 *David Dalton* | The Ukrainian Oligarchy After the Euromaidan. How Ukraine's Political Economy Regime Survived the Crisis | With a foreword by Andrew Wilson | ISBN 978-3-8382-1740-6

261 *Andreas Heinemann-Grüder (Ed.)* | Who Are the Fighters? Irregular Armed Groups in the Russian-Ukrainian War since 2014 | ISBN 978-3-8382-1777-2

262 *Taras Kuzio (Ed.)* | Russian Disinformation and Western Scholarship. Bias and Prejudice in Journalistic, Expert, and Academic Analyses of East European, Russian and Eurasian Affairs | ISBN 978-3-8382-1685-0

263 *Darius Furmonavicius* | LithuaniaTransforms the West. Lithuania's Liberation from Soviet Occupation and the Enlargement of NATO (1988–2022) | With a foreword by Vytautas Landsbergis | ISBN 978-3-8382-1779-6

264 *Dirk Dalberg* | Politisches Denken im tschechoslowakischen Dissens. Egon Bondy, Miroslav Kusý, Milan Šimečka und Petr Uhl (1968-1989) | ISBN 978-3-8382-1318-5

265 *Леонид Люкс* | К столетию «философского парохода». Мыслители «первой» русской эмиграции о русской революции и о тоталитарных соблазнах XX века | ISBN 978-3-8382-1775-8

266 *Daviti Mtchedlishvili* | The EU and the South Caucasus. European Neighborhood Policies between Eclecticism and Pragmatism, 1991-2021 | With a foreword by Nicholas Ross Smith | ISBN 978-3-8382-1735-2

267 *Bohdan Harasymiw* | Post-Euromaidan Ukraine. Domestic Power Struggles and War of National Survival in 2014–2022 | ISBN 978-3-8382-1798-7

268 *Nadiia Koval, Denys Tereshchenko (Eds.)* | Russian Cultural Diplomacy under Putin. Rossotrudnichestvo, the "Russkiy Mir" Foundation, and the Gorchakov Fund in 2007–2022 | ISBN 978-3-8382-1801-4

269 *Izabela Kazejak* | Jews in Post-War Wrocław and L'viv. Official Policies and Local Responses in Comparative Perspective, 1945-1970s | ISBN 978-3-8382-1802-1

270 *Jakob Hauter* | Russia's Overlooked Invasion. The Causes of the 2014 Outbreak of War in Ukraine's Donbas | With a foreword by Hiroaki Kuromiya | ISBN 978-3-8382-1803-8

271 *Anton Shekhovtsov* | Russian Political Warfare. Essays on Kremlin Propaganda in Europe and the Neighbourhood, 2020-2023 | With a foreword by Nathalie Loiseau | ISBN 978-3-8382-1821-2

272 *Андреа Пето* | Насилие и Молчание. Красная армия в Венгрии во Второй Мировой войне | ISBN 978-3-8382-1636-2

273 *Winfried Schneider-Deters* | Russia's War in Ukraine. Debates on Peace, Fascism, and War Crimes, 2022–2023 | With a foreword by Klaus Gestwa | ISBN 978-3-8382-1876-2

274 *Rasmus Nilsson* | Uncanny Allies. Russia and Belarus on the Edge, 2012-2024 | ISBN 978-3-8382-1288-3

275 *Anton Grushetskyi, Volodymyr Paniotto* | War and the Transformation of Ukrainian Society (2022–23). Empirical Evidence | ISBN 978-3-8382-1944-8

276 *Christian Kaunert, Alex MacKenzie, Adrien Nonjon (Eds.)* | In the Eye of the Storm. Origins, Ideology, and Controversies of the Azov Brigade, 2014–23 | ISBN 978-3-8382-1750-5

277 *Gian Marco Moisé* | The House Always Wins. The Corrupt Strategies that Shaped Kazakh Oil Politics and Business in the Nazarbayev Era | With a foreword by Alena Ledeneva | ISBN 978-3-8382-1917-2

278 *Mikhail Minakov* | The Post-Soviet Human | Philosophical Reflections on Social History after the End of Communism | ISBN 978-3-8382-1943-1

279 *Natalia Kudriavtseva, Debra A. Friedman (Eds.)* | Language and Power in Ukraine and Kazakhstan. Essays on Education, Ideology, Literature, Practice, and the Media | With a foreword by Laada Bilaniuk | ISBN 978-3-8382-1949-3

280 *Paweł Kowal, Georges Mink, Iwona Reichardt (Eds.)* | The End of the Soviet World? Essays on Post-Communist Political and Social Change | With a foreword by Richardt Butterwick-Pawlikowski | ISBN 978-3-8382-1961-5

281 *Kateryna Zarembo, Michèle Knodt, Maksym Yakovlyev (Eds.)* | Teaching IR in Wartime. Experiences of University Lecturers during Russia's Full-Scale Invasion of Ukraine | ISBN 978-3-8382-1954-7

282 *Oleksiy V. Kresin* | The United Nations General Assembly Resolutions. Their Nature and Significance in the Context of the Russian War Against Ukraine | Edited by William E. Butler | ISBN 978-3-8382-1967-7

283 *Jakob Hauter* | Russlands unbemerkte Invasion. Die Ursachen des Kriegsausbruchs im ukrainischen Donbas im Jahr 2014 | Mit einem Vorwort von Hiroaki Kuromiya | ISBN 978-3-8382-2003-1

284 „Alles kann sich ändern". Letzte Worte politisch Angeklagter vor Gericht in Russland | Herausgegeben von Memorial Deutschland e.V. | ISBN 978-3-8382-1994-3

285 *Nadiya Kiss, Monika Wingender (Eds.)* | Contested Language Diversity in Contemporary Ukraine. National Minorities, Language Biographies, and Linguistic Landscape | ISBN 978-3-8382-1966-0

286 *Richard Ottinger (Ed.)* | Religious Elements in the Russian War of Aggression Against Ukraine. Propaganda, Religious Politics and Pastoral Care, 2014–2024 | ISBN 978-3-8382-1981-3

287 *Yuri Radchenko* | Helping in Mass Murders. Auxiliary Police, Indigenous Administration, SD, and the Shoa in the Ukrainian-Russian-Belorussian Borderlands, 1941–43 | With forewords by John-Paul Himka and Kai Struve | ISBN 978-3-8382-1878-6

288 *Zsofia Maria Schmidt* | Hungary's System of National Cooperation. Strategies of Framing in Pro-Governmental Media and Public Discourse, 2010–18 | With a foreword by Andreas Schmidt-Schweizer | ISBN 978-3-8382-1983-7

*ibidem*.eu